Twentieth-Century South Africa

The twentieth century has brought considerable political, social and economic change for South Africa. While many would choose to focus only on the issues of race, segregation and apartheid, this book tries to capture another facet: its drive towards modernisation and industrialisation. While considering the achievements and failures of that drive, as well as how it related to ethnic and racial policymaking, Bill Freund makes the economic data come alive by highlighting people and places. He proposes that South Africa in the twentieth century can actually be understood as a nascent developmental state, with economic development acting as a key motivating factor. As a unique history of South Africa in the twentieth century, this will appeal to anyone interested in a new interpretation of modern South African economic development or those in development studies searching for striking historical examples.

BILL FREUND is Professor Emeritus of Built Environment and Development Studies at the University of KwaZulu-Natal, and Visiting Professor at the University of the Witwatersrand. His previous books include *The African Worker* (Cambridge University Press, 1988), *The African City: A History* (Cambridge University Press, 2007) and *The Making of Contemporary Africa* (2016).

Twentieth-Century South Africa

A Developmental History

BILL FREUND
University of KwaZulu-Natal

CAMBRIDGE
UNIVERSITY PRESS

CAMBRIDGE
UNIVERSITY PRESS

University Printing House, Cambridge CB2 8BS, United Kingdom

One Liberty Plaza, 20th Floor, New York, NY 10006, USA

477 Williamstown Road, Port Melbourne, VIC 3207, Australia

314–321, 3rd Floor, Plot 3, Splendor Forum, Jasola District Centre,
New Delhi – 110025, India

79 Anson Road, #06–04/06, Singapore 079906

Cambridge University Press is part of the University of Cambridge.

It furthers the University's mission by disseminating knowledge in the pursuit of education, learning, and research at the highest international levels of excellence.

www.cambridge.org
Information on this title: www.cambridge.org/9781108427401
DOI: 10.1017/9781108604222

First published 2019

Printed and bound in Great Britain by Clays Ltd, Elcograf S.p.A.

A catalogue record for this publication is available from the British Library.

Library of Congress Cataloging-in-Publication Data
Names: Freund, Bill, author.
Title: Twentieth-century South Africa : a developmental history /
Bill Freund.
Description: New York : Cambridge University Press,
2018. | Includes bibliographical references and index.
Identifiers: LCCN 2018015238 | ISBN 9781108427401 (alk. paper)
Subjects: LCSH: Economic development – South Africa. | South
Africa – Economic conditions – 1991– | South Africa – Economic policy.
Classification: LCC HC905 .F748 2018 | DDC 330.96807–dc23
LC record available at https://lccn.loc.gov/2018015238

ISBN 978-1-108-42740-1 Hardback
ISBN 978-1-108-44615-0 Paperback

Contents

Figures and Maps

Figures

Maps

Tables

Acknowledgements

I have tried my best to respond to the very useful critical remarks provided by Cambridge University Press's anonymous readers in creating a final version of this book. Over a good ten years, I have made use of a variety of friends and colleagues in thinking about and collecting material on this subject matter. The first paper I can remember writing towards this end was probably for an international conference organised by Monash University, irresistibly held in the town where my father was born, the Tuscan Renaissance city of Prato, Italy.

However, I would give pride of place to the Corporate Strategy and Industrial Development (CSID) MA programme at the University of the Witwatersrand's School of Economics and Business Sciences. There I found for a time an intellectual home that correlated with my own ideas and interests in the material I cover here. My role in the school was partly organised by my friend Nicolas Pons-Vignon, but the director, Seeraj Mohamed, was a very welcoming and supportive figure in every way. Through the CSID MA I participated for several years in the African Programme on Rethinking Development Economics (APORDE), which supported postgraduate students from South Africa and elsewhere with an impressive array of guest speakers focused on development issues. Here too I was stimulated as well as honoured to be a participant. I finally need to thank Ben Fine of the School of Oriental and African Studies, who was an inspirational figure and frequent visitor to the programme. Ben's work on the mineral and energy complex in South Africa was co-authored by Zav Rustomjee, who also made an important unpublished paper of his own available to me. Their landmark book is currently being updated and should appear in a new edition. I could hardly have written this book without their platform existing. Amongst the teachers in the programme were Samantha Ashman, Sue Lewis, Lotta Takala-Greenish, Rex McKenzie and my old student and friend Firoz

Khan of Stellenbosch University. Nimrod Zalk, an associate from the Department of Trade and Industry, kindly gave me an almost complete version of his London doctoral thesis. All these people formed a community of intense commitment and interest to the development project in South Africa which was exciting to join.

One area that is touched on in this book is the Industrial Development Corporation (IDC). I am very grateful to them for access to their library (the Infocentre) and files. For his assistance, I would also like to thank Jorge Maia, head of research and also Raymond Majozi, the Records Department Support Services manager. An IDC official and former student, Nnzeni Netshitomboni, now working on his PhD on the history of the organisation under my supervision, has been a great colleague and host at this important institution. On the history of the Centre for Scientific and Industrial Research, I profited from conversation with Professor David Walwyn of the University of Pretoria.

Some parts of this book depend on research in the National Archives in Pretoria where I found a helpful staff. In Pretoria I enjoyed the hospitality of, and many great discussions with, Rasigan Maharajh. At home I have made use of our library at the University of KwaZulu-Natal and occasionally at the Killie Campbell Africana Library special collection. The National Research Foundation made funds available for travel to Gauteng. On visits to Johannesburg, I made use of the Wits library system. In particular, I have consulted several documents kept at the Cullen Library of the University of the Witwatersrand, with its very friendly and knowledgeable staff. An important part of this was the material about planners active in the formation of the parastatal towns. Here I enjoyed the invaluable help of Professor Alan Mabin, who had himself interviewed Roy Kantorowich long ago and knew much about his story. Indeed, Alan must know as much or more than anyone about urban planning and urban history in South Africa; he also pointed me in the direction of a son of Vanderbijlpark, Professor Mark Oranje of the Town and Regional Planning Department of the University of Pretoria, who returned to his home town with me on a memorable visit. Victor Munnik is not a Vaal Triangle native but he is the author of a great University of the Witwatersrand sociology thesis on Steel Valley and ecological problems there. I learnt a lot from meeting him and reading his thesis. I am also indebted to Steve Sparks of the University of Johannesburg and his thesis on Sasolburg, from which I learnt so much. I am waiting for Steve to turn this University of Michigan thesis into a published work which should attract considerable attention. Eddie Webster indicated in conversation that his first book, *Cast in a Racial Mould,* and allied research was actually partially set in the Vaal Triangle and thus of particular value to me to rediscover. Frank Sokolic produced my clarity-enhancing maps.

I spent a month as a guest of the Institute of Social and Economic Research at Rhodes University and Professor Robert van Niekerk, the director, was not only a very pleasant host but also the author of an Oxford thesis of which I made use. This work made me think about the attempt to create a national health system in the 1940s and I also must thank Simonne Horwitz of the University of Saskatchewan for giving me access to her then unpublished Canadian thesis on Baragwanath Hospital. I also found at Rhodes the papers of Douglas Smit, Smuts' Minister of Native Affairs, who had much to do with the creation of a homeland textile industry in the Eastern Cape and was a key figure in the old United Party. Dr Johan Fourie hosted me at a seminar at Stellenbosch University and Professor Anne Mager, for whose excellent Economic History programme at the University of Cape Town (UCT) I served as external examiner for some years, made a big contribution to this book by pointing me towards the unpublished UCT Andrew Marquard thesis on energy policy. In general, this project has been a great chance to meet and learn from a wide and very impressive range of South African intellectuals. Amongst the seminars I have addressed with reference to my expanding ideas on the old South Africa and its development trajectory, I should note a new impressive Iranian/German friend, Kaveh Yazdani, who spent a couple of post-doctoral years at the University of the Witwatersrand. My paper for his workshop was actually the basis of the first chapter of this book.

1 *White-run South Africa as a Developmental State*

An Interpretive Economic History of Twentieth-Century South Africa

For many years as a historian increasingly taken up with issues in political economy, my thinking was powerfully influenced by dependency theory. In brief, dependency theory proposes that deeply wrought structurally one-sided relationships mark the economic interactions between the West and the rest of the world. These interactions, if one followed the work of Andre Gunder Frank or Immanuel Wallerstein, changed in detail considerably over time but retained their dominance over the centuries, basically from the first intrusion of Europeans into the wider world (Brewer 1980, chapter 4; Frank 1969; Wallerstein 1976).

Dependency theory was in several respects an awkward fit to Marxist political economy, with its emphasis on the dynamism of capitalist accumulation and the potential for elites to look into the mirror, observe the early phases of the Industrial Revolution and promote the same processes in their own backyards. It was associated with the Economic Commission for Latin America and the Argentine economist Raul Prebisch, who headed it, and it seemed apt to explain the limited and frustrating development experience of Latin America, where episodes of slow growth, dominance of foreign capitalists and debt crises prevented a 'take-off' of the Rostovian kind. Africa ranked on average far behind Latin America and experienced a more modern form of colonial conquest and rule, yet was it not in line in the same queue? To what extent could we blame post-independence African development problems on the structural fix that the *dependencistas* delineated? Claude Ake's work, not without subtlety and refinement, seems to make the strongest case for this sort of approach (Ake 1981). There was one obvious link to the writings of socialists: as the history of the Soviet Union or China appeared to demonstrate, a high degree of isolation or delinking was essential for a set of rulers determined to build an economy structurally very different from that of the capitalist

West, one that could build 'socialism in one country', even if this formation itself created a substantial number of problems.[1]

After a time, however, doubt set in. Did dependency interrelationships completely counter the free trade advocacy enshrined in Adam Smith's *The Wealth of Nations*? Isn't the evidence largely in the direction of seeing economies flourish when wide-ranging intercourse between them takes off? Don't capitalists do best when this intercourse is most favoured, most possible? It is true, of course, that interest groups may prefer a fixed set of interactions that benefit particular businesses and individuals.[2] This is a commonplace and demonstrably very largely the case in the heyday of colonial rule in Africa, but didn't independence allow for a redirection of the economy in new ways that underscored growing complexity, higher consumption levels, internal structural change as well as the holy grail of growth?[3] A determined state could surely preside over a learning process in which the pupils could even potentially overcome the impediments that affected their teachers and surpass them.

To a historian, two further contradictory realities seemed to intrude. After the first few years of mere neo-colonial forms of development, many, probably most, sub-Saharan African countries drifted into chaos and economically incoherent situations. The treasured primary products that Africa sold to the world, notably the ex-colonial powers, for the most part lost value compared to the complex consumer goods such as automobiles and airplanes, as well as the machinery for producing them, which Africa imported, causing deep problems in the world of international trade. This kind of chaos actually echoed to a degree the problems of Latin America in the first decades of independence in the nineteenth century (or the situation of the self-liberated slaves of Haiti). However, there, with time, so-called 'neo-colonial dependency relationships' reasserted themselves or took off once

1 For a recent and convincing re-examination of the Soviet economic experience without any apparent ideological spin, see Allen 2003.

2 For the rather shameless French case, see Marseille 1984.

3 For a defence of the view that African states in the first decade of independence in the 1960s and into the 1970s had at least an important developmentalist component and some features of the developmental state, see Mkandawire 2001 and Freund 2016. Mkandawire, however, does not even mention South Africa. For a current view that suggests a few African states, especially Rwanda and Ethiopia, are once again to be seen from this perspective, see Kelsall and Booth 2010.

again in the second half of the century, although only to a very limited extent in the case of Haiti. Would this also happen in Africa eventually? To what extent did the situation within Latin America rather than the dependency relationship, the built environment and the infrastructure but also the social situation, the class structure, the values and orientation of the continent's dominant men, determine things in fact?[4]

Moreover, and secondly, imperialism and colonialism, these bugbears, generated not just oppression but its very opposite, where settlers from the metropole were numerous and strong enough to present coherence and eventually dominate new nations: Australia, Canada and above all, the USA. The USA was, of course, not merely a success story; it had become the very core of world capitalism, the most successful state of them all. It is also a truism that the USA as a system witnessed the flourishing of capitalism without having to deal with the historic residue of earlier social and political forms, as was true even in Britain; colonialism was the platform for spectacular long-term development in this case (Moore 1966). Yet it was also a basic historic fact that the southern states before the Civil War, characterised by the widespread presence of plantation slavery and given over to selling plantation-grown crops, especially cotton, lagged behind, even though the dominant group were also settlers with British origins. At first this was the richest and most economically important part of the new nation but with time it gradually fell behind the rest of the country.

At this point, although it came later in my intellectual trajectory, it seems most useful to take this further and refer to the work of British and Dutch historians considering, as they do (usually with some self-satisfaction), how capitalism arose in early modern times (Landes 1998). I would refer particularly to the work of Berkeley historian Jan de Vries and his conceptualisation of 'industrious' society, in effect of the capitalism emerging from below, from the endeavours and values of the middling sorts of men and women over many centuries (de Vries 1994; Luiten van Zanden 2012; Brenner 1993). Such people found the establishment of new societies through conquest and the often ruthless elimination of native peoples an ideal setting for success along these lines. In both the Netherlands and Britain, it was the state that in time adapted to the needs of this kind of society and encouraged it to flourish

4 For an early critique along these lines, see Laclau 1977.

(Hobsbawm 1968). In other words, the Industrial Revolution itself emerged, in stages (albeit in the last stage increasingly rapidly), as a process with unpredictable consequences out of many centuries of social change. The Netherlands and Britain were great colonial powers but what is striking was their ability to correlate imperial culture, imperial dreams and the thrust for conquest, often very brutal conquest, with enabling economic actors to move in directions that promoted capitalist growth. Imperialism itself was not a sufficient condition. This trajectory was far less true of the legacy of the Spanish conquistadores and particularly less true of those imperial pioneers, the Portuguese, who never developed an impressive industrial society and who came out of imperialism and colonialism startlingly poor. Even wider reflection, considering the Romans or the Vikings or indeed China, lends one to thinking that empires can be 'successful' in many ways but these ways reflect the social dynamism within the imperial society first and foremost whatever the wealth that may be uncovered overseas. Imperialism is not irrelevant but itself it does not explain remotely enough.

If one explores the European dimension from the inside, the historic picture, as the early modern historians frequently insist, is one of stark divisions. There is no superior form of development to be correlated to 'whiteness'. It is only in this north-western corner of Europe that capitalism took off at first. Even today, much of eastern and southern Europe displays, even to a fairly casual visitor, signs of relative historic backwardness.[5] At some point, of course, more and more parts of Europe benefited from capitalist growth both through conquest and learning processes albeit without forgetting that the European world 'we have lost' was regretted and resisted everywhere – at times through radical cultural and political resistance. At every stage, there were losers as well as winners. Every example of European success one can give is matched by much larger examples of failure elsewhere within Europe and, indeed, partial successes need to be considered as well. Within Europe there is the halfway house of France, the

[5] When I spent a day in a car in the rural western Ukraine, it came to me that I wished I had some African company to show that company the poverty in a region where somatically the people were just as white as I am, just as white as the population anywhere in western Europe. Backwardness has nothing to do with skin colour as they might mistakenly deduce from their own perceptual world.

spectacular late bloomer, Germany and the late industrious transformation in Scandinavia for starters, as well as the problematic south and east.

Returning to the colonial world and to Africa in particular, it is striking that there seems to be one country, dominated by white settlers primarily with Dutch or British origins, which was a relatively dynamic success story. This was South Africa. The most thoughtful and comprehensive writer on dependency in Africa, Samir Amin, in his major work *Accumulation on a World Scale*, is disturbed by, and denotes, this South African example (Amin 1974). In my view, Amin is perceptive in seeing the importance of this example but it upsets his whole picture (Amin 1974). Capitalism structures dependency, but white settlers are the ones who can modify this so extensively as to open the door to impressive forms of economic development. In effect, they are in a position to make dependency work for them with beneficial effects on their own living standards in particular. This settler exceptionalism seems to me an important thread to retain. Donald Denoon, an expatriate South African historian settled in Australia, has proposed the idea of a 'settler capitalism', even though his work is descriptive rather than theoretical. It continues to resonate, though, as one platform for finding a key to explain South Africa (Denoon 1983).[6] In my view, settler capitalism, which brought to this region a version, limited as it was to be sure, of the Industrious Revolution of de Vries, was important in creating instruments which a purposeful developmental project, partnered and managed by the state in the twentieth century, could use before its contradictions in terms of racial exclusion created increasing problems.

Into this conundrum came a new literature to which I began to be exposed and which has inspired me. This literature has focused on what is termed the developmental state. If the *dependencista* literature was mainly forged by Latin American, African or South Asian writers, the developmental state literature has been the handiwork of East Asian scholars and sympathetic Westerners. It is, moreover, radically divorced both from the shadow of Communism and its dream of political and sociological development counter to 'the West' or

[6] Denoon is under-theorised but he cites writers such as Louis Hartz, historian of the US frontier, who expounded on the particular social advantages of US development, the master theme for settler capitalism.

Europe – *socialism in one country*. Classic studies are those of Chalmers Johnson on Japan and Alice Amsden on Korea (Johnson 1982; Amsden 1989). Perhaps the most striking populariser of this paradigm is the Cambridge based Korean Ha-Joon Chang (1992). However, amongst other writers, one should perhaps mention particularly Peter Evans and his concept of embeddedness as a way of exploring state-capital relations in Brazil (Evans 1995). One of the more successful applications of this paradigm has been in pointing not merely to early capitalist development but to the role of planning in the *reconstitution* of capitalism, a far more dynamic capitalism, in post-Second World War France and Japan. And, of course, Chang is particularly forthright in insisting that Britain itself only 'kicked away the ladder' of protection, imperialism and mercantilism on which wealth and power were necessarily built before taking on (some of) the Smithian virtues of the self-regulating market.

What are the main tenets of the developmental state literature? The developmental state is conceptualised as one where close relations exist between a significant part of the capitalist class, sections of the state apparatus and key political figures. This relationship goes beyond alliance. 'The common thread . . . is that a developmental state is not an imperious element lording it over society but a partner with a business sector in an historical compact of industrial transformation' (Woo-Cumings 1999: 4). A key defining element is *agency*, the existence of a state-formed body that transcends bureaucratic rules; in Weberian terms, this means bureaucratic rules *plus* charisma. Such agencies are capable of directing capital and defying the logic of market forces which may constrain structural transformation.

Also crucial, therefore, is the capacity of the state to discipline capital and in so doing affect the direction of investment and innovation. While the state may tolerate large-scale corruption, favourites are channelled in such a way as to ensure economic results, not simply to result in private rent-seeking activities. Such negatives are counterbalanced by the state's ability to override dominant existing interests in pre-capitalist forms of power and wealth. Capitalists and government officials, perhaps in the military as well, come together to form an elite, probably moulded through social associations, common educational background and personal ties. Peter Evans, in his noteworthy study of Brazil, proposes that members of such an elite 'are embedded in a concrete set of social ties that binds the state to society and provides institutional channels for the continued negotiation and renegotiation of goals and policies' (Evans 1995, 12). Chalmers Johnson's original Japanese model was the Ministry of Trade and Industry, which drove development as well as trade (Johnson 1982). They thus fulfil the requirements suggested by Ronald Coase's Nobel Prize winning theory: costs are reduced to a minimum where economic interactions are embedded in social forms and cease to rub against them (Coase 1937).

For Korea, Alice Amsden has insisted that the willingness existed to drive economic policies beyond the logic imposed by the market price mechanism (Amsden 1989). *Getting prices wrong* and defying the logic propounded by the Washington Consensus institutions proved in fact to be crucial to the successful outward drive of Korean industry in the 1970s and 1980s. If we look back at W.W. Rostow's stages of economic growth theory, we can find it governed by an assumption that the same rules apply to all. Japan – one of his case studies – industrialised essentially along the lines of universal stages that would apply anywhere (Rostow 1960). In fact Japanese officials were so annoyed at the World Bank formulae for approved national economic behaviour thirty years ago that they insisted on writing up an alternative economic historical model for how Japanese industrialisation actually took off. The Japanese state defied market rules in crucial phases to promote a drive for industrialisation, fundamental to the Meiji Restoration of the late nineteenth century, and then to deepen and widen it after the catastrophic events of the Second World War. It is not only the future rules of the Washington Consensus that were rejected here.

Developmental state analysis might be seen as also part of a process of provincialising European history and casting it as a deviant, if interesting, historical model rather than the model for all successful nations to follow, the first flying goose pursued dutifully by the rest. Of course, to take things this far is to forget that the economic history of European countries, taken as a whole and as already noted, itself contains failure as well as success and considerable deviation from any norm (Chakrabarty 2000). The developmental state narrative has been increasingly attractive to contemporary regimes that wish to consider themselves developmental and look for a way forward where other models seemingly have led to blockage (Chibber 2013). Indeed, it really found its feet in the teeth of the ideological triumph of neoliberalism with its reification of market forces and its hostility to the state as a director of economic initiatives. South Africa after 1994 endorsed neoliberalism controversially but the limited success of that agenda led President Thabo Mbeki to embrace, perhaps half-heartedly, what he called the 'democratic developmental state' (Freund 2007b).

Having put this forward as a way of making sense of South African successes under the segregation and apartheid regimes, I would like to suggest two obvious limitations to the developmental state literature in order further to understand the circumstances for the real developmental states to have emerged historically. These limitations clarify, but do not eliminate, the value of the approach. The one is marked by the typical presentation of the developmental state in an abstracted form as virtually a Weberian ideal type. When one casts one's eye around, there are very few historic examples of such a state. Even these few do not necessarily suggest that particular countries will carry on in this way permanently. The developmentalism of the developmental state paradigm can, in fact, in this sense be seen as a more spectacular and deeper means of overcoming teething problems, as an extension of the classic economic protectionist defence which sees tariffs and other forms of preference to local manufacture as a crucial but finally temporary measure until a competitive environment can be entertained, and the props eliminated, just as in the classic studies of Hamilton or List (Hamilton 1934; Selwyn 2009). However, it is interesting that some of the most critical cases are not about the emergence of modern industry but about its adaptation and re-launching at a different phase, notably France and Japan after the Second World War (Johnson 1982; Woo-Cumings 1999). This surely needs to be set against what had already taken place earlier in those same countries.

A modified view would stress the importance of continuing to consider the model for examples of partial success or even failures. This is the only way in which the developmental state concept can be integrated into a broader understanding of economic development, certainly of capitalism. Here there are many cases to consider indeed. One of the most interesting writers on development today is the Indian Vivek Chibber. Chibber sees newly independent India as a developmental failure and explains very clearly why this position can be justified apart from the slow measured growth rate, the infamous 'Hindu growth rate' India experienced for up to forty years after independence (Chibber 2003; 2013). For Chibber, above all, it is the considerable power and influence of the actually existing Indian industrialists and the class they represented compared to that of the nationalist politicians by the time of independence who caused the failure after an initially promising start at a brief historic moment. In the early 1940s, however, the Indian business elite reasserted themselves decisively. While Chibber's views on the relationship between industrialist (or bourgeoisie) and state are unexceptionable, it is not so clear that this marked complete failure unless one insists on applying an ideal type of developmental state to the story. It can also be argued that the interventions of the state into industry, the growing emphasis on infrastructure and heavy industry and the ties with the Soviet Union, which broke the old links to Britain substantially without creating the same sort of dependence, were actually impressive achievements – achievements, moreover, on which further transformations were built in the late twentieth and early twenty-first centuries. In fact, as I have earlier pointed out, the relative levels of development of India and South Africa have over the whole period changed dramatically (Freund 2014). Even today, Indian development has various limitations, compared say to China. Yet today it is India which trades to South Africa through a variety of sophisticated industrial products on a big scale and invests more than China. This is not so easily to be dismissed as failure on the part of India, while richly illustrating the flaws from the point of view of equity and democracy of the Indian example.

When we move in eastern Asia beyond ex-Japanese colonies and countries or territories with a very strong Chinese social influence, there is less success than in Taiwan, Singapore or Korea but, in fact, a mixed picture that partly reflects the continued commercial importance of rich natural resources in the former (Thailand, Indonesia). Understanding these mixed bag cases, rather than concentrating only on the flaws in order to dismiss them, may be more helpful. Brazil, Evans' prototype developmental state for Latin America, is also a case in point.[7] From the perspective of development, we should not dismiss any of these but rather focus study on them. China, with its often harsh history, its immensity and particular Communist foundational decades,

[7] The currently disastrous state of the Brazilian economy makes one wonder what we make today of the embedded structures Peter Evans highlighted in his analyses. The circumstances of a decade ago have dramatically shifted for the worse already. For a careful and circumspect look at Argentina, see Brennan and Rougier 2009; Hurtado 2010. Other Latin American countries seen from a developmental focus are studied in Coronil 1997 and Hamilton 1982.

also needs consideration and study and this must involve moving the deck chairs around for a somewhat different view. The task of integrating Pomeranz' very long-term historic comparative perspective, comparing parts of China, especially the Yellow River Delta to northwestern Europe, with an assessment of early Communist and contemporary China, is a huge and important, if very daunting, one (Pomeranz 2000).

The second stricture I want to introduce is the socio-political one. The idealisation of development in general, and certainly any portrayal as a shining image of the developmental state, can lead us to forget or gloss over the context. The big political battles in early Meiji Japan were over the choice between invading and conquering Korea or focusing on borrowing and indigenising European industrialisation techniques. When Japan's export orientation was stymied in the years after the First World War, the ruling elite turned to militarism, brazen imperial conquest and borrowed fascist ideas, going into alliance with the Axis and initiating the Asian side of the Second World War. Korea and Taiwan, for example, were not merely dictatorships as they turned on the juice economically; they were also committed crucial junior allies of the USA in its Cold War, and keen participants in the Vietnam War. It can be argued that the USA was not going to insist on imposing an economic model on countries where stability and military commitment to the cause of anti-Communism were crucial; a reactionary foreign policy gave these states some policy freedom to defy metropolitan shibboleths.

A final subject which needs to be taken up is indeed Communism itself. How can we evaluate the development trajectory of the Soviet Union? A recent study of the Soviet experience, which seemed dispassionate and convincing to me, gives a far more nuanced account of this very difficult history. Allen's recent study, with considerable quantitative methodology applied, vindicates in large part the classic assessments of Deutscher and Carr. This is a huge lacuna in most of the developmental state literature. In the Soviet Union we confront on the one hand dramatic advances in industrialisation accompanied by big improvements in human welfare indicators and a massive shift in urbanisation with little unemployment after the first decade, plus, of course, the remarkable victory over Germany in the Second World War. On the other hand, there is both the abusive history in terms of human rights on a staggering scale but also a subsidence after half a century, never corrected, into long-term stagnation. How do we compare this to the somewhat different stories of the former so-called 'satellites' in eastern Europe? What of not merely China, but also Vietnam, Mongolia and North Korea? This is far too big a part of human history to push aside. So far left-wing experiments in the Americas, such as the Bolivarian revolution in Venezuela, have led to great achievements in social assistance and greater equality, notably in Cuba, but these have not been developmental success stories, and in particular success in altering historic dependency structures has been fairly limited.

I have tried to understand a little about contemporary Israel. Here is what seems like almost a model success story albeit with even the Jewish population increasingly affected by growing levels of inequality – a small country with a limited consumer market and little scope for heavy industrialisation but with a spectacularly successful military-industrial complex operating under the US penumbra and a striking proliferation of so-called start-ups based on information science expertise, a perfect exemplar for what seems to be happening technologically in the emerging twenty-first century (Senor and Singer 2009). However, here we have once again a country that it is too politically incorrect for the development literature to touch. The point here is not to celebrate the Israeli achievement but to point out that developmental success may well require nationalist commitment on the part of insiders; it is hardly essential to link it to a liberal or socialist notion of political or social emancipation for all. On the contrary, for the most part, Israel, as with mid-twentieth-century Japan or France, might be a site for developmentalism pursued by dedicated agencies in which the state and business collaborate within a formal democracy, but one's notion of democracy then needs to be qualified. If anything, Israel probably needs to be positioned as a somewhat distinct and contemporary version of the successful settler states.

We might finally turn from Israel to what might seem to be its opposite, the oil-laden Gulf states. Here we have shrewd rulers presiding over arid territory and small populations, completely lacking in orientation to many aspects of modern society. Creating a modern infrastructure is heavily dependent on foreigners so numerous that they outnumber the locals. Given that the ruling class has no intention whatsoever of creating cosmopolitan commonwealths and that there is little in the way of potential capitalist 'partners' with local credentials, the answer has been a policy of infrastructural growth and shrewd investments along with the patronage of Islam in whatever official version is orthodox. Favoured foreigners are certainly well rewarded. The scale of these countries makes industrialisation virtually an irrelevance. Oil, of course, provides for the foreign exchange. Developmentalism without industrialisation? Yet on this basis for decades these emirates have become the site of a different but not contemptible kind of success (not forgetting the often scandalous treatment of unorganised contract workers from elsewhere in Asia). Are these not developmental states cut to the cloth? A concluding comment must be that, if the developmental state literature is to have a future as more than a fad – as more than a journalistic device – it will have to be integrated into a broader historical view of economic development and the relationship between economic development and the state in different and specific conjunctures.

To place the old South Africa, one has to cast aside the idea that developmental states are particularly democratic or indeed democratic at all. At this point, taking on-board these considered limitations, I initiate the project of writing a new kind of economic history of South Africa that follows from these premises. Having outlined some of the ideas suggested through taking in this new paradigm, in what follows I wish specifically to pursue South Africa as it existed between the Union of 1910, after which it was essentially an independent country, and 1990, when negotiations began that created a deracialised citizenship and an inclusive democracy.[8]

During these 80 years it will be argued that South Africa achieved considerable success from the point of view of economic development.[9] Deep structural furrows were ploughed. The historiography of the country during these decades revolves around its inequities and the unfair treatment of the black majority, descendants of those people who lived in the region before the coming of Europeans. The origins, development and contradictions in the segregation and apartheid systems, together with the resistance movements that tried to undermine them, are the subject of a great many distinguished historical works

[8] For preliminary approaches see Freund 2007a; 2009; 2013b.

[9] There are various South African writers on political economy who do not use the same paradigm proffered here but have written not so differently in essence.

written by liberal and radical critics. In general, the economic structure of the country and how it altered has usually been a backdrop to this dramatic story.[10] In this book, without wanting in any way to take away from the importance and value of this historical tradition, I wish instead to put the racial system somewhat in the background and place the economy, and in particular the relations that linked state to economic development, to the centre of the picture for once. The racial definition of the citizenry and the emergence of the Bantustan system were of course part of the conception of this state and loomed large in the intensification of economic contradictions.

Viewing South Africa as a developmental state does not make it any nicer or less problematic than it seemed before. However, it creates another lens which is particularly interesting because the economic inheritance of those times, of that history, may no longer contain much coherence but it is still there both in terms of concrete and bricks and in terms of what sits in the heads of South Africans. Mbeki's proclamation of the democratic developmental state as the goal of the African National Congress (ANC), essentially still bruited by his successor Jacob Zuma, needs to be evaluated critically and with a view to the past.[11] For an historical understanding, it is also valuable to grasp that in terms of the possibilities available in the 1940s, the United Party government under General Jan Christiaan Smuts and the policies it pursued following wartime exercises in planning fitted the criteria of a developmental state remarkably well at a crucial time in the history of South Africa. Social policy, which has received some attention from historians, formed an important part of the planning thinking of this period and I have myself written on the formulation of health policy in this light, but here I propose to say relatively little about this except as it fits a broader developmental canvas.[12]

In what follows, a hopefully graceful understanding of developmentalism in South Africa is proposed by identifying three distinct thrusts

[10] For an example, Ivor Chipkin (2016: 216) recently noted Marks and Trapido's *The Politics of Race, Class and Nationalism in South Africa*, I would say by its very title, as putting forward the central themes dominating South African historiography.

[11] I have tried to do this elsewhere at two different junctures: Freund 1997; 2008.

[12] Much of the scholarly attention has been directed to independent thinking and initiatives about society and race, for which there was some space in this historic phase although the limits to which such approaches were tolerated as serious policy projects must also be stressed (Freund 2012).

whose trajectories will recur in this book. The first of these is usually identified with the idea of Reconstruction after the Boer War. One could compare this to the developmental efforts of Britain in its African colonies after the Second World War, but in South Africa the stakes were much higher and the commitment much greater. South Africa was effectively put together as a working operation by the British. The infrastructural and economic aspects of this process were critical to what followed in fact. However, undoubtedly the imperial interests came first and the slant was towards Britain as guardian and guiding leader of Reconstruction as well, of course, as a substantial beneficiary.

The second thrust is to be associated especially with Smuts' second phase as prime minister between 1939 and 1948. As we shall see, the state and its relationship with business at a period of severe crisis for Britain was able to, and did, function to a large extent along the lines of a nascent developmental state. The top planners with Smuts' approval placed critical emphasis on heavy industry.[13] After 1948 (but not immediately afterwards), Afrikaner Nationalists changed significant elements in the model in order at first to give priority to their own sectional interests, which especially involved promoting Afrikaners as businessmen and as government officials. This can be singled out as a third distinct thrust, with a vision that contrasted with that of Smuts – but by no means entirely. As Hendrik Verwoerd became more powerful as Minister of Native Affairs and eventually premier, there was also the increasing commitment to racial partition as an ideal, which certainly distorted the model in a new direction previously only developed sketchily and of very secondary importance. In the later apartheid period, significant reform initiatives were juxtaposed with the growing salience of security issues and big-scale militarisation as well as the threat of sanctions, which became gradually more serious. This third thrust, the apartheid thrust, as we shall see at first enjoyed some major successes but eventually fell into conflict and contradiction.

However, if one compares contemporary South Africa to a developmental ideal only to dismiss the outcome as a complete failure, the picture is in danger of being shaped more by moralistic precepts

[13] It is not perhaps uninteresting that Samir Amin also believed that heavy industry tied to mineral production, rather than the conventional light industrial model, should be central in West African development planning (Amin 1973).

than a full consideration of the situation. The 2016 figures record a manufacturing workforce that, despite deindustrialisation, still exceeds 1,600,000, impressive by African standards. Heavy industry has far from disappeared; in fact, industrial decline has arguably been more dramatic in consumer goods industries such as clothing. Post-apartheid South Africa has also witnessed the remarkably successful material adjustment of whites, the intended beneficiaries of previous development planning, despite their large-scale departure from state employment and certainly from official preference. This is not just a question of so-called 'white monopoly capital', the corporate wealth and economic power largely dominant and in the hands of a relatively few. The percentage of young whites receiving higher education and training is much higher than ever before, perhaps today a majority, and it reflects capital built up in households during the apartheid era. The build-up of skills and education as well as capital has in fact had a long-term positive effect and looks like an effective platform despite overall economic stagnation or very slow economic growth, depending on the years used to assess statistical change.

It thus places the emphasis in terms of negative impact of the social system not on conquest or loss of land but on exclusion from the benefits of industrialisation. This is remarkable in the face of the common wisdom in black society that secure state employment based on formal educational criteria is itself overwhelmingly the road to a better life. State employment certainly played a beneficial historical role for whites, notably for Afrikaners, but it was accompanied by other advantageous processes nurtured by the state. Instead of simply deploring this, perhaps one should rather learn from it.

This book reads as follows:

- Chapter 1: White-run South Africa as a Developmental State: An Interpretive Economic History of Twentieth-Century South Africa
- Chapter 2: The Conflicted Foundations of Industrial Policy
- Chapter 3: Industrial Development in South Africa up to the Second World War: Some Figures and Some Business History
- Chapter 4: A (Near) Developmental State Forms 1939–48
- Chapter 5: The Impact of Apartheid 1948–73
- Chapter 6: The Parastatals ISCOR and SASOL
- Chapter 7: Key Institutions: The IDC, the CSIR, the HSRC

- Chapter 8: The Company Towns of the Vaal Triangle
- Chapter 9: Energy and the Natural Environment
- Chapter 10: Developmentalism Dismantled
- Conclusion: The Developmental State Today

Chapter 1 is projected as an introduction with a theoretical discussion. An exposition of the first, second and third trajectories respectively will dominate the following chapters. In the second and third chapters, we shall look at foundations and assess the strengths and weaknesses of the economy before 1940. This already involved important state interventions. It is important to build an analysis on what did exist at this time rather than assume a *tabula rasa* as might be assumed in a purely economic assessment of development à la Rostow.

However, industrialisation, while it found a local market, largely remained confined to consumer goods manufacture and to economic activity that relied on agricultural/pastoral activities. Primary product exports from such activities were overtaken by gold mining. Trade in gold dominated South Africa's relatively extraverted economy. Yet society was experiencing rapid urbanisation and decline in self-sufficiency as consumer purchases became fundamental to life. In Chapter 4, the second trajectory kicks in and an account of the attempt to found something like a developmental state is made. This is an attempt that does not negate either the racial exclusivism of the white electorate or the dependence on gold, which it now aims to harness to new purposes, and on cheap coal-based energy applied on a huge scale. Chapter 5 takes the story beyond 1948 to look at the third trajectory, and considers to what extent apartheid carried through on this impulse up to the mid-1970s. Chapters 6 and 7 will look critically at some central institutions associated with the developmental state prospectus and their history and significance. Chapter 8 is urban history; it concentrates on the Vaal Triangle cities, which were established to service new parastatals and how they developed up to 1990. This chapter contains a strong element of social as well as institutional history. It at least opens the door to adding the human dimension to the picture. How did developmentalism impact on people's lives and vice versa? Chapter 9 considers the key question of energy and key linking formations within South African capitalism. It really follows particularly from the 1996 book of Fine and Rustomjee that proposed to understand the economy in terms of a Minerals and Energy complex (Fine and Rustomjee 1996). Their study is the most important relatively recent critical analysis of the South African economy and in fact has been a platform on which the unfolding picture below is constructed. Chapter 10 looks at the crisis of the 1970s, where initiatives associated with the developmental state's further articulation and growth hit the rocks and led to problematic adjustments. The Conclusion considers contemporary perspectives relatively briefly. I have elsewhere tried to explain the circumstances under which the policy framework of the 'New South Africa' emerged (Freund 2013a) and, of course, other studies considering this by the likes of Patrick Bond and Hein Marais, amongst others, exist.

The academic foundation for this study is variable. In some areas, notably the energy-related pages or considerations of the military build-up of the late apartheid years, I am reliant on the work of others very largely. For institutional histories particularly I have delved into the state archives substantially and, for instance, the library holdings of the Industrial Development Corporation (IDC). On the Vaal Triangle towns, I have also used more wide-ranging sources including contemporary interviews. I also rely here, in the case of Sasolburg, on the University of Michigan PhD of my colleague Steve Sparks of the History Department, University of Johannesburg and, for environmental issues, on the Wits PhD of Victor Munnik. This is an approach which permits the methodological approach associated with the use of quantitative evidence as well as the tools of a social historian with a particular interest in economic structures. The deductive unfolding of economic laws or correlations would not fit this trajectory given the emphasis that will be placed on institutions and on structural changes within economic processes. Here there is some relationship to the new institutional economic history associated with Douglass North and his many followers, albeit not on their method stressing quantitative deductions. As such, it is an argument for the value of a more holistic understanding of economic history.

There is room for far more research in this area and I hope this book will inspire more writing that considers the issues at hand. As the narrative in preceding pages indicates, the developmental state model seems to me valid and a useful way of discussing South African economic growth in the twentieth century. However, this model was only to a very limited extent democratic and its social context was both noxious and in a profound way contradictory over time. This does not necessarily mean discarding the developmental state trajectory entirely, however. In the words of Mushtaq Khan, one of my favourite currently active writers in the development field, '[t]he first part of the policy challenge is to identify the main contracting failures blocking a particular goal'. He adds another challenge which hopefully I begin to address here: 'Economics can't be done by people who don't know history.'[14]

[14] APORDE lecture, 4 September 2014, Hilton Hotel Johannesburg. For a way of overcoming the shallow and unsatisfactory conventional liberal view of corruption in development studies, see Khan and Sudaram 2000.

2 *The Conflicted Foundations of Industrial Policy*

Preliminary History

There is little to suggest from cultural studies, social structure or the history we know that pre-colonial African societies, in what is today South Africa, were heading for the development of a market society. Certainly there was a strong notion of wealth, largely defined in terms of livestock and ultimately access to the labour of people, some specialised economic activity and exchange, but organised commerce on a professional basis or coinage is not known to have existed. States in the sense of structured bureaucracies did not exist nor did any form of literacy. There were some larger human agglomerations on the edge of the Kalahari, mainly in what is today Botswana, but they lacked most of the features we would call urban. Indeed, the cattle outposts actually engaged the most critical economic activities even in these societies. This is not to say that they did not have scope for the exhibition of creativity and art or for providing human beings with multifold forms of satisfaction. There is reason to see this as related to a long-term stability as kin and clan created and recreated themselves in a continuous relationship with the available natural resources. European visitors in the age of Enlightenment were often charmed and impressed by the people they met. With the decline of Romanticism and the dominance of calculation and material progress in valuing culture, these same people were dismissed as backward and troublesome by Westerners, in need at least of being taken in hand, if not pushed away entirely.

From the end of the fifteenth century, however, ships from Europe hoping to circumvent the Muslim-controlled eastern seas began to use the very long Cape Route and introduce South Africans to new forms of wealth and commerce. In 1652, the Dutch East India Company, representing perhaps the most economically advanced corner of Europe, took possession of Table Bay. In the next century and a half, Dutch rule came to encompass more or less the present-day Western Cape Province. In this corner of the African continent, economic life had almost entirely hinged on the ownership of livestock plus some foraging and hunting. As a result, while an agricultural potential was there, it was almost entirely unused and the population density was thin and made thinner through devastating new disease and the violent eruption of Dutchmen armed with muskets. The older population was driven out or incorporated as servants in a context of almost total dispossession over several generations. Here a new kind of society was born and, in Marxist terms, a new mode of production emerged, eventually enveloping and overtaking what was there before.[1]

There are probably two key features to the Cape Colony that need to be mentioned, even in this very brief summary. The first is that this was a colony attached to a global commercial system with its other main links in Asia – Indonesia, Sri Lanka, etc. in modern terms – and to Dutch trade with Asia. The dominant social milieu, including ideas about race, derived from this system even though its economic prowess was in definite decline from the early eighteenth century onward. A striking aspect of this was the demographic weight of the capital – Cape Town, Tavern of the Seas, with its large garrison and sea traffic – where there was little other urban life at all. Servicing that traffic and the needs of the garrison were paramount and an economic stimulus in good times. The second aspect, which was different from the situation in eastern seas, was the dominance in society and economy of the institution of slavery. Slaves soon came to outnumber free individuals. Although slavery and racial hierarchy were not identical through the Dutch period (and the slaves came in large part from Madagascar or from southern Asia and were thus not exactly African at point of capture), they did underline a powerful association that would have struck all residents.

This was not a plantation system geared towards the production of a desirable commodity. The temperate climate of the Cape and its distance from Dutch markets prevented such a system. Cape Town can in this sense be compared to contemporary New York or Buenos Aires, where many slaves also lived. Cape agriculture was focused on

[1] Although its use as a term has some limits due to the high level of abstraction, it is in my view a shame that the conceptual strength of the mode of production has been abandoned by Marxists themselves (Freund 1985).

growing grain and tending vineyards; soldiers and sailors were key customers. A large part of the slave population lived in the town and numerous slaves actually were fitted out by masters for commercial purposes and able to keep a fraction of the earnings from any sales.

The wealthy colonists often had their hands in a multitude of activities. They kept inns, sold a variety of goods to those coming off the ships, owned agricultural farms outright and possessed vast loan farms deeper in the interior where they kept cattle and sheep acquired from the inhabitants often by questionable means. The beautiful houses of the Boland are testimony to successful accumulation on the part of some. From early on, a settler community developed a sense of common purpose and their own economic ideas. For instance, a few dreamt by the late eighteenth century of harnessing ships to go east and fetch slaves. Commandos of frontiersmen raided native people, seizing children as client workers, taking over herds of livestock and hunting for game. The state (for one now certainly existed) was frustrated at the autonomy of these settlers and their penchant for making war and alliances as they liked, but in the end depended on their growing numbers and prosperity. Before 1800 there was already a recognisable, if modest, settler capitalism although it had no pretensions to challenge the European-derived commercial impetus. At the same time, settler society included significant numbers of poor property-less whites as well as much larger numbers of people of colour, many of whom were desperately poor. The colour line was not very well defined. The most far-seeing administrators, by contrast, wanted to replace the slave system with something securer and more in line with commercial capitalism. This meant finding an export outlet for Cape produce; the best candidate for such an export lay in the flourishing vast sheep population in the dry country of the interior.[2]

The history of nineteenth-century South Africa and its neighbours is so complex in terms of political history, deals and conflicts that exploring it in any detail is inappropriate to the story being told in this book. Adventuresome colonials found space and strength to establish themselves as they looked for autonomy, but also economic possibilities, spilling out of the old colony in the Great Trek which gathered strength from 1834 to 1835. In time wars brought about the subordination of

2 Based on research done long ago for my dissertation, I have summarised my own perspective on this era in Elphick and Giliomee, 1989.

numerous local African populations, which became payers of tribute or shareholders on the land, or were driven off entirely with somewhat different outcomes in different regions. Some of the land in the well-watered eastern half of the present-day South Africa remained in the hands of chiefs who accepted colonial authority in the end and controlled distribution to followers; these gradually became, with each generation, more dependent on cash incomes but rarely succeeded in any kind of capitalist accumulation. The white frontiersmen were attracted to products of the hunt, to income as transport riders and to ownership of cattle and sheep more than to agriculture. They formed a succession of political units that slowly stabilised where white racial self-consciousness drew ever-deeper lines in terms of privilege and access to resources, although whites formed barely one-fifth of the population at the time of Union in 1910. Some of this occurred within the emergent interior republics of the Orange Free State and the South African Republic and some of it under British aegis in the coastal colonies, which had expanded so as to isolate the autonomous republics from international connections.

Once the British secured the Western Cape from the Dutch – permanently in 1806 – a kind of prosperity ensued, partly to the benefit of a new generation of British immigrant merchants, through the opening of the British market to Cape wine. This short phase ended when cheaper wine from Portugal and elsewhere could again enter that market after the close of the Napoleonic Wars and subsequent commercial treaties had been signed. With the import of white wool sheep whose fleece could be washed, sorted and made available for cloth manufacture, the arid parts of the country did acquire a significant export market, and in mid-century, the Cape Midlands and Port Elizabeth began to rival the Boland and Cape Town as the economic centre of the country. However, the climatic scope for this was less extensive than in Australasia or southern South America; it was a limited development. The British did indeed abolish slavery. While the ex-slaves had very little access to land and thus were in a poor position to bargain for better wages, abolition did not lead to a flourishing of free labour-based capitalist production, as the ideologues would have it. While the economy did not collapse, it went through a long phase of slow growth in which property tended to shift around between family members (Dooling 2008).

In the final third of the nineteenth century, this situation was radically transformed by what a wide consensus of historians label as the 'Mineral Revolution'. The discovery of a massive deposit of diamonds in Kimberley, quickly and firmly claimed by the British as part of the Cape Colony in 1867 (Turrell 1987; Worger 1987), was a prelude to the far more spectacular and consequential discovery of a reliable long seam of gold in the Witwatersrand ridge of the southern South African Republic in 1885. Once this seam could be technologically accessed and the gold separated out systematically, this revolution put South Africa on the world map of the rapidly emerging globalised capitalist economy as the major producer of these commodities, true notably for gold, the basis for the valuation of the money system, by the early twentieth century (Allen 1992; Johnstone 1976). It had massive implications (van Onselen 1982). The mines required great concentrations of labour, skilled and unskilled, access to a large capital market and a very broad range of infrastructure, notoriously at first dynamite but also metals, wood and other raw materials. In addition, railways had to be built and urban sites, above all the new city of Johannesburg, developed from nothing. Spatially, the economic heart of South Africa shifted from the line of coastal ports to the British conquered province of Transvaal, somewhat north of the centre of the country as determined in its established twentieth-century borders.

The old century ended with a war – by far South Africa' s bloodiest – in which the backward South African Republic, so undeserving of this windfall discovery, was conquered by the British, whose core position in global capitalism was increasingly focused on the strength of London as a financial centre. The Anglo-Boer War can be interpreted in two ways, to make a very long story short. It can reflect the impulse on the part of the British Establishment to modulate and control economic and social development in the southern part of the African continent based on establishing a firm system for securing the needs of this gigantic new mining industry in a stable way. If even large mining operations often eventually lead to ghost towns after a raw history in which urban amenities are few and expensive, South Africa was the classic case of the mines becoming the core activity of a new and complex society, attracting immigrants from all over the world as well as dispossessed, and ambitious, locals of all colours and backgrounds. Controlling this required a multifaceted, experienced state which the British were prepared to initiate. This story has been given classic form by two iconic figures from South African historiography: Shula Marks and the late Stanley Trapido (Marks and Trapido 1979). However, one could also create a somewhat different story whereby the South African Republic might gradually have played this role itself, led by new and more sophisticated leaders such as the young Jan Christiaan Smuts and linked, perhaps via the Mozambique rail connection, to Britain's competitors and rivals. This was the plausible hypothesis of J.S. Marais, a historian of a previous generation – and it was certainly feared by the post-war proconsul, Lord Milner (Marais 1961).[3]

Some of the challenging issues of the day were very directly economic. Thus the mines needed ore to be crushed, sifted and shipped to the coast. Where originally there were no lines of rail, several competing ones were developed and their claims had to be sorted out, ideally by a dominant state, and suitable ports developed. The mines were massive consumers of materiel such as timber, but in addition, the workforce, which reached six figures by the time the war broke out and doubled again a decade later following peace and Reconstruction, needed food, shelter and clothing. The interior provinces favoured low tariffs on foreign imports, expensive enough as they were, to allow needed supplies into their workshops and ultimately lower wages, while the coastal provinces had railway rates and customs duties as the main source of revenue and inclined towards protectionist measures.[4] Unskilled workers had to be recruited and inured into work practices that were extremely dangerous to life and limb. Organisation had to be instilled that could cope like a military force with thousands of workers at a time. Skilled workers had to be brought from overseas, their skills had to be nurtured, but their outsize wages also needed to be reduced. In time, some were followed by their wives and children. This meant producing the basics more cheaply and

[3] Some such as Lord Selborne believed however that this would require some kind of deal between the republican President Kruger and the largely British mining capitalists or Randlords and their *uitlander* leaders on the Rand (Headlam I, 1931, letter from Selborne to Milner, 21 January 1898). Marais contains an interesting discussion of the Transvaal Industrial Commission of 1897 towards which British views were ambivalent. It was not really possible for the ZAR state, however, to put its policies into practice.

[4] This interestingly is the one economic issue Leonard Thompson took up in his standard work on the unification of South Africa, 1960. It was obviously a major bone of contention in negotiations.

systematically, which was at first completely beyond the capacity of the regional economy. Throughout South Africa, this was a call for a more productive agricultural surplus but also offered opportunities to crafts and urban businesses. Here, too, law and order, tussled over between those workers with the rights of citizens and their bosses, had to be worked out and installed.

From the point of view of this study, Reconstruction after the war contained both positive and negative elements. In some respects, the idea involved an indigenisation of development according to the latest Western norms that could only ultimately transform South African society. Even the arch-imperialist Lord Milner was a fervent believer in the value of enskilling and educating South Africans. He was also a strong proponent of the modernisation of agriculture and its technical development as fundamental.[5] It was in Milner's time that the South African Association for the Advancement of Science was founded in 1901 and helped transform what Dubow calls 'South Africa's rudimentary scientific infrastructure' (2006, 168). He was a strong supporter of the creation of a residential teaching university in Cape Town and especially anxious to promote knowledge of the flora of the country and scientific methods in agriculture, notably through the foundation of the Botanical Gardens at Kirstenbosch and the impressive veterinary establishment that arose in the Transvaal at Onderstepoort (Dubow 2005, notably 77, but see also Nell 2000 and Brown 2005). A look at his papers reveals a powerful overall concept of what Milner felt was needed to make a unified South Africa into a growing proposition.

However, with his general contempt for local knowledge, he saw all this in terms of the benefits that would accrue to Britain. He would become, as with the former Colonial Secretary Joseph Chamberlain, a strong supporter of free trade within the British colonial orbit of a global Commonwealth economy. This was a vision which could easily lend itself to a situation where the metropole Britain produced the industrial goods and offered finance as well as situating the highest

[5] '... Milner, who oversaw the early years of reconstruction, was determined to make the Transvaal a prosperous colony by promoting gold mining on the Witwatersrand, as well as making agricultural production, primarily by white, and preferably British, settler farmers. Milner believed in the imperial ideal that the empire should pay for itself' (Brown 2005, 516).

level of skills while the colonies efficiently produced the raw materials Britain needed.[6] It fitted the thinking of a Britain where free trade was considered to be, if ideally, a desideratum, under threat from more or less under-handed competitors – the USA, Germany and even Japan (Kaplan 1976, 79). On the other hand, Milner also thought the South African gold mines should cough up a large bounty in taxes to pay for some of the reforms he thought critical (Headlam, v. 2, 1933). Thus Reconstruction and Milner's so-called 'Kindergarten' of top advisors were both arch-imperialists and promoters of state assistance to key forms of economic development.

This is not, however, to take away from what has always made Milner notorious, his attempt to quash Afrikaner nationalism, built up to a new level by the war and his British chauvinism. He hoped that mounting immigration would lead to a British male voting majority where in fact the war ushered in a period of recession on the mines, overwhelmed at first by structural problems once the Republic disintegrated. With Milner's return to England, however, it is the very plausible view of Saul Dubow that Lionel Phillips and other members of the Kindergarten (or Kitchen Cabinet) aimed instead to reconcile with moderate Boers and create a way forward that they would find acceptable. Here the defeated Cape-born general, J.C. Smuts, was to play a critical role initially alongside Louis Botha, the first Union prime minister, in what Dubow calls 'South Africanism' (Dubow 1997). Although Dubow tends to skirt around economic issues, South Africanism certainly was firmly embedded in ideas about economic progress and capitalist development as the means to forge a new nation, the nation which the Liberal government in Britain was prepared to preside over in negotiations after 1906. He has also given us our main serious study of the history of science in South Africa, unfortunately with too little emphasis on technology (Dubow 2000; 2005). Here again he views South Africanism as an outlook which created a bridge between Briton and Boer. Building local knowledge fitted the continuous development of South African expertise and initiatives, not at all the Milnerite view of subordination and assimilation to a British norm. However, in

6 This kind of mood did not dissipate for a long time. Thus naively as late as 1930 as the Great Depression started to kick in, *The Round Table*, 21, 82, 1930, pointed out that the best advantage for South Africa in the Commonwealth preference system lay in the access to Britain of relatively expensive sugar exports, 462.

considering Smuts and his intellectual lieutenant J.H. Hofmeyr, later a critically important University of the Witwatersrand vice-chancellor, he notes that this development could and did develop under what was still a British penumbra. As a young man after the war, Smuts still believed that the mines should really be 'the heritage of the workers of South Africa' (Smuts, v. 2, 1966, 313). At this point he still posed the interests of the country against the 'money power' but he came to support the dictates of the mining industry, notably against the militant actions of workers, both black and white, and to feel that a South African vision should transcend the Boer versus Briton bifurcation of good and evil.

South Africanism would have, perhaps in theory, been an ideological opening to a yet broader conception of the South African people, but this would have worked directly against the common sense of almost all white South Africans and notably of Smuts.[7] An editorial in *The State* even before Union laid out this view, citing a commission report for the once again self-governing Transvaal on the mining industry in 1909:

> . . . the other great issue, remote as it appears to-day, namely, whether the vast expanses of South Africa, so eminently adapted to white occupation, shall be the home of a great white people or be the habitation and breeding place of

[7] For a single sample from an influential voice, see Selborne to Smuts, 'No one can have any experience of the two races without feeling the intrinsic superiority of the white man' in Smuts v. 2, 1966, 379. Smuts himself, beyond the prejudices of his youth and his lifelong distaste for political perspectives from sources beyond the white community, was a pragmatist in terms of white values and tended to go with what would secure a reasonable electoral majority if possible. Thus in 1908 he wrote to the anti-imperialist economist Hobson that '[t]he political status of the Native is no doubt a very important matter but vastly more important to me is the Union of South Africa'. Smuts strongly favoured the compromise which kept the non-racial franchise in the Cape, but only in the Cape (Smuts 1966, 441, Smuts to Hobson, 13 July 1908). His own vision was one of exclusion and segregation (Smuts 1917). He endorsed Rhodes' opinions in this regard (Smuts, 19, v. 5, 1973, pp. 368–70, Smuts to Leo Amery, 13 February 1928). He certainly had a vision of South Africa as a 'great white civilisation', leading a colonised and very large portion of the African continent on a highly racialised basis (Smuts to Amery, 22 May 1928, in Smuts, v. 5, 1973).

He was very hostile to British proponents, such as Lord Lugard, who saw East Africa, for instance, as being held in some sense in trust for black Africans (Hancock 1968). His belief in what Dubow has called 'scientism' and the application of scientific expertise to African development was widely shared by people such as Joseph Chamberlain, Milner and Leo Amery (Hodge 2007). The British created a department of Research and Industry to this end in 1917 (97).

masses of natives and other coloured people of mixed races, in all degrees of semi-barbarism and semi-civilization (10 September 1909, 300).

No question as to which of these was desirable for the makers of the Union and indeed their ideas about territories further north.

Even in Britain and certainly amongst English-speaking white South Africans, this was the view of most and the British government was unprepared to stand in the way of South African racism. The Cape establishment believed in retaining the voting rights that existed in the new parliament (but only for white representatives) but that was the one limitation imposed before Union came into being in 1910.

Development Issues in the Interwar Years

The remainder of this chapter will be far narrower in scope, focusing on the characteristic but important debates of the time. These debates took developmental ideas further than before. It will be left to the following chapter to describe the character of the actual economy. During the first generation after the formation of the Union of South Africa, national industrial-cum-economic policy focused on the levying of tariffs on imported goods. Tariffs were a major public question openly debated both in policy circles and by academics. Shortly after Union, Parliament convoked the Cullinan Commission, which reported back in 1912 (UG 10 1912). The Commission took for granted the need for the state to take measures to protect agriculture and to extend tariff payments to a variety of imported goods which needed to be evaluated. It recommended the creation of a suitable Advisory Board to deal with such matters. The Commission was headed by Sir Thomas Cullinan, whose Transvaal Refractories family business built on urbanisation and mining needs. One vice-president was the ambitious industrial pioneer Sammy Marks. Both of these individuals will receive more attention in the following chapter.

The Commission was aware of the situation at the time, whereby early industries were one-off propositions substituting for specific widely used import categories and lacking in any sort of integration into national frameworks. There was already (p. 61) an interest in the possibility of iron and steel manufacture in South Africa (the key to David Landes' view of a Second Industrial Revolution internationally), noting that a small metal manufacture already existed in Natal. In fact, the state envisioned itself as a purchaser of much of the production of the iron ore mines that had begun production outside the national capital of Pretoria (Schirmer 2008, 41, 17). Tariff considerations also needed to be joined to discussions about critical railway rates, so crucial as the Witwatersrand, far from the coast, took off as the centre for industrial growth. Tariffs and railway rates also had to differentiate between finished products and the raw materials required for manufacture. There was also an awareness of the need for the creation of plausible national economic statistical data and for the accumulation and availability of investment capital.

The food requirements of the urban population were not yet being met by South African farmers and substantial amounts of grainstuffs, sugar and sugar products, pork products and even dairy products were being imported (Schirmer 2008, 41, 17). Thus the whole question of the modernisation of agriculture was at stake. The notorious Land Act of 1913 which followed was not merely an attempt to oust small-scale African cultivators from fertile land as it is conventionally considered; it was also aimed at cutting down on dysfunctional white hired help (*bywoners*) and those whites who simply extracted rent from black tenants, destroying their livelihoods and bringing them into towns where they could better be put to work in industrial concerns. This was essentially a continuation of the Reconstruction project and views that went back to Milner – a process which, it could be argued, has still not run its course today.

If there was a distinctive and unusual feature to the Cullinan Commission's view of tariffs, it lay in the emphasis on using protection against imports in order to prop up the situation of white workers. These appeared to need land reform programmes that would benefit them and technical education to train them to become skilled industrial, or indeed mines, employees, skills that barely existed amongst South African-born individuals in 1912. The advantages held by the coastal provinces of Natal and the Cape were reckoned not so much in terms of transport costs, but because of the substantial Indian and Coloured populations (but particularly the latter), more skilled than Africans and well able to compete with white workers from the point of view of costs given the racialised systems that prevailed. Not only was it foreseen that industries should be forced to hire a particular percentage of whites, but bounties were proposed to those that exceeded that percentage. These eerie racist ideas are a striking parallel to the post-1994 ANC so-called 'BEE [Black Economic Empowerment] strictures' on land reform and employment, strictures that depend on the continuing definition of all workers in South Africa by race, just as before, but now to benefit the disadvantaged blacks.

In fact, opinion about tariffs was very divided in the government itself and little transpired at first (Kaplan 1976). On the one hand, business interests dependent on large-scale importing wanted a free trade regime especially within the British Commonwealth, while others were more orientated to building up a national economy. This latter group fitted very well the ideological construct of a South Africanist identity and loyalty that has been so well explored by Belinda Bozzoli, as well as Dubow (Bozzoli 1981; Dubow 1997). After 1919 as premier and then after 1924 in opposition, Jan Christiaan Smuts tried to balance these two sides.[8] Smuts was also specifically concerned that protection would benefit weak industrial endeavours that could only be costly; it was the potentially strong who needed support. Smuts specifically supported 'discriminating protection for those industries especially suited to the country' when campaigning in 1924 (Hancock 1968; Kaplan 1976).

In fact, Steven Schirmer has recently argued that, rhetoric aside, the more serious protectionism came before 1924 and before the tariff system was generated. He argues that it had led to more rapid industrial growth (albeit that was partly in fact simply a response to international economic rhythms). By this token, Smuts' view that Pact policies privileged undeserving individuals and made little sense broadly speaking was correct (Schirmer 2008; 2009).[9] In particular, he notes the growing public presence of protectionist W.J. Laite, whose writing Smuts certainly liked. Smuts no doubt helped Laite's appointment to the First World War Munitions Committee.[10]

[8] Bozzoli 1981 is probably right that, just as emerges from Vivek Chibber's research on India, in this period, business hoped that the state would more or less do what it wanted. She also suggests that in post-Second World War South Africa, Anglo-American, with its towering economic importance, found a chief executive in Harry Oppenheimer, a man who lived and died in South Africa, who embraced a considerable part of the 'South Africanist' ethos that assumed autonomy from, if not conflict with, British interests, and a wide-ranging attitude to economic development of the country.

[9] But see Martin 1990 for the opposite view.

[10] Thus in 1920 Smuts wrote to Laite that 'I need your services in connection with the large policy of industrial development which both you and I have been

He led the Industries Advisory Board during the war years, when it was restructured into the Tariff Committee and then the Board of Trades and Industries (Kooy and Robertson 1966). Laite is a key figure for Bozzoli as ideologue, and a family biography exists that recollects his ideas (Laite 1943).

Laite was himself a British immigrant. Unusually, he became sympathetic to the struggles of workers over the course of a big London dockworkers' strike, but also for the losers of the great South African war. It was only after war's end that he moved to South Africa, hoping to recover his health. Instead of joining the Labour Party, Laite stayed with the South African and later United Party while keeping an open door to Afrikaner Nationalists. It was Smuts who authorised the creation of the Board of Trade and Industries in 1922, which he envisioned as a key regulator on these issues; it began to be more forthright than its predecessor Advisory Board of Industry and Science (Martin 1990). The Ministry of Mines and Industries got along well with and co-operated with the Federated Chamber of Industries formed in 1917.[11] The Chamber was founded and headed by Laite, failed businessman but remarkable protagonist for the cause of secondary industry, who had discovered the potential of protectionism (Laite 1943).[12] Its predecessor, the increasingly influential Transvaal Chamber of Industries, had certainly favoured protection and tariffs for South African produced industrial goods (*Transvaal Chamber of Industries 1910–1960*). Laite noted especially the dominance of British imperial interests in banking and stressed the importance of South Africa acquiring its own domestically sourced national bank(s); he regularly denounced the importers, Cape Town's 'merchant princes'.[13]

advocating' (Laite 1943, 57). Laite equally became friendly with Sammy Marks, the pioneer industrialist discussed in Chapter 3, who also can be said to have shared much of this outlook. Interestingly Laite stayed with Smuts politically rather than join with the Pact. His atypicality is striking; his two attempts at running for a parliamentary seat failed.

11 This was particularly true when F.S. Malan with his close links to Graaff and Cape capitalists was minister. Hertzog's financial guru, Nicolaas Havenga, was by contrast, notorious for his parsimoniousness.

12 He had previously been head of the South African Manufacturers Association, established in 1905.

13 Indeed one of his election losses was against J.W. Jagger in Cape Town who certainly qualified as royalty of this sort (Kooy and Robertson 1966).

He believed that

> no country has ever become prosperous that did not produce, and by that I mean manufactures as well as undertake farming and mining. (Laite 1943, 35)

> South Africa must manufacture goods for itself, or be doomed to perpetual under-development, or rather lop-sided development until the mines give out . . . (36)

Like Smuts, Laite had a sub-imperial view of Africa and was a strong proponent for the development of central and eastern Africa at least as an outlet for South African manufactures.[14] He reconnoitred in Africa already in the days of his Munitions Committee activities.

Renfrew Christie has argued that the ticket towards a major industrialisation drive in South Africa had to be electrification. This was at first the task of the Victoria Falls and Transvaal Power Co. Ltd, formed by Cecil Rhodes' British South Africa Company, although largely engineered by AEG (Allgemeine Elektricitäts-Gesellschaft AG) and more advanced German technology (Christie 1984, 20). By 1914, when the war broke out, these were the 'world's largest power works' (Christie 1984, 43). However, the VFTPC (Transvaal Power Company) system was thoroughly dominated by the need to service the mines, although it was also expanded to help power trams in Johannesburg, for instance. With the coming of the Union, Lord Selborne sponsored a Commission of Inquiry into the Power Companies in his new role of first governor-general leading to the passage of the Power Bill of 1910. Under Smuts' leadership, Sir William Hoy then played a critical role in electrifying the state-run railway system, which Renfrew Christie argues was a key step (Christie 1984). Hoy formed a kind of triumvirate in Christie's opinion together with Robert Kotze as Government Mining Engineer and Sir Thomas Price in charge of the railways (note again the importance of railway rates in a country where both agricultural and industrial interests, as well as mining, were focused well into the interior of the country) in the first days of Union. As Dubow emphasises, further economic development hinged very directly on effective state intervention (Dubow 2006, 206).

[14] Hodge (2007) proposes that Smuts' view, insofar as the need for development in Africa to be posited on scientific study as a basis for investment and economic decisions, was actually very similar to those percolating in Britain by people such as Leo Amery and Joseph Chamberlain. There was some acceptance that inevitably whites resident in Africa would play a big role here.

The Smuts government was also successful in creating the Electricity Supply Commission (ESCOM) in 1922 through the Electricity Act. Here the young brilliant scientist Hendrik van der Bijl, a family friend for Smuts, was enticed back to South Africa from America in 1920. His career belongs really to discussion in Chapter 4, but he was already primed to be what he became in time, the great economic czar and industrial promoter of the mid-twentieth century in South Africa. A Scientific and Technical Committee leading to the appointment of an Advisory Board of Industry and Sciences, as well as a permanent science advisor to the prime minister was also a feature. The old South African Party government presided over the formation of a government Office of Census and Statistics (1917) and a Public Service Commission. A *Journal of Industries* was in this context created (Christie 1984, 54). However, the Smuts impetus towards the creation of a national grid was stymied. This was an unwanted potential white elephant as far as the mining interests were concerned and the VFTPC held on to a virtual private monopoly position for a generation. To create ESCOM, Smuts had to struggle against them for two parliamentary years, 1920–2 (Christie 1984, 82). In the biggest ESCOM power station located in Witbank in the eastern Transvaal, the state did in the end secure profitable co-operation from the VFTPC. However, the idea behind ESCOM was to make it as independent as possible both from private capital and from any political interest within the state.

Through the 1924 election, in the wake of the bloody suppression of the white Rand Revolt, Smuts was ousted from office in favour of a Pact between Afrikaner Nationalists and the Labour Party. At one level, the pendulum now swung towards more protection. A blue-ribbon commission, including H.S. Fremantle and A.J. Bruwer, was now instituted to consider the tariff question, and produced report 26 of 1924 (Botha 1973). Fremantle was an ardent Nationalist and Bruwer had recently written a dissertation on industrial protection for the University of Pennsylvania (Bruwer 1923). With Germany, the USA was the spiritual home of economists with a nationalist and protectionist outlook that had important policy effects. The sometimes far-sighted but eccentric Bruwer can be considered the leading light of the commission, whose findings led to the Tariff Act, passed in 1925.[15] M.H. de Kock,

[15] Bruwer (1896–1983) is now a forgotten figure. Like Verwoerd, he was trained academically in the USA. With the Great Depression, he turned to fascism as an

a University of Cape Town economist, was an influential voice in favour of some kinds of economic protection (Christie 1984, 613). He was also American trained, although considerably more guarded in breaking with orthodoxy. De Kock was prepared to tweak railway rates to extend business and to support the work of the Land Bank, which sat behind the poor white problem as one potential solution, but he saw government ownership generally as a 'necessary evil' and can hardly be said to have had a decisive developmental view (de Kock 1922).

The change in government brought about a paradox. Industrial development continued to mount and had greater support in tariff legislation. However, the forces that governed the country were precisely those that most businessmen, largely English speakers and usually tied to British interests, most disliked. This was both true of the Labourites and the Afrikaner Nationalists. This meant that business interests as they actually existed had little purchase on the government in the days of the Pact. At most they adjusted to the new climate of opinion (Christie 1984, 98). Instead of all-round dedication to promoting industrialisation, the government was most enthusiastic about assisting its numerous voting followers – the so-called 'poor whites' – who favoured measures such as job reservation that would benefit themselves exclusively (Kooy and Robertson 1966, 214; Feinstein 2005). Agrarian interests tended to support protection indifferently; they were not yet strong consumers of industrial products and exported little (Kaplan 1976). At the same time, the opposition was strongly

inspiration and combined an interest in radical rejection of capitalism (writing admiringly of Mussolini, Hitler, but also Stalin) and the political dominance of rich old men in decadent democracies, with the mainstream Afrikaner nationalism of his generation. He directed himself very narrowly to Afrikaners, poured scorn on the Carnegie Commission which he saw as soft on capitalism and advocated racial separation vis-à-vis Africans that foreshadowed later apartheid policy. Apart from being an extreme protectionist and enemy of free trade and mainstream economics, he was focused on financial rather than industrial issues and widening access to capital on the part of ordinary whites. Curiously he was a diehard supporter of the foolish policy of keeping to the gold standard before the fall of the Pact government. His critique of the narrow policies of the Reserve Bank (and de Kock) is probably the one prescient element striking a contemporary reader (Bruwer *c.* 1934). In time he re-joined the mainstream and headed the IDC under Smuts during the Second World War. Later again he could be described as a typical racist Nationalist, with a hobby interest in the supposed non-African origins of the ruins of Great Zimbabwe.

dependent on British-orientated business interests and had difficulties in forging a different path. While the state was determined to let any profits in the financial sector accrue to South Africa rather than to Britain, the creation of the Reserve Bank and its early functioning steered towards maximizing profits for the country in gold sales, rather than any overall part in development and industrialisation (Ally 1994).

Martin reports during this period, and the Fusion government that followed from 1933, that one objective which had some impact was the gentle decline in the role of Britain as a trading partner. In 1929 on the eve of economic meltdown, South Africa signed a trade treaty with Germany (Martin 1990, 80). Whereas in 1920–4, 55 per cent of imported goods on average came from Great Britain, this figure fell to 46 per cent in 1924–9. In 1920 and 1924, no less than 46 per cent of all South African exports went to Britain, a figure that rose to 49 per cent in 1928 and 47 per cent in 1938. But this was hardly an earthshattering shift. Rhetoric in this department far outweighed reality on the ground.

In responding to Martin's embrace of protectionism, Renfrew Christie, taking a slightly different tack than Schirmer, has simply stressed that the 1925 tariffs simply were not stringent or extensive enough to make much difference; they were lower in fact than were contemporary Australian tariffs, where a comparable national debate was active (Christie 1984, 589). International perturbations benefited South Africa in isolation, such as the World Wars, which allowed industry to expand with little competition when resources were available, and the Great Depression, which quickly had a positive effect on the gold mines but hardly elsewhere at first. In quieter years, Christie stresses that economic and industrial growth tended to proceed at a fairly regular moderate clip independent of policy.

S.H. Frankel, the future Oxford economist who was so influential in the 1930s when protectionism was put into question, saw this as an inexplicable 'series of miracles', a notion which David Kaplan once derided (Kaplan 1976). Yet it is true that government intervention remained fairly limited. Moreover, the Fusion ministry in 1933 certainly brought about the powerful influence of those close to gold mining, South Africa's main export. With South Africa off the gold standard, mining boomed and was poised to take advantage of major new discoveries in the Orange Free State, which would be developed after the Second World War. Frankel was a powerful voice against protectionism and another influential one was that of the former Administrator of the Transvaal and vice-chancellor of the University of the Witwatersrand, J.H. Hofmeyr, who had been a key critic at the time of the 1925 tariff decision. Equally important in this camp was the Wits economist C.S. Richards. British interests continued to plump for imperial preference free trade which benefited both British manufacturers and South African producers of raw materials such as sugar (*The Round Table* 21, 82, 1930, 462).

These rival perspectives came out when tariffs were again considered by a major government commission – the Holloway Commission – in 1935.[16] Richards was a member and retrospectively could be seen as cancelling out the influence of his colleague Laite, industry's great protagonist.[17] This Commission addressed at length, but critically, the unskilled white labour question which was so intensively linked to tariffs.

> In such industries as lend themselves to a large employment of native labour, the chances of competing on an even footing with European countries is generally much better. These are, generally speaking, industries of a heavy type where muscular exertion is more important than skill, judgment or initiative. The question of replacing natives by Europeans in such industries must be carefully considered in relation to the additional costs involved which might increase their economic difficulties (p. 95).

This was exactly the point stressed in 1920 by the Kotze Commission (UG 24/1920) in response to those who dreamt of white labour exclusively on the gold mines, which helped precipitate the Rand Revolt soon after. The historian David Duncan has considered Kotze, the Government Mining Engineer and a close associate of Smuts, as a particularly determined defender of the racist status quo, not a liberal in aid of black advancement, which he considered a necessity for profitable and orderly gold mining (Duncan 1995, 40).

Thus the report stressed that nothing in the economy was more central than gold mining, then on a roll, and it recommended keeping things much as they were with an eye to the substantial state revenues that came directly from tariffs. Here we have a sense of growing teeth linked to finance and gold mining hostile to industrialisation and diversification that might prove a drain on the business world. In this

16 Customs Tariff/Holloway Commission 1934/35 UG 5/1936.
17 For Laite see Bozzoli 1981.

period, the Board of Trade and Industries also came to veer towards a critical perspective on protectionism (Kooy and Robertson 1966). The importance of developing an industrial economy that might supplement or surpass mining was muted where it existed at all. The debate was reduced to the basic issue of job creation, what policy was to create the most jobs – and the question of who would get the consequent jobs (as in the *Transvaal Chamber of Industries 1910–1960*, naively put). For a short while the more muscular debate of the pre-1924 years was lost. However, in one direction, the liberals represented an advance; they pointed to the modest size of the white population, its higher wages than comparative workers elsewhere in the world and the improbability of economic advance on this racialised social platform, which in so doing, pushed vital questions about the need to build up black labour and black consumerism to the periphery.

The most daring thing the Pact authorised (actually opposed by the Smuts-led opposition) was the Iron and Steel Corporation of South Africa (ISCOR), formed in 1928 but only instituted in Pretoria as a manufacturing concern in 1934. Government manufactured steel was strongly opposed by the mining industry and was lucky to find a somewhat renegade British manufacturer, Charles Merz, prepared to sell know-how and machinery. In its first years, ISCOR, also chaired by van der Bijl under Fusion, required considerable protection against imports and grew relatively slowly. It was forced to abandon the initially proudly vaunted reliance on purely white labour.

The Pact government presided over an economy that recovered very well from the Great Depression, powered by gold. But it was not a structurally transformed economy in the spirit of nationalist visionaries. Bruwer's dream of a textile industry based on South African cotton goods had not taken hold (Bruwer 1923). Cotton textile users depended still on imported fabrics. The state had, as we shall explore later, created ISCOR but this was only a relatively modest beginning for this other Bruwer vision. To the great frustration of its key executive, E.C. Reynolds, the National Bank of South Africa, instead of intruding effectively on the British-run banking scene and introducing some kind of national financial planning, was allowed to die with the Great Depression (McDowell 2000, 52–3). Things would change when the Pact government, expressing the sentiments of Prime Minister Hertzog, who wanted South Africa, like Ireland, to stay out of the Second World War, collapsed in 1939 and Smuts with his wider vision of development came back to power in force and in a stronger position than as Hertzog's subordinate or trying to balance the forces as he had done behind the old South African Party.

The hesitancy of using social policy to embrace the needs of industrialisation, urbanisation and social change was also notable under the Pact. Saul Dubow, but also a range of others such as Jeremy Seekings, have also looked at whether social policy that fitted the needs of an industrialising state was being put into place by a development-minded government under the Pact and afterwards (Seekings 2008). Sue Krige has, for instance, written incisively on the contradictions in policy towards 'Native education'. If some began to realise how important it would be, now that mission education was clearly inadequate to the task of building up skills amongst an African population beginning to urbanise on a big scale through mass education, others were unwilling to face the white public with the political and economic implications (Krige 1997; 1999). There were some steps, modest and racialised as they were, in this direction under the Pact, notably the Old Age Pensions Act of 1928, the Blind Persons Act of 1936 and the Children's Act of 1937, as well as the creation of a government department of social welfare. The Slums Act of 1934 did lead to a modest expansion in public housing on a segregated basis but not only for whites (Duncan 1995; Parnell 1987). Seekings has held that these reforms still had the stamp of Victorian ideals of religious charity and self-help, which was particularly the gist of the US-generated Carnegie Commission report into white poverty which reported back before the Fusion ministry came into being in 1933 (Seekings 2008).

The cleaning up of entry into public service for white South Africans led to the gradual rise to responsible posts of thoughtful figures such as Holloway. In his impressive look at the bureaucracy, David Duncan, in contrast to Seekings, stresses that a number of liberals were rising in state service after the creation of Fusion and becoming convinced that the narrow ideas of the Pact government needed to be shelved and replaced with thinking that would speak for a sense of the total South African population and to the growing social needs of an urban and industrial country (Duncan 1995). As a result he argues that the tone of government changed after 1933 away from the obsession with white jobs and towards considering social transformation, especially on the part of a network of forward thinkers like Holloway or Herbert Cooke. Cooke, Chief

Native Commissioner for the Witwatersrand, pushed the mines (eventually successfully) on considering tuberculosis as an occupational disease, believed health and safety legislation should be extended into agriculture and supported old age pensions for Africans as early as 1931 (Duncan 1995, 70).

The outbreak of the Second World War in September 1939 created a dramatically different dynamic. On the one hand, Prime Minister Hertzog, deeply committed as he was to staying out of Britain's wars, for him the critical mark of achieving real independence and making good the terrible war that had raged as the century began, was out and Smuts was in. On the other, the previous Fusion coalition atmosphere was to change during a fascinating period. The voices of defenders of British economic interests via free market strictures were now drowned out by the obvious necessities of waging the war and the powerful allure of national state-inspired planning and consequent rapid economic and social development. However, before we shift into that period, we need to examine the actual conditions of industrial development up to 1939, having considered the public debates about economic policy of the era.

3 Industrial Development in South Africa up to the Second World War

Some Figures and Some Business History

Quantitative Evidence

In supplement to its predecessor to which it is really a companion, this chapter consists of two parts intended to buttress its portrait of the political economy of South Africa particularly in the first three decades after Union studied historically above. Up to now we have focused on the vagaries of policy and the intention of the state in building up or transforming the nature of the economy with a focus on industry. This chapter by contrast tries to explore the economy from within and in particular the industrial economy of South Africa as it then grew. In other words, it considers the level of economic development at the point before one could talk about a state commitment to prioritise structural changes.

It consists of two parts. The first looks at the figures. By 1917, when the first annual survey of manufacturing activity was taken, industry was estimated at representing 22 per cent of national income (*The Round Table,* 15, 1924–5, 193). Where was the key quantitative growth of secondary industry to be found in the first four decades of the twentieth century between the Anglo-Boer War and the Second World War? What were a few of its characteristics? These can perhaps be discerned from the data accumulated by the celebratory volume of Union Statistics released in 1960 (Union Statistics 1960). The picture we are drawing is not, however, a revolutionary one and the tables below are based on the figures in that volume.

First, let us examine the number of workers in private industry as measured for the following years: 1915/16, 1919/20, 1924/25, 1929/30, 1933/34 and 1939/40 (see Table 3.1). These dates, albeit not ideal, are selected deliberately. The first is simply the earliest count available. The second represents the end of the First World War boom when industry was in a strong position to replace imports. This was followed by a serious

Table 3.1. *Numbers of Workers in Private Industry with the Percentage of those Workers who are Considered White*

1915–16	101,178	39
1919–20	155,008	33
1924–25	169,676	35
1929–30	162,329	36
1933–34	176,510	40
1939–40	282,779	36

recession, which had ended by 1924/25 as the Pact government came into place. In 1929/30 a phase of relative growth internationally and government stability in South Africa concluded. An election brought the National Party into power again with its Labour Party partner securing few votes. However, at this point, the Great Depression began to be felt. In the next years, industrial stagnation and decline, together with serious problems in commercial and subsistence agriculture, were coupled with mounting gold prices. The good fortune of gold accelerated from 1933/34 when the Fusion ministry was created and South Africa went off the gold standard. Fusion collapsed as South Africa entered the Second World War in 1939.

Growth between 1924 and 1934 was halting and limited despite the introduction of protectionist legislation although the percentage of white workers increased somewhat. By contrast, employment growth in industry between 1915/16 and 1919/20 was 53.2 per cent in four years only and between 1933/34 and 1939/40 37.6 per cent over six years, a more moderate but still substantial increase. These figures confirm what some of the previous discussion has proposed. State policy had only a very limited effect on industrial growth, at least as measured by the increase in the workforce. The downturns at the start of the 1920s and again in the conjuncture of the Great Depression were more marked while the conditions created by wartime isolation in the first decade of Union and then by the movement off the gold standard in 1933 (with global recovery, especially in natural resources) were considerably more significant in their impact.

State policies were obsessively concerned with the employment of whites. During this period, the percentage of the labour force considered

Table 3.2. ***Workers in South African Railways and Harbours (with White Percentage)***

1910	52,595	51.8
1915	61,402	51.6
1919	75,497	48.0
1924	86,181	45.3
1929	100,095	58.0
1933	77,653	63.9
1939	123,421	55.5

white fell from 39 per cent to 36 per cent but in fact this modest decline was characterised by ups and downs. Noticeably the percentage of whites at work in industry fell during the phases of rapid growth and increased again, no doubt propped up by policy consequences, during the phases of lower growth peaking at the end of the Pact. These increases were not, however, substantial enough to give the sense of policy shaping the direction of growth beyond a point.

It may be interesting to compare these figures with workers employed by the state through South African Railways and Harbours (see Table 3.2). Here we see the relative impact of state intervention where the state itself was the employer. The impact on employment during the years of the First World War was moderate. After the war, employment was allowed to grow substantially. When the Pact came into power in 1924, more workers were taken on and the gradual decline in white labour very considerably reversed. With the Great Depression, the workforce was massively cut back. Whites were disproportionately retained but their absolute numbers also fell noticeably back, albeit not to earlier levels. Then the good years of the 1930s saw unprecedented numbers of workers taken on. The proportion of whites fell back to the level of the early Pact years but not to those typical of the first Union decade. This tends to confirm the picture that white protection (this was primarily whites hired at lower skill levels or unskilled workers) cut into economic growth as a whole and protection of white labour, and indeed the tariff regime introduced largely to back that up, were at best moderately positive in economic terms. The counter evidence suggests that good times brought an increase in black workforces – and concomitant urbanisation, more or less despite what the state would have desired.

Table 3.3. *Size of other Workforces in the First Thirty Years of the Union of South Africa*

	Retail	Wholesale	Services	Agriculture	Mining	*of which* Gold
1910					291,337	224,347
1914					277,979	202,385
1919				17,482,062	288,623	203,610
1925				589,165	300,554	208,236
1930				749,195	349,031	236,305
1934					362,710	299,954
1939					464,359	393,967
1946/47	142,169	71,113	82,522	45,649,992		

Without worrying about the problems (of which there are many) in these statistics, they do reveal that secondary industry came to employ more South Africans than the tertiary sector of the economy in this period (see Table 3.3). However, in 1939 agriculture was still a vastly more significant employer of labour and the 1945 figure below under-estimates this dimension considerably especially if we consider agriculture and livestock holdings in the so-called 'Native Reserves'. Black urbanisation in particular was still at a relatively early stage. Mining also outdistanced industrial employment before the Second World War and by quite a lot, given its expansion during the post-Depression years (note that employment in mines other than gold was actually relatively stagnant, taking this period as a whole although it fluctuated). However, if one counts alongside industry the SAR and H workers, the gap narrows. By all accounts, though, this dominance of mining in non-agricultural employment is very striking, particularly if making any international comparisons.

We can enhance our sense of what this meant in terms of money values as they altered, also based on annual economic statistics (see Tables 3.4 and 3.5).

These figures, broadly speaking, show a pattern that correlates with the figures for labour. Agriculture as a business stagnated in the interwar years despite the concerns of the Pact and did not quite equal the value of 1919 production in 1934 after fifteen years. It, of course, remained a major source of work but in economic terms less productive. Thereafter moderate growth ensued. Thus in value terms the moderate

Table 3.4. *Money Values for the South African Economy*

	A	date A	B	C	date B and C
1910			28,933	93,196	1911
1914	35,699	1915–16	33,131	85,543	
1919	76,849	1919–20	55,725	80,090	
1925	66,295	1924–25	60,695	76,130	
1930	78,425	1929–30	51,143	70,267	
1934	95, 373	1934–35	55,089	85,536	
1939	161,671	1939–40	68,023	113,144	

A = value of industrial output gross in '000 pounds. B = value of agricultural (field and livestock) products in '000 pounds. C = capital issued for mining investment.

growth of industry under the Pact left agricultural values behind substantially, a gap that grew in the Depression years and then spectacularly under Fusion. In 1919 industrial and agricultural production were valued as approximately the same. By 1939, industry was valued at about 2.5 times agricultural value despite the fact that a vastly greater number of people were employed in agriculture; it was less productive by far in money value. During the equivalent period, money investment (and gold sales) was down. Gold sales modestly increased through the second and third decade of the twentieth century.

However, the situation became far more positive after the Great Depression created a hunger for security – and gold – especially, but not only, once South Africa went off the gold standard in 1933. Nonetheless even in 1939, the *annual* value of gold sales was more than half the total valuation of all private industry placed together. Thus mining, and particularly gold mining, continued to play a pivotal role in economic life. South African economic life was moving away from classic dependence on agriculture and the secondary and tertiary sectors were growing, but mining very much remained king and the movement was a gradual one. This chapter does not try to give a definitive valuation to the role of the Pact government in its succession of tariffs and its attempt to racialise the labour force in the economy, notably in industry. It is arguable that these two drives cancelled each other out. At the least, it is possible to say that government intervention was not a targeted factor leading successfully to overall economic growth. The rapidity of growth was more marked during

Table 3.5. *Gold Sales in '000 Pounds*

1911	35,049
1914	35,664
1919	39,280
1925	40,768
1930	45,520
1934	72,311
1939	98,943

the First World War and again once South Africa went off the gold standard. These were indeed important factors. In the 1920s and early 1930s, however, economic growth was modest.

These figures reflect the official categories into which industrial production was divided in the interwar period (figures were not consistently produced for the first post-Union decade) (see Table 3.6). There are only two clear patterns that emerge of real significance: the category food, beverages and tobacco systematically fell in percentage value while the metal-working category increased substantially, particularly in the prosperous years of the 1930s which saw the opening of South Africa's steel industry. The category of textiles and apparel, while increasing systematically until those years, is surprisingly small given its historic role in the Industrial Revolution and the industrialisation of many other countries. Metal-working is strikingly extensive, indeed taking over as the largest category by 1939. This illustrates the point made previously that some sectors of industry actually expanded under the impulse of gold mining rather than being crowded out. Yet these sectors did not necessarily achieve a wider purchase through consumer goods production or export as a result.

Secondary industry grew substantially between the time of Union and the advent of the United Party government (in coalition with Labour) that came to power in 1939. This growth was uneven in time. There was rapid advance at the time of the First World War when South Africa was isolated from its main trading partner, Britain, up to a point. However there were also periods of stagnation and decline during the post-war recession and again in the Depression years after 1929. The character of industry was also not precisely what one might expect of a 'new nation'. This was not the classic Rostovian pattern of stages of economic growth.

Table 3.6. *Industrial Output in Value by Sectors (in Percentage)*

	Food, beverages and tobacco	Textiles and apparel	Wood and furniture	Paper and printing	Chemicals etc.	Non-metal minerals	Metal, machinery and transport equipment	Other
1924–25	32.7	9.3	6.9	11,3	12.1	6.9	17.7	3.6
1929–30	31.0	11.1	7.0	11.7	10.8	7.3	17.6	3.5
1933–34	29.3	13.7	6.0	10.4	10.7	7.1	19.5	3.3
1939–40	24.0	12.5	6.1	8.6	9.5	7.6	25.8	4.8

The typical consumer goods industries expanded slowly and became dependent on the post-1925 tariff regime when they did grow. In contradiction to the conventional *dependencista* wisdom, the sheer scale and complexity of gold mining itself engendered a wide range of auxiliary activities including some relatively advanced heavy industry linked to metals. This was to the advantage of the dominant mining interests themselves and it thus had a kind of service character. The advantage here lay in the accrual of skills and skilled workers. However, there was little interest in export, particularly outside the region which itself constituted only a fairly small cross-border market.

Men and Firms

The second part of this chapter is brief as text but it is really based on the descriptive appendix which follows. These are historical accounts of businesses, which are clearly significant but have also been the subject of substantial studies that allow for comments. South African industry in 1940 was already quite a significant economic feature as noted already. The chief obvious weakness was the very limited role of heavy industry. Apart from a couple of theses, the studies in the appendix are all based on secondary sources and mainly accounts supported by the firms discussed themselves. These are qualitative assessments which can complement the quantitative data provided up to this point. Moreover, and crucial for our purposes, most consider the relationships of lines of businesses that did succeed to the state and to the mining industry. In this way, this section is a qualitative appendix as a supplement to the quantitative data provided earlier.

What are the general lessons we can learn from this set of narratives, culled from available business histories? There are perhaps three key roots of South African manufacturing: the direct needs of the massive mining industry (2, 9, 10, 11, 12, 13, 14, 16), the potential for making use of South African agricultural products and notably livestock (2, 4, 5, 6, 13, 16, 17) and following from that, the market created by the rapid urbanisation process taken forward so quickly by the Mineral Revolution (1, 2, 3, 4, 7, 8, 9, 11, 12, 15, 16). In some cases, linkages developed between the three.

Pioneer industrialists were often Jews, of outsize importance in the business world, sometimes Afrikaners but almost certainly whites.

Accumulation by Africans, a very marginal phenomenon by the twentieth century, was confined to services and agriculture. There were a small number of Indian manufacturers by 1940, primarily in Durban, but the more ambitious Indian capitalists seem to have been discouraged by the wall of white racism they encountered in South Africa and thinned out very substantially by the onset of the First World War. They had been primarily linked in any event to commerce (Morrell and Padayachee 1991).

The entries above indicate the personal links which also transcended ethnic if not racial boundaries. Successful capitalists formed myriad ties that linked them as suppliers and collaborators even while they competed with one another. They were highly attentive to state policy. Protectionist tariffs seem already to be less critical than personal ties with officials and politicians with a common vision. Before the Second World War this was primarily confined to infrastructural improvements and much debated tariffs on imports, but it was precisely the individuals who seemed to profit from the more intense protectionist policies pursued after the Second World War, especially under National Party rule. Some key business figures established close personal relations with politicians (1, 2, 5, 6, 8, 9, 17). Yet it is instructive to turn again to van Onselen's famous essay on the grain distillery, which was the Transvaal's 'first factory' as it was grandly named (van Onselen 1982). Protection, monopoly, links to the state and to agrarian capital, all were there but the effect of strong liquor on mine workers was considered to be so noxious that it was closed down (with compensation to Marks, however) at the end of the Boer War!

A wider spin appears in the pioneering study of Belinda Bozzoli (1981), however, at the rather abstract level of what she terms, following Gramsci, 'hegemony' of an ideological 'South Africanism'. In some respects, the appendix confirms this approach and fleshes it out. By the time of the formation of the Hertzog-Smuts Fusion ministry of 1933, it does seem possible to talk about an interlocked 'national capital' where the state was directed to serving its interests, not, of course, without contention and struggles, where business operated on a national basis and where the chief figures crossed ethnic lines to the annoyance of ethnic politicians and more parochial figures. She is right that what she terms 'mercantile dominance' surviving from the nineteenth century was being seriously challenged if not overcome.

'South Africanism' however on the one hand took for granted the privileging of whites and virtual exclusion of the people of colour, who made up a massive army of workers defined as low skill and only reluctantly being tolerated as urban residents. On the other, it meant businessmen's collaboration with competitors to fend off foreign competition through close ties to the state. Exports were mostly significant to nearby colonial markets in the southern third of Africa; systematic massive gold exports propped up the system, usually effectively in terms of the international terms of trade. The Rupert interests (15) in their outward thrust were an interesting exception but rather late on. However, as other examples show, the interest in export did become more significant in the last years of apartheid as the value of the Rand fell compared to other currencies (16). Yet here there was a dramatic contrast with the developmental states of east and south-east Asia, where global export markets have been absolutely central. In the post-Fusion United Party government after 1939 we shall see in the next chapter a further level of state intervention that can be compared fruitfully to classic developmental state exemplars. It also led to the formation not merely of alliances but of monopolies and semi-monopoly conditions in many lines of business. The examples discussed in the appendix were mostly written in order to provide a virtuous history of progress but they also reveal structural features and particular orientations that give a sense of the choices open to successful businesses.[1] Moreover, key features did not die away after 1940 but continued to be of considerable importance despite some important structural innovation in the course of the following half-century.

Appendix

In the following pages, we wish to highlight a number of companies and white businessmen important in the development of South African industry, separate from mining proper, during this period. These miniature analytical narratives, culled from a variety of published and unpublished sources, give a strong sense of key

[1] In his very impressive economic history of South Africa, Charles Feinstein captured the major elements discussed in this chapter and its predecessor (Feinstein 2005). Our analysis so far is really intended to reinforce his assessment.

elements in the rise of South African industry. What kinds of men and what kinds of businesses came to the fore in the decades before the Second World War?

1. Sammy Marks (1843–1920) was a remarkable industrial pioneer (Mendelsohn 1991). His numerous ventures seem to foreshadow how twentieth-century South Africa was to develop. Famously, his first industrial investment was the Eerste Fabrieken (First Factory) Hatherley monopoly distillery which served the thirsty men of the Witwatersrand but could be described as strongly counter-productive of the disciplined needs of mines management and closed down after the South African Republic went down to defeat (van Onselen 1982).

'While acknowledging his courage and vision, it must be admitted that Sammy Marks was a premature industrialist', writes his biographer (Mendelsohn 1991, 85). Marks' vision brought him an interest in a wide range of business possibilities, most of which were developed after his time by others. From the import of foods and local agricultural activities, he sold meat and grain, he took an interest in the jam business, helping to inspire Rhodes Fruit Farms and diversified into bottle and glass making. The sale of blankets led him to contemplate their local manufacture. He was interested in building up Lourenço Marques, now Maputo, the capital of Mozambique, as a port for the Rand. He promoted the railway link of Pretoria to Vereeniging, where he owned massive properties – 32,000 acres – around the Vaal river and then on to the sea (Trapido 1986). He discovered the coal deposits around Vereeniging, which developed later and planned the manufacture of steel (Mendelsohn 1991, 223) through Union Steel, not quite yet in operation at the time of his death. Vereeniging was also the site of a major transmitter which signalled the use of coal for electrification. In this sense, he was the father of the Vaal Triangle industrial complex, which will occupy us further on.

Marks had close links to top politicians, notably key figures in the South African Republic – President Paul Kruger and General de la Rey especially. He also established a friendly relation with Laite, the great champion of industrial protection in the first generation of the Union of South Africa, discussed in the previous chapter (Laite 1943). A pioneer Jewish immigrant from the Russian Empire, his descendants essentially dropped the Jewish association as best they could.

2. David Graaff (1859–1931) perhaps came next in importance after Sammy Marks as a capitalist in early twentieth-century South Africa outside the gold mines (Dommisse 2011; Morrell 1986). He was reckoned to be the richest man in the Cape upon the death of Cecil Rhodes. Graaff was an Afrikaner, a poor farm boy who was virtually adopted by a bachelor uncle. The uncle was a prosperous Cape Town butcher, Jacobus Arnoldus Combrinck, wealthy partly due to his abattoir investments and his purveying to the military, who eventually entered the Cape parliament.[2] Graaff made his fortune as the first local master of refrigeration techniques through the meat trade. While he sometimes exported refrigerated products, he got rich through supplying British troops in the Anglo-Boer War with meat – despite his opposition to the war as an Afrikaner Bondsman – and thereafter by selling meat to the gold mines. He diversified into other businesses such as diamonds, but he is not considered to have had a strategy for industrialisation. He was above all 'the pioneer who brought large-scale cold storage to South Africa and made a fortune out of frozen meat and the refrigeration of fruit and other products' (Dommisse 2011, 302). In his last years, for instance, he established links to Max Sonnenberg, who pioneered the manufacture of khaki trousers in Cape Town alongside Morris Mauerberger and Louis Berman. However, this business failed in 1929. Sonnenberg's importance would lie rather in commerce; he was the founder of South African Woolworths, today the chain store selling clothing and food to the national urban middle-class.

In the first years of the twentieth century, Graaff was forced to compete with Union Castle in the shipping trade. He succeeded in winning a deal that broke their monopoly. However, Graaff did not clear the way for other competitors, who remained frozen out of the 'shipping ring'. Marginally it might perhaps be said that this was a victory for national over imperial capital. However, the virtual meat monopoly he had was looked at very much askance by the Pact government after 1924. Indeed, his key firm, Imperial Cold Storage, was effectively controlled by Sammy Marks and associates for some

[2] Combrinck followed here in the footsteps of some of the wealthiest Cape burghers of the eighteenth century.

years when Graaff had little to do with its management (Mendelsohn 1991, 175–6). Graaff's investments were generally less successful in the 1920s.

Graaff (and his two brothers) were cabinet ministers and he was particularly close to Louis Botha, the Union's first prime minister. In that sense he could be described as a very political businessman who kept close ties to the state. In his early years, he was a reforming mayor of Cape Town in the mould of urban reformer contemporaries such as Joseph Chamberlain in England. As a young man, Graaff did much to create a modern system of sanitation and electrification (via hydroelectric power) in Cape Town.

3. I.W. Schlesinger (1871–1949). Schlesinger was one of the principal figures in business on the Rand in the interwar years. His business interests hardly involved industry. He concentrated on the consumer world of urban South Africa, including the press. 'His empire included insurance, real estate, theatres, cinemas, amusement parks, catering, hotels and real estate' (Bozzoli 1981, 208). His Colonial Banking and Trust Company was 'well known for small loans to Africans' (Swanson 1996, 279). Schlesinger was a Jewish immigrant from the USA attracted to the Rand soon after the foundation of Johannesburg.

4. Lever Brothers. This famous British firm (later on through merger, Anglo-Dutch Unilever) had strong links to west Africa through the import of palm oil to Britain. Opening up in Durban in 1911, it became a major industrial firm. The locational advantage of Durban had to do with the import of soap and margarine ingredients and their manufacture via the port, not export. However, Lever Brothers did make use of South African groundnuts, sunflower seeds and marine oils and thus can be linked to internal market orientated agribusiness and transport as well as fishing (Rosenthal 1961). Thus its importance must be linked to urbanisation and the emergence of consumer society in South Africa together with the links to agriculture.

5. Tiger Oats (Frankel). This classic business was the subject of a memoir by an unusually astute and articulate businessman, Rudy Frankel (Frankel 1988). Frankel was the brother of Solly Frankel, a key economist in South Africa before his emigration to Britain in the

1950s.[3] The heart of the business lay in the purchase of maize but this became the platform for a whole variety of food related investments, a great fortune based on the internal consumer market with little interest in export and of the greatest importance to the rise of organised agribusiness.

> Maize was our pillar even before we acquired a plant to process granulated mealie meal for human consumption ... Today wheat milling and bakeries play a very important part in our activities but had we not gone intensively into the former we could not have been the leading balanced feed manufacturers in South Africa, for wheaten bread is an irreplaceable factor. (Frankel 1988, 268)

Maize in turn fed into the feedstock business, instrument for the mass market rearing of South African poultry. It brought Tiger into links with I&J and the fishing industry as another source of animal feeds. The growing interest in refrigeration brought him into contact with Imperial Cold Storage (ICS) and the world David Graaff (2, above) had created. At the same time Tiger Oats moved into flour milling and baked goods (Frankel 1988, 242). The mills were often the site of conflict between the miller and the white farmer co-operatives who had to sell to him in effect.

The mines were massive purchasers of maize and maize products and from the 1940s this brought close links between Tiger Oats and the Anglo-American mining empire that rested on gold and diamonds with which the firm was effectively complementary from the 1940s (Frankel 1988, 126). However, these links were also based on financing. Frankel commented very interestingly about networking. His dense but wide networks included fellow Jews, so prominent in South African capitalism, but also other white South Africans such as the key Afrikaner financial figure Fred du Plessis or Stanley Methven, founder of Rainbow Chickens.

Some of this had to do with Frankel's sympathies as a young man for Afrikaner nationalism, perhaps natural given his German roots and identification and his leanings towards the formation of a national economy. However, after 1933 his German sympathies disappeared and by the outbreak of the Second World War, he was strongly pro-Allied and a backer of Smuts. He was disturbed at the National Party

[3] Solly Frankel fitted poorly into the interventionism of the post-1939 regime and eventually drifted into the international right-wing liberal think-tank, the Mt. Pelerin Society, associated with Friedman and Hayek.

victory of 1948, which inspired him to develop business interests north of the border in Southern Rhodesia (Frankel 1988, 179ff).

Probably the most striking element in Frankel's consideration of the business, admittedly with growing salience from and after the Second World War, was the fundamental importance of oligopoly, the dominance of a very small number of firms if not actual monopoly and of prosperity behind the walls created by tariff and other forms of protection. The war here was critical for Tiger Oats.

> The Marketing Act and its sequel, which led to fixed prices from the 1941–42 season, removed most of the speculative element and gave us a chance to concentrate on productivity, keeping costs down and watching margins. Finally, with the introduction of one channel marketing through the Control Board in 1944 as well as fixed prices, the whole speculative element in the domestic trade was removed. (Frankel 1988, 110)

As the post-war years developed, Frankel gives the sense of a huge firm or in theoretical terms *Konzern* that invested in a myriad of local opportunities without any non-financial connection and the growing importance of technical expertise and its implications in terms of staffing and linkages.

6. Premier Milling. This was Frankel's chief rival, whose success came a bit earlier. It was also the work of a Jewish family – in this case, the key figure, Joffee Marks, built a fortune having come to South Africa as a poor Lithuanian immigrant peddler. His was the classic route from selling bread to flour retailing and eventually manufacturing. The key here was milling. Premier began operations as a mill in Newtown, central Johannesburg on the eve of the First World War. In ten years Marks owned three mills (Jaffee 2001). Marks' East European Jewish networks (significantly with Schlesinger as in 3, above) were crucially important but, like Frankel, he established key relationships with a variety of figures, such as the Durban-based German Jewish immigrant shipping magnate Karl Gundelfinger (1871–1935, who had close links to the Pact government) and the trusty Scots general manager Alex Aiken. In 1918, the state authorised the baking of bread mixing wheat with a fixed maximum amount of maize. Jaffee does not suggest that Premier had important state links but awareness of a key piece of legislation was critical to its rise to fortune.

7. **Morris Mauerberger** (1890–1974) was yet another Lithuanian Jewish immigrant who was a pioneer of the clothing business. Like others, Mauerberger moved from sales of imported goods to manufacture of very basic and then more varied fabrics and clothing. He founded the major retail firm of Ackermans and supplied clothing made in South Africa to it. Mauerberger linked up significantly with Graaff and Frame (McDowell 2000).

8. **Philip Frame** (1904–79). Frame was par excellence South Africa's textile manufacturer. While he could be described as a Lithuanian Jew, in fact he came from independent Lithuania's future port, the Baltic town of Memel (Klaipeda today), just within the German empire until the Treaty of Versailles. Moreover, he learnt the textile business formally at the Technische Hochschule in Zittau at a time when German textile technology led the world. After Zittau, he effectively apprenticed at the great Russian textile centre of Lødz (today in Poland) where much of the business was Jewish owned. When Frame was ready to establish the backward link from cloth to textiles, he returned to Germany to buy equipment and confirm mastery of the technology.

A Lithuanian relative introduced him to the sale of clothing, and above all blankets, to Africans in Vryheid, Natal. Frame had extensive social networks that linked up the business with others. Mauerberger, Harris and perhaps other family members represented important connections from a familiar milieu as well as competition but a critical creditor was B.J. Balladon, a Durban-based Swiss immigrant entrepreneur who helped finance him and Johannes van Leen, his chief engineer, who was presumably Dutch.

Links to the state loomed especially large for Frame as with Gundelfinger. His empire really took off after the institution of apartheid, where he established close links to the state. His obsession was tariff protection. Inauguration of production was kicked off by the establishment of a tariff protection regime for textiles in 1925, when African Textile Manufacturers (Afritex) was established in Durban. On this basis, blanket manufacture took off in South Africa. Even early on, Frame diversified a bit into other operations and areas. He struggled and almost went under early in his career when the Depression hit. The Consolidated Textile Mills, when formed in

1934, had a board that included Gundelfinger and Mauerberger, and other Jewish manufacturers and merchants (owners of the major commercial retail firm of OK Bazaars). As Frame's wealth grew, he bought out creditors and partners. Recovering from debt, he tended to try to use private shareholders' investments rather than return to the state of a debtor (McDowell 2000, 129, 132–3). However, he well understood the need for organisation and was crucial in founding the National Association of Textile Manufacturers in 1946 (McDowell 2000, 120).

His position in the port city of Durban as a capitalist was especially powerful although he did have investments in Johannesburg and outside the province of Natal. During the Second World War, the business expanded substantially based on state orders servicing the troops and McDowell reports that he would later informally design the detailed tariff schedule to be established by the state together with the relevant Minister Nico Diederichs, ironically notorious for his anti-Semitism in the heyday of Afrikaner radical nationalism (McDowell 2000, 122). He was probably a substantial contributor to the National Party by this phase. Thus his commercial success fitted particularly well the developments which we shall examine in the next two chapters. He also established excellent relations with the state-run IDC. At peak, he employed more than 30,000 people in the 1970s and made more blankets perhaps than anyone in the world. At times, Frame did diversify – into rubber soled shoes or underwear or, after the war, into manufacture in booming Southern Rhodesia, but in pursuit of the same sort of market behind the same protectionist wall. Frame seemed uninterested in export or international competition but was very focused on apartheid spatial policies that fitted cheap labour strategising. He was never concerned to develop cotton as a crop in South Africa and was a major importer from the USA and the British Empire. His import bill was estimated at R39 m. in 1939 and R117 m. in 1945 (McDowell 2000, 136, 163). His customers were par excellence the poor but cash dependent black population of the country, consumers who made up in numbers for their very limited spending power. Frame was significant especially in the decades after the Second World War but he deserves attention here because the pre-war foundations laid were so characteristic and important.

9. SARMCOL (Rosenthal 1981) was another major Natal based enterprise. Despite its use of cheap black labour (it owned a 'labour farm' where workers could graze cattle and their families could raise produce for their own use during the off-season), the chief reason for this was the benefit of hydroelectric power from the waterfall around which the town of Howick grew, above the provincial capital of Pietermaritzburg. The SA Rubber Manufacturing Co. Ltd (SARMCOL) had two other different characteristics that are worth bringing forward. First, they focused on rubber made products, with imported raw materials, above all intended to service the immense mining industry while also feeding the consumer market for tyres as well as providing for other largely white consumer products such as garden hoses. The automobile was certainly fundamental to the affluent consumer market but also of course to all commercial undertakings. Second, was the link, especially via British Leyland (the 'overseas parent', Rosenthal 1981, 177) to British industry, where it continued to have substantial strengths. Here was the experience and know-how. In time, SARMCOL had rivals such as Goodyear, General Tire and Dunlop, which were clearly branches of foreign firms. Rubber based manufacture also had to contend with imported competition and early on got into the business of lobbying for tariff protection. It was behind the tariff walls that foreign firms entered in order to manufacture in South Africa and they did so primarily in coastal cities near harbours. However, SARMCOL and others also sold to (British) colonial firms from 'the Congo to the Cape'. Here the crucial element was mining and its interconnections. The Copperbelt boom from the later 1930s was a great fillip here.

10. Mining-Generated Manufacturing: Bateman. It has already been pointed out that the expanding metal related industries were directly linked to the immense world of mining. Mining on the scale of the Witwatersrand did have a very significant secondary multiplier effect in stimulating manufacturing. Bateman Equipment Ltd was a typical British firm founded directly to equip mines in 1919 (Nel 1982). Even in the late apartheid era, when Bateman was exporting to a limited extent, the mines bought 85 per cent of its product. Protectionism may have helped Bateman grow (although it was a firm that certainly had expertise in its specialised market) but it also generated a problem, industrial verticalism standing on the platform created by the consolidation of very big firms behind the protectionist wall so that Coa Equip, owned jointly by General Mining and Anglo-American, became a very serious competitor in the local market. Other firms based on the Witwatersrand were, however, created by entrepreneurs settled in South Africa.

11. The Wits Chamber of Commerce was set up by Sammy Marks, whose importance we have noted, and Thomas Cullinan, who started Cullinan Refractories Ltd (*Transvaal Chamber of Industries 1910–1960*). Cullinan's fortune was made in construction contracts extending into brickworks, fire clay, tiling and piping manufacture. Refractories (the name was only adopted in 1955) line furnaces. This was a big employer using a variety of raw materials, some local and with a significant business in colonial Africa north of the Limpopo. Cullinan serviced both South African urban consumerism through the construction industry and mining directly.

12. **Reunert** is another major firm that has some of the same characteristics. Despite the German name, it was created by German immigrants to Yorkshire, Theodore Reunert and Otto Lenz, and also had very strong British links. It was a family firm for a long time (Kok 2009, 248ff). Reunert made electric linked machinery from lightbulbs to locomotives at different times. It both manufactured and supplied firms but especially the mines. In the late apartheid period, it was Reunert that gobbled up through mergers various competitors pursuing disinvestment strategies, such as African Cables and Panasonic.

13. Perhaps the most basic product needed for mining was dynamite. The question of the dynamite monopoly in the days of Paul Kruger was a major incentive for British capitalists to want to put an end to the pretensions of the South African Republic and thus to the Anglo-Boer War. In time De Beers, the diamond monopoly company that generated Anglo-American and Nobel, came together to form AECI (African Explosives and Industries, later African Explosives and Chemical Industries) in 1923, thus unifying three explosives companies already formed in the neighbourhood of what had become the three key metropolitan centres of the country: Johannesburg, Durban and Cape Town (Scerri 2009). By 1932, AECI was manufacturing synthetic ammonia and thus tying up to agribusiness (107).

14. Seemingly in the same category was Metal Box. However, this British-run company, founded in 1932, was more orientated, especially at first, to growing white consumerism and to agribusiness/fishing, with its main market in canning. Imperial preference was a key incentive for its foundation and its early history was riven with competition from South African management with a more national orientation driven down in the end by Sir Robert Barlow.

Later on, under National Party rule, this major company, which had various international branches, with the South African one being the biggest, re-orientated itself to a significant degree. This conflict over outside vs. inside control highlighted in the company history (Reader 1976) is instructive. From 1956, Metal Box became more diversified and more linked up to the concentrated companies that were attuned to state protection and orientated to selling to a local market.

15. The consumer market for tobacco followed on the rise of a match making manufacture (Kok 2009). That began as early as 1885 in Port Elizabeth, a typical pioneer industry in a late industrialising country. Matches and tobacco have in common that there are links of potential importance with agribusiness. The match business diversified into timber and the major tobacco company, UTC (United Tobacco Company), diversified from the 1960s into food production. Cigarette making in the prosperous wartime years was the basis of one of South Africa's great fortunes, that of Anton Rupert (Kok 2009). Rupert, an Afrikaner at first attracted to right-wing student politics, was able to combine an awareness of the importance of state legislation, the consumer market and an array of linkages with Afrikaner national organisations. In 1945 Rupert established himself as a cigarette manufacturer supplied by Rothmans, a big English firm but he eventually bought Rothman's South African interests out. However, he was an unusual (and pioneering) figure in shifting into international marketing, manufacture and sales from the 1960s onward. This could be described as the model of a South African firm that turned into a multinational operation.

16. Cape Gate (Kaplan 1979). This narrative concerns a business with many of the same characteristics noted above. Founded by immigrant Jews in Johannesburg in 1923, the key figure, Mendel Kaplan, was a metal scrap dealer. It initially specialised in making metal fences, wire works and chain links. These were certainly used in mining but also extensively in the South African consumer market and, in time, chain links would also tie into bottling and into fruit and fish extractive industries. This part of the business would stay in Cape Town where the initial Cape Gate was formed and used originally imported metal as raw material. In 1979 Davsteel opened its melt shop and manufactured specialised purpose steel directly under Cape Gate auspices; Cape Gate remained the wire and mesh netting specialist.

However, Cape Gate's interests become tied into the development of steel manufacture in South Africa by ISCOR. When, as we shall learn below, ISCOR opened a huge new plant at the start of the Second World War on the Vaal river near coal mining sources, Cape Gate also focused manufacturing on the new town of Vanderbijlpark after 1960. Its relationship to ISCOR sometimes involved smooth relations of customer to client but also included direct competition. ISCOR also made wire but, in the view of Cape Gate's historian, it did not have the know-how in terms of finished products to compete despite its obvious advantages as a very large state corporation. As Cape Gate developed, dependence on technical staff became more significant but also the company moved into oligopoly mode to fit the South African market. A deal with the main competitor, van Thiel, in 1962 involved distribution and sales. In 1970 however van Thiel was itself bought out by an ISCOR affiliate. A quality product, Cape Gate by then had begun to export significantly, a feature of only the most advanced industrial firms in South Africa. However, it is noteworthy that the machinery it used was itself largely imported or perhaps manufactured on licence.

17. Afrikaner Capital. Hermann Giliomee has pointed out both that some Afrikaners were able as farmers and landowners to take advantage of the growing urban consumer market for agricultural products in South Africa and that they formed a small class faction together with networks of professional men and their families (Giliomee 1979). From early on in the history of the Union and noticeably in the Cape Province, they formed organisations, such as agricultural co-operatives, to build up their businesses. Right at the close of the period covered in this chapter, the *Reddingsdaadbond* was created and its funds were in fact, despite, as the name suggests, the official purpose of 'saving' poor Afrikaners, meant to make funds available to expanding Afrikaner business. While there were few significant Afrikaner capitalists on the Rand, in the Cape there were not just agriculturalists but the growing insurance empire of SANLAM-Santam that became a major source of capital aimed at Afrikaners.

4 A (Near) Developmental State Forms, 1939–48

During the 1930s, while some steps were taken by the South African government that could qualify as developmental, on the whole movement in this direction was stymied.[1] The core developmentalists, notably General Smuts, were part of the South African Party coalition but not its dominant element. On one side were the former Afrikaner Nationalists, including the premier J.B.M. Hertzog. While Hertzog was very concerned to show his independence from Britain and stress South Africa's different destiny and, while his supporters remained enthusiastic supporters of ameliorative measures to relieve the 'poor white' problem, they did not have the vision or the talent to sustain an overall developmental thrust (Koorts 2014). Hertzog probably saw his most important follower as Minister of Finance Nicolaas Havenga, whose fiscal policies were consistently conservative in the best traditions of orthodox economic theory.

At the same time, the forces Smuts brought into the South African Party included Anglo South Africans who represented either the strong mercantile interests that linked the country to Britain such as Stuttaford and Jagger, both of whom had been cabinet ministers earlier, or the enormously important mining industry in which the great firm of Anglo-American, reaching out from its original base in diamonds to dominate gold mining, set the tone. Mining interests were concerned to build up some kinds of industrial concerns that were essential to their operations, ideally under their control directly or indirectly. However, they were consistently hostile to any independent state initiative.

A divided economics profession certainly did not abandon its cherished disciplinary principles in order to support developmentalism under Smuts (Nattrass 2005, 22–3). Indeed, most hammered away at two obvious weaknesses which remained. If industrial growth did

[1] Several pages of this chapter are taken from my article, 'A Ghost from the Past: The South African Developmental State of the 1940s' (*Review of African Political Economy*, 2013, 86–114).

promote employment, foreign sales rested on gold mining in that industry hardly exported manufactured goods at all. Additionally, the market for manufactured goods amongst consumers in South Africa was small if growing. Industry remained technologically very dependent and was not accompanied by an equivalent rise in the availability of skilled labour (*The Round Table*, 33, 1942–3, 186; 34, 1943–4, 180; Oppenheimer 1950). Economists S.H. Frankel and C.S. Richards at the University of the Witwatersrand were articulate and voluble enemies of state intervention in the economy (*South African Journal of Economics* 2002), Richards wrote a book attacking ISCOR and state intervention in the iron and steel sector sponsored by the Chamber of Mines, in which Richards pointedly presented the figures on the dominance of mining as the most important customer for steel (Richards 1940).[2] He considered one of the key wartime commissions to be discussed below as 'the Blue Print of the New Order in South Africa' formulated by 'enthusiastic but untrained amateurs' (Richards 1942, 48). Solly Frankel wrote under commission *Capital Investment in Africa* (Frankel 1938), a classic still of value for consultation. He was often considered the doyen of South African economists and tasked with important jobs during the war but excluded from the policy framework afterwards (Frankel 1992).[3]

The result was a mixed bag of initiatives. The Pact government had succeeded in forming a state iron and steel industry, ISCOR, in 1928 with a plant in Pretoria although its growth was slow. Smuts, then in the political opposition, had actually opposed its formation. Eric Rosenthal, in his commissioned history of the IDC, claims that its private sector enemies tried to ensure that it was starved of funds and dependent on Treasury handouts (Rosenthal 1960). Agro-business had a smoother path. The Marketing Act of 1937 was an important state intervention into the troubled agriculture sector of the economy (Feinstein 2005, 142). It encouraged the formation of big co-operatives that came to control storage and the emergence of a major agro-industrial sector (R. Frankel 1988).

[2] Meyer 1952, presented a more reasonable assessment.

[3] See Botha 1973, 353 for his views on tariffs. He was offered a chair at Oxford University in 1945 and Hofmeyr advised him to take it. As Frankel 1992 makes clear, he became very right-wing in Britain, hostile to decolonisation and later a luminary of the Mont Pelerin Society. For another such libertarian South African with a similar trajectory, see Hutt 1943.

The 1935 Holloway Commission on tariffs was a major battleground in the 1930s and it included sympathisers and opponents. In the end it opted for keeping things much as they were in line with the Pact legislation aimed at protected local industry without any wider sense of linkages or any real interest in export. An underlying factor was undoubtedly state dependence on tariffs for revenue (Botha 1973). The background however was different than under the Pact. After South Africa went off the gold standard in 1933 and the Fusion ministry formed, the economy took off. In particular, middle-class urban white consumerism advanced and, to cater to that end in part, industrial operations spread. Gold mining itself was very lucrative and expansive with the prospect of massive new developments in the Orange Free State to come.

Then in September 1939 the Second World War began and the political configuration changed entirely. Hertzog failed to carry parliament to support his bid for South African neutrality. Smuts became prime minister again. Not only did the National Party go into opposition, and became thus irrelevant to the policy framework, the imperatives of mobilisation strongly favoured breakneck industrial development. Pro-British and pro-mining qualms in this regard could for years be set aside. Wartime also encouraged all the belligerents, very much including the Allies, to abandon any pure free market fantasies and embrace the need for state intervention in key areas and in planning, a kind of open sesame that would bring forth economic development theorisation in the following era.[4] Suddenly the possibilities for a state orientated to large-scale qualitative economic development could now go forward with limited opposition. This initiated a phase where economic policy moved very sharply in the direction of what we have termed a developmental state.

The Industrial and Agricultural Requirements Commission of 1940, largely motivated by war demands, was an early example of the new generation of thinking. Ringing words called for 'a society where every individual would have a right to develop himself [sic] to the best of his

[4] For imperial thinking, it is interesting to note that *The Round Table*, a voice for imperial opinion, found the formation of the IDC perhaps understandable but pointed out the 'ominous reference to self-sufficiency' (30, 1939–40, 710). Yet elsewhere it could not but point to the value of South African manufacturing build-up for imperial interests more generally (33, 1942–3, 92).

abilities and to a decent living standard and the state, where necessary, should intervene to support this right' (UG 40/1941). The state would inevitably be 'the largest investor' and stabiliser through its investments in the economy, with Sweden held out as a model (UG 40/1941, 26, 67). This remarkable report really was a charter for a new wave of industrialisation. The Commission called for rationalisation and a more efficient industry that did not depend on protection for its existence long-term (Feinstein 2005, 131). It affirmed the centrality for industrial development focused on the Rand, of 'a cheap supply of electrical energy generated from coal' (UG 40/1941, 8). Investment in machinery would counterweigh the poor quality of skills and weakness of social protection in South Africa. However, there was scepticism about the beneficial effect of aid to agriculture, which had already come some way (31ff).[5] Smuts initially hoped that this commission would be the advance notice for the formation of a powerful planning unit, a capitalist equivalent of the Soviet Gosplan, that would synchronise the work of ministries and provide 'for the development and progress of this country . . . a scientific planning body' that would be the key to the development of all of Africa.[6] There was also an assumption that the Allies would preside over a planned world via the coming United Nations Organisation. South Africa would fit well into those developmental plans and the goals they aimed to achieve.[7]

However, other documents of the era also deserve mention. Industrial decentralisation, which would loom large in time, was the focus of the Rural Industries Commission and will receive more attention below (Clark 1994, 145–6; Mager 1999, chapter 2). The Factory Act of 1941 (preceded by the Shops and Offices Act of 1939) was aimed at establishing acceptable work conditions in secondary industry (Duncan 1995, 57). The 1942–4 Social and Economic Planning

[5] The desirable future for farming was spelt out more clearly in a commission under the aegis of van Eck. Here what was stressed as problems to overcome were pre-existing low levels of investment and productivity, a lack of farmers' education, the prevalence of soil erosion and the importance of extending electrification. This added up to a programme of building up capitalist agriculture with inevitably large-scale elimination of inefficient white farmers and unnecessary black labour that could be replaced by machinery (NA UG/10 1945 Social and Economic Planning Council, #4 The Future of Farming in South Africa).

[6] Smuts Address, 9 June 1942, NA SEC 3.

[7] NA, HEN 2927, Post-War Planning.

Commissions series, chaired by H.J. van Eck (Clark 1994, 108) which differed in quality and importance, were of overall significance as well. They were notable for the absence of the mainstream university economists, incurring Richards' ire as we have seen. The new spirit was classically modernist in its belief in scientific surveys and the potential of statistics to assist social change.[8] A key area here was the planning of space, urban and rural.[9]

Institutional formation both went along with and followed debate. The Board of Trade and Industries, critical from the point of view of tariff determinations, became far more active in the new era (Kooy and Robertson 1966). The 1939 Research Commission can be seen as a new rung in the effort to co-ordinate and further scientific research to the benefit of industry following the creation of the National Research Council Board (Dubow 2005, 237; Cartwright 1971). The IDC was created in 1940 in order to assist new business activities as well as promote the expansion, better organisation and productivity augmentation of existing firms (Cartwright 1971, 5; Nattrass 2005, 32). Its first head was H.J. van Eck, who was really to shape it (Clark 1994, 130).

Various other agencies such as the Fuel Research Institute and the Forest Products Research Institute and various bodies linked to agricultural development were amalgamated under the overall care of the Council for Scientific and Industrial Research (CSIR), a formative body for developmental concerns. For the CSIR there were precedents. H.J. van der Bijl had advocated for such an organisation as early as the 1920s and Jan Hofmeyr, as Minister of Education, was in fact a key figure behind its formation (Kingwill 1990). In addition to the CSIR, once the war ended, the National Council for Social Research was

[8] NA, UOD 2812, E296/ v.1/Social and Economic Planning Council.
An intellectually quite impressive effort that developed on this basis and was not closely tied to apartheid policy was the multi-volume Natal Regional Survey, which was probably inspired by Ernst G. Malherbe when he served as vice-chancellor of the University of Natal. See NA UOD 2812, E296/ v.1/Social and Economic Planning Council, 4 January 1944, Memorandum for Discussions of Social Surveys and their Optimal Use. Professor Batson of the University of Cape Town, considered the inventor of the poverty datum line, was called in as advisor.

[9] NA, BTS 01,132/5/5 v. 8, Summary of Report 5: Town and Regional Planning.
The 1948 planning report came right as the United Party was pushed out of office and its thrust lent itself very well to the coming apartheid spatial planning of the following era.

Figure 4.1. Portrait of H.J. van der Bijl

formed. Eventually it would evolve into the Human Sciences Research Council (Dubow 2005, 243).

In the case of ESCOM and electrification, the battle was to wrest the electric grid from British interests tied into gold mining, nationalise the VFTPC – the 'largest electric power supply in the British Empire' (Scerri 2009, 119) – and tie it into a national power system, in other words to turn it from an essentially regulatory non-profit body to a major stimulus to the growth of heavy industry as a national grid. It was right at the end of Smuts' period in office in 1948 that the largely British-owned VFTPC, unwillingly but profitably, was finally bought out (Marquard 2006, 123).[10] Scerri has reminded us that this outcome was 'a great victory' for Smuts' top industrial advisor, H.J. van der Bijl, who had focused on the construction of big coal-based power stations (Christie 1984, 145ff; Clark 1993). The VFTPC had in fact been especially lucrative during the war years as a business concern but the priority of Smuts and his inner circle, above all

10 Marquard (2006) points to this being acceptable to the gold mining industry because the VFTPC costs had become so excessive, 151.

van der Bijl, was industrialisation based on cheap electricity (Clark 1994; Dubow 2005; Fine and Rustomjee 1996). This in turn would depend on the exploitation of coal mines at very economical rates (and, of course, so benefit the gold mining industry) but led to the extension of secondary industry requiring power as well as to the electrification of farms (Christie 1984). ESCOM now had an irreplaceable niche amongst the mining interests, notably Ernest and Harry Oppenheimer's Anglo-American Corporation. Harry Oppenheimer came to accept the link to the state corporation. A concomitant was to shift taxation away from the gold mines and tariff collection to income levies guaranteeing the state a certain independence.[11]

With regard to the other extant parastatal, ISCOR, Feinstein's economic history of South Africa gives an impression of how it expanded in efficiency and scale during the war, providing another foundation for industrial expansion based on steel (Feinstein 2005). According to Clark, 'van der Bijl's plans to expand ISCOR's market control, were largely successful, turning the state corporation into the country's major supplier of steel' (Clark 1993, 150; Cross 1994a; Meyer 1952). Van der Bijl induced manufacturers to buy from ISCOR. And the end of the war would be accompanied by new parastatal plans, although the most substantial and long-lasting, South Africa Synthetic Oil Liquid (SASOL), would only get going after the fall of Smuts in 1948 under National Party auspices.

The institutional foundations of an industrial developmental state had been laid by 1948. However, the paradigm also requires the presence of a determined and tightly linked elite with a plan. The next pages are intended to suggest that for a time such an elite existed. Smuts found in particular a small number of committed Afrikaners who rejected the vision of the Nationalists as too narrow, were at the least much less obsessed with the problem of British hegemony or dominance in the business world and had a common world-view. One was the faithful Louis Esselen, closest to the prime minister of all. However, here we will devote a couple of pages to the individuals crucial in the field of economic development. J.H. Hofmeyr, former principal of the University of the Witwatersrand, occupied several important wartime ministries at once and is often assumed to have been the deputy figure of Smuts and his future successor. Smuts certainly admired his intelligence (Paton 1965). However, he was out of the loop on the economic issues.

[11] NA, SEC 48, Report 7. Taxation and Fiscal Policy.

He did though play an important role in his promotion of scientific research.[12] Indeed, improving South African technical education particularly was a significant part of the developmental package given the obvious skills deficiency. However, the dominant tone was that stepping up technical education would be basically something aimed almost exclusively at white boys.[13]

The czar of the economy during the war years was the Director-General of War Supplies, Hendrik Johannes van der Bijl – Hennie to Smuts and H.J. to almost everyone else (see Figure 4.1). He was a remarkable man whose career has struck a number of academic observers although it can be argued that his importance in shaping modern South Africa has been neglected (Christie 1991; Clark 1993; Dubow 2005).[14] He was a family friend not only of Smuts but his predecessor as premier General Louis Botha and Smuts' rival Hertzog as well as of Sammy Marks, the pioneer Jewish industrialist discussed in Chapter 2. His father, a successful Pretoria businessman, took a special interest in South African industrial potential even before the Anglo-Boer War when H.J. was a boy. Van der Bijl was a brilliant university student in imperial Germany where he was the rare foreigner invited to take up a university post himself. Thereafter he went on to New York and Bell Laboratories with his American wife where he authored an important early textbook on electronics ('thermionic vacuum tubes') and was one of the pioneer developers of long-distance telephony. It was Robert Milliken, the second American to win a Nobel Prize for physics, who spirited him west from Dresden (van der Bijl Memorial Lectures, Address by P.E. Rousseau 1972). After the end of the First World War, Smuts persuaded him to come back to South Africa in 1920 (Clark 1993, 49), initially to rather frustrating beginnings under the pre-1924 government and thereafter, where he became the key champion of state intervention on behalf of industrialisation. In 1922, he remarked that

[12] Dubow, however, questions his willingness to spend and his enthusiasm in this regard (2006, 237).

[13] NA, UOD 2812, E296/ v.1/Social and Economic Planning Council, Principal, Free State Tech College to Secretary, Union Education, 2 December 1942.

[14] There exists a short biography by his daughter (Jacobs 1948) and a brief, adequate summary in Bozzoli 1994. Christie 1984 and Scerri 2009 discuss his importance.

the dependence of the country on a wasting asset, i.e. the Gold Mining Industry, is what struck me most forcibly on my return to South Africa after many years' absence. It is time that every South African should take this condition of affairs to heart and assist in doing whatever can be done to get away from [it] ... (T.P. Stratten address, van der Bijl Memorial Lectures 1963)

Van der Bijl actually came back to South Africa in 1920 when he was thirty-two or thirty-three. The great engineer was never trained as an engineer but actually in science, which is what he studied in Leipzig and Halle. He loved classical music and art as well as architecture and English literature, golf and bowls. Van der Bijl was also the first chairman of ISCOR and before that he brought van Eck into ESCOM in thinking already about the potential of turning coal into oil. ISCOR depended on training raw men from rural South Africa but the top team was taken from the mines.

Van der Bijl headed ESCOM from the start and later ISCOR and was a decisive figure in the wartime commission structures. After the war and before his early death from cancer in 1949, he (with his great influence on Smuts) looked forward to South African exploration of nuclear energy based on its uranium deposits and its capacity to build a commercial national shipping fleet. It is not surprising that Nazi Germany tried to secure his services in the 1930s and Britain under Clement Attlee's Labour Party brought him over to negotiate between state and business in the discussions leading ultimately to the nationalisation of steel (Jacobs 1948).

Van der Bijl can be said to have anticipated the debate on the developmental state and democracy with considerable acumen:

The best thing that can be said for dictatorship is that in some cases it has resulted in more expeditious material development but the same can be achieved by democracy more suitably constituted. I do not see why it should not be possible to form a democratic constitution that will enable a country to be run more like a business concern (Jacobs 1948, 224).

The core activists around van der Bijl, who had Smuts' ear, represented just the kind of small, personally close, elite circle that developmental state theory claims is critical. Frederik Meyer, with a background in steel, and a German doctorate, and H.J. van Eck, perhaps van der Bijl's chief lieutenant, would remain significant figures in the National Party era (Cartwright 1971, 7).[15] Basil Schonland, a geophysicist who helped in the applied development of radar, was a wartime advisor of importance. He succeeded in bringing a range of autonomous state-initiated research organisations into the more centralised CSIR penumbra. He left the CSIR in 1950 and emigrated to Britain in 1954 (Kingwill 1990; Dubow 2006, 242). Another Afrikaner (Schonland was not one) was Ernst Malherbe, an educationist closely associated with the Smuts era. Malherbe's interventions in the sphere of education were not always very successful but perhaps his finest hour, according to Dubow, was his adult education efforts aimed at the military during the war (Dubow 2001; 2006).[16] Van der Bijl and van Eck were used as key speakers and Malherbe's opinion polls of soldiers (polling was an area where he was a pioneer in South Africa) indicated a very wide acceptance of the role of the state in promoting economic development (Malherbe 1980).

By contrast, the end of the war marked a return to the mining based hostility to state intervention in the economy, or at least a desire to see it thoroughly tamed (Cronje 1952; Richards 1949; Oppenheimer 1950; Palmer 1954). As these critics inevitably pointed out, despite a slight shift, South African involvement in international commerce continued very heavily to depend on exports of gold and diamonds. The main exception here was the rise in other mineral exports such as coal and asbestos.[17] This was far from van Eck's dream of a more sophisticated and dynamic manufacturing sector linked to international markets, to building skills and to mopping up unemployment (Clark 1994). There

[15] At the end of his career, van Eck (1902–70) was called by the leader of the opposition, Sir de Villiers Graaff, himself the grandson of David Graaff discussed in Chapter 2, 'the father of our Industrial Revolution'. Van Eck studied chemical engineering in Leipzig so, like van der Bijl, he held a German doctorate. He did know the British and American applied science scene first hand but was brought back to South Africa by van der Bijl to work at ESCOM. He was afterwards head of technology at ISCOR in its early days and then in 1934 shifted to Anglo-Transvaal. He was also heavily involved in wartime planning and early on took a special interest in the possibility of converting coal into oil (*South African National Biography v. 4* Hendrik Johannes van Eck 1902–70).

[16] His colleague here, Leo Marquard, was decidedly more liberal and an influential enemy of apartheid in later years.

[17] For a considered government assessment, see NA HEN 29, 28, 477/2/6/1 v. 1/2, Formation of Tariff Policy Desiderata. In fact, exports remained a small share of manufacturing activity but were increasing from 4 per cent of production in 1939 to 7.7 per cent with a more diverse package of exported products by 1950 (Palmer 1954, 154).

was much concern in the commission reports for the danger of large-scale post-war unemployment, a factor that weighed heavily for those with memories of the First World War and its aftermath. In fact, it was clear after some time that this was not really an issue. African unemployment was many years away from even being considered or measured.[18]

Moreover, there were other areas where it is possible to point to key deficiencies from the perspective of development state theory. First of all, the hopes from 1942 of a supreme planning body that would exclude the economist doubters were not realised. The relevant advisory structures lacked power and there was even a lack of conviction in Smuts' favoured circles that there should be such structures superseding normal cabinet responsibilities.[19] Second, there was no real financial centre that offered credit for bold new experimentation. There was no national bank and the IDC was not given the resources to play this role and especially not as an independent force.[20] This is not to say, however, that the spirit had died. The final ESCOM report under Smuts certainly captured somewhat breathlessly the moment. South Africa was

> still a young and vigorous land in a world grown old and perhaps weary, South Africa produces abundant resources which her virile people will not leave underdeveloped. (1948 ESCOM Annual Report)

In Smuts' view, 'We have thus the conditions for great industrial advance' (Smuts, V, 1972, 502, speech to the United Party, 11 October 1944).

18 UG 40/1941 3rd interim report, Industrial and Agricultural Requirements Commission; NA, BTS 132/5/5 v. 1, 'Aspects of Post-War Planning', 1942; Review of Economic Conditions 1947, BTS 01, 132/5/5 v. 8 Minutes, 21/22 October 1948; BTS 01/132/10/30, Full Employment in South Africa, 1949.

19 NA, SEC 2, Correspondence, Social and Economic Council 1946 Extract from meeting: 25 February 1946; Memorandum from Smuts, 21 October 1948.

20 An example of this sort of experimental thinking was J.E. Holloway's proposal under the inspiration of Keynes to create a South African equivalent of the New Deal Tennessee Valley Authority focused on the Caledon river (NA, BES 5 v. 1, Memorandum to the Prime Minister, 15 November 1945). For the decisive rejection in 1948 of a national bank to be created, see NA, BTS 01/132/10, 1948 Report on Banking (12). Wallis (1953) discusses the unsuccessful mounting of a National Finance Bank. The one exception here was the already extant Land Bank, which did play a significant role in lending for agriculture, UG 40/1941 3rd interim report, Industrial and Agricultural Requirements Commission; NA, BTS 132/5/5 v. 1. In fact this report demonstrates that development capital already was dependent on the state.

Modernity Confronts Segregation

It is a commonplace of the historical literature that an apparently liberal turn in connection with the outbreak of war and the fear of a Japanese invasion transpired for some time in South Africa, a turn which flopped back to normality once danger had passed (van Niekerk 2007, 73ff). While this may have some truth at the level of ringing Churchillian rhetoric, notably the famous and often-quoted speech by Smuts to the Institute of Race Relations stating that 'segregation had fallen on evil days' at a time when the pass laws were in abeyance, in fact it is argued here that intensified social planning was intended to go hand in hand with intensified industrialisation and that debates about social policy were ongoing through the middle 1940s.[21] This book does not seek to incline readers towards feeling South African history would have taken a better turn if only the 1948 election had not gone as it did or that there really was a 'world of possibilities' as one recent volume has proposed (Dubow and Jeeves 2005).

Rather than viewing this interest in social planning as a humanitarian liberal intervention, which may have been the case for a few contemporaries, it was rather that planning for deeper and more thorough industrialisation, building a modern society, went together with a great deal of establishment thinking about social policies and about issues that touched on race such as urbanisation.[22] The 1944 Commission on Social and Economic Planning Reports put it succinctly: the coupling of social welfare and economic development was essential in creating 'an internally logical system where social welfare is coupled with economic investment and growth' (39). Indeed the early planning documents seem actually stronger on social than economic cogitation. Van Eck and even van der Bijl passed over at times into social planning. However, as against this, three years earlier, the Deneys Reitz (another key Afrikaner Smuts supporter) Commission into Native Affairs, in the heyday of the Japanese scare, had still emphasised the need to combine industrialisation with segregation/

[21] A full reading of the speech indicates primarily that Smuts wanted to drop the watchword of segregation, borrowed from the US South earlier in the century, and replace it with the more British sounding and respectable term, trusteeship. See the Address to the South African Institute of Race Relations in Smuts 1973, 556–68.

[22] NA BTS 132/5/5 v. 1, 'Aspects of Post-War Planning', 1942 [van Eck?]; Posel 2005; Seekings 2005; Seekings and Nattrass 2005, 84ff; van Niekerk 2007.

trusteeship, to focus on the development of the Reserves and to avoid social integration where possible (UG 41/1941). As Seekings and Nattrass have noted, social welfare was meant in particular to serve the needs of a bounded, urbanised population with little interest in the rural residue (Seekings and Nattrass 2005). Within these limits, areas such as education, health, housing, pensions, unemployment and school feeding were all discussed and shifts made towards provision particularly aimed at black workers.[23]

A major part of this thinking focused on health care (UG 40/1941). The miserable state of health provision, the prevalence of tuberculosis and venereal disease and the scale of malnutrition arrived on the agenda.[24] As the Reitz Commission put it frankly in 1941, '[i]t is a commonplace that a healthy Native population is necessary to the well-being of Europeans'.[25] This commission stressed the need for rural clinics serving Africans to focus on infectious diseases. However a more benevolent figure, Douglas Smit, grandson of missionaries, also reminded white South Africans that no less than 20 per cent of black babies died as infants in Pietermaritzburg, a medium-sized South African city.[26]

In 1942 Dr Henry Gluckman, South Africa's first Minister of Health, convened a committee to look into the formation of a National Health Plan. I have written critically about this Plan elsewhere and I will not reproduce the detailed argument here (Freund 2012). However, an outline would mention the following. The commission interviewed dozens of people, including representatives of the ANC and the Communist Party of South Africa. It sponsored the impressive work of Doctors Sidney and Emily Kark, a pair of doctors pioneering a health care system through their Institute of Family and Community Health at Polela in rural Zululand (Jeeves 2005).[27]

[23] NA, SEC 2, Memorandum from Smuts, 21 October 1948.

[24] UG 9/1943 Social and Economic Planning Council Report 1, Re-employment, Reconstruction and the Council's Status.

[25] Native Affairs Commission/Reitz, UG 42/ 1941, 55.

[26] Douglas Smit Papers, Speech to Rotary Club, Pietermaritzburg, 13 November 1941. For even more horrific figures, see NA UOD 2812, E296/ v.1/Social and Economic Planning Council, Social and Economic Planning Council, 17–19 September 1947, Summary of Planning Report 9 on the Reserves, 1947. Here it was claimed the figures show most Transkeians died before reaching adulthood.

[27] The Karks and another married pair of doctors, the Sussers, would go on to become international pioneers of community medicine. George Gale, their key backer in the bureaucracy, would play a central role in the creation of a medical

The commission recommended that this work be extended throughout the country with 400 health centres particularly in poor rural communities (Seekings and Nattrass 2005). However, one has also to look at the limitations of this scheme. Gluckman had a bee in his bonnet about hospitals, which he detested. His emphasis lay on better health practice and the employment of black health 'visitors' instructing the population on better diets, hygiene and the like. The limited medical care offered would fall far short of what nationalised medicine meant in developed countries. The civil servant F.A.W. Lucas pointed to the need to address 'freedom from want and poverty' in his statement to the Commission.[28] Yet the problems of sheer poverty and consequent malnutrition were not addressed.

In the event, Smuts quickly rejected the Gluckman proposals as financially unrealistic.[29] School feeding was an area, however, that could be expanded, notably to rural black children (UG 53/1948). This and other discussions about food in rural areas were more interested in subsidised shipments of food, no doubt to the benefit of large-scale white farmers, than raising wage levels, clearly not an element in forward planning.

Another set of issues debated focused on black education. Here the question lay around skills shortages. Towards the end of the Fusion ministry, it was reported that blacks had no capacity to learn sophisticated skills on any scale in an influential report by M.L. Fick for the South African Bureau for Educational and Scientific Research. This was now challenged. Simon Biesheuvel was the principal figure advocating for the potential Africans had to learn skills of economic value that could be unleashed (Biesheuvel 1943). There clearly was an enormous skills shortage in South Africa, a shortage whites could hardly fill on their own. Nattrass (2005) argues for this particularly as a phenomenon that became more observable in the war years. However, there was entrenched and adamant resistance to passing skills on systematically to black people. Van der Bijl, also a proponent of attracting skilled immigrants, took the situation as

school in Durban for non-Europeans before going off to found a medical school in Uganda, the first in East Africa. The achievements of the Karks (on a shoestring) were positively noted by Smuts himself.

28 3.8 Statement to the National Health Services Commission, F.A.W. Lucas Papers and see also Wylie 2001.

29 *The Round Table*, 34, 1944–5, 185.

a fait accompli. He suggested both that massive housing construction could become an important component of the economy but that this would be best effected by coming up with a construction system that could manage with a very low level of skills (Scerri 2009, 117–18, 125). Van Eck thought that the answer to the skills shortage lay in intensified mechanisation (UG 40/1941). Probably the most typical answer lay in the growing frequency in reference to 'semi-skilled' work which left an ambiguous place for large-scale black industrial workforces that seemed inevitably to be the way of the future.

In 1944 Hofmeyr was allowed to take money from the General Budget for black urban education, an apparently bold step (Posel 2005). However, institutionally the issue was still really one of a wider diffusion through state involvement of mere primary education where very limited skills were actually on offer. The Social and Economic Planning Reports called for universal primary education, a big change but within these limits.[30] Anything more than that was exceptional (Krige 1997).[31]

Other reforms lay in the inclusion of people of colour in the award of state pensions[32] and disability grants, albeit on a racially calibrated, unequal basis (Duncan 1995, 78; Seekings 2005).[33] Sagner argues that with regard to pensions, which were not much subject to black demands: 'without adopting a narrowly instrumental view, it can be argued that the broadening of the national pension scheme in 1944 was indirectly related to the needs of the economic structure' (Sagner 2000, 538).

These did not, however, suit the mine owners, who had also opposed the legalisation of trade unions organising black migrants tooth and

[30] NA UG 9/1943 Social and Economic Planning Council Report 1, Re-employment, Reconstruction and the Council's Status, 6.

[31] Krige rightly insists on the postulate of racially segregated education. It is true that during the war years, the English medium universities begin to accept a few non-white students.

[32] NA, UG 4/1944 Social and Economic Planning Council Report 2, Social Security, Social Services and the National Income; Pensions Law Amendment Act of 1944.

[33] For disability grants see NA, UOD 2812, E296/v.1/Social and Economic Planning Council, I, van Biljon, Secretary, Council to Prime Minister, Secretary, 29 October 1943. The Social and Economic Planning Commission in Report 2 had approved the idea of provision of assistance for those suffering from disabilities, work injury, to help in the costs of births and funeral and to help the mothers of young children.

nail. Mining was in fact exempted from this novelty in the proposed pre-election reform plans (Duncan 1995, 80). The Natives (Industrial) Bill, intended to legalise black unions, was never put to a vote and David Duncan believed that Smuts was a very lukewarm supporter at best (Duncan 1995, 202). During the war years, the pass laws were largely in abeyance and the government, which used the wage council system to improve black wages, dithered over granting recognition to black – or even perhaps integrated – trade unions (Lewis 1984; Duncan 1995, 179; Nattrass 2005).[34] Harry Lawrence, wartime Minister of Labour who eventually would join the Liberal Party, favoured negotiations aimed at regularising and improving workplace conditions and wages, notably through the intervention of Lynn Saffery, an employee of the Institute of Race Relations, a stalwart fortress of the Johannesburg white liberals, to this end (Hirson 1989; Duncan 1995).[35] Trade unionists such as Max Gordon and Ray Alexander were able to negotiate effectively on behalf of workers of colour with Saffery and Lawrence, who wanted to limit the number of strikes and appreciated the wartime prevalence of inflation. Politically this would be accompanied by recognition for local equivalents to the Native Representative Council, formed in 1936 as a result of the passage of the Native Bills, and an inherent element in the removal of any participation in the core political system by Africans.[36] Deborah Posel has

[34] The best study of the history of the pass system is by Doug Hindson (1987). See Duncan 1995, 92, for the system as it functioned in the 1930s. Industrial reformers such as Reitz and van der Bijl found the pass system inconvenient and unnecessary. This was also the view of the commission report chaired by van Eck: UG 53/1948 Social and Economic Planning Commission, Report 13. Economic and Social Conditions of the Racial Groups in South Africa.

[35] However, once Alfred Rheinallt-Jones returned to the harness at the Institute of Race Relations (IRR) and rendered Saffery ineffectual, this phase ended for Gordon (Hirson 1989).

[36] It is very well known that in consequence of the repression of the African gold mine workers' strike of 1946, the ANC dropped out of the Native Representative Council (NRC), which effectively collapsed. It is less well known that a plan existed to revive the Council, eliminating white representation entirely and giving it revenue-raising power. This may be seen as a more generous arrangement but it certainly looks like a prelude to apartheid and racial partition. Smuts at the end of 1947 was considering giving the NRC executive powers – *within the Reserves alone* [my emphasis] – as well as contributing to better social welfare policies (Douglas Smit Papers, Notes on Future Development of Native Councils, 24/3/47 and ff; the manager of Non-European Affairs in Johannesburg was talking of giving the vote to Coloured and Indian residents and creating an NRC for segregated black areas, *South African Outlook*, 1 January 1947).

thoughtfully summed up the whole picture as a 'racialised welfare state ... white supremacy albeit one with a much more human face' (Posel 2005, 66).

Smuts and those around him had not the slightest intention of destroying the structures created apparently definitively in the 1930s – the 'Native Bills' – or of meddling too much in the harsh racial regimes propounded by the gold mines or the substantial white-owned farming enterprises. It followed that there was a general absence of consultation with people of colour who could in any sense be described as militant (van Niekerk 2007).[37] This was not exactly because no possible critique existed. A small articulate fringe of white thinking was increasingly aware of the contradictory nature of the position of the state. Nattrass highlights, for example, the position of economist Ellison Kahn who denounced 'the "Reserves" and their maintenance as a kind of workhouse strategy' that got to the heart of the dual economy (Kahn 1943; Nattrass 2005, 37).[38] S.D. Threllfall pointed beyond the skills question for the need to develop the black population as a consumer market in the interests of overall economic development (Threllfall 1946). This argument is a major thrust in Bozzoli's consideration of the history of economic thought in the Union of South Africa (Bozzoli 1981).

Smuts himself understood very well that, whatever the success of programmes encouraging white immigration to South Africa from Europe (quite considerable between 1945 and 1948) there would inevitably have to be an acceptance of black urbanisation as part of the broad industrialisation project. This perspective can even be confirmed by the most famous of all the wartime and post-war reports, the Native Laws Commission Report chaired by Judge Henry Fagan (UG 28/1948). It is true that the Commission unequivocally calls for the recognition of black urbanisation but most of its recommendations (more effective and inexpensive transport, African-built public housing under white supervision, modification and eventual phasing out of pass laws, institution of labour bureaux and other measures aimed above all at 'stabilising' black labour), while following from that principle, are still marked by the assumption of racial separation. If the Fagan

[37] See, for instance, Smuts' contemptuous dismissal of A.B. Xuma of the African National Congress, van Niekerk 2007, 103–4.

[38] Another economist's voice particularly concerned to promote black enskilling was that of R.J. Randall (Randall 1942, 124).

Commission sought to end the anarchic and unpredictable regulatory regime, it affirmed that the 'South African combination of races differ ... so radically from each other that there can be no question of assimilation' (UG 28/1948, 50).

The thrust of United Party thinking was to separate out the urban areas and provide housing and amenities there for a black population that could not nevertheless expect political rights while rural locations needed economic development in good part to staunch the flow to the cities and keep more of the black population settled away from white residents.[39] One of the van Eck led commissions of 1944 envisioned blacks being divided into an A population, covered by social welfare legislation at some level and a B population, where there would be little social welfare and the Minister of Native Affairs would be in charge of policy, but this line of thinking was not pursued.[40]

Douglas Smit, when Secretary of Native Affairs under Fusion, had addressed an African audience in 1937 as follows:[41]

> The idea is that the urban areas are European areas in which the Natives shall in future only be permitted in so far as they serve the needs of the European ... At the present moment there are on the Witwatersrand many thousands of Natives who do not work, and whose numbers are gradually increasing by the influx of newcomers from the kraals, and the problems of how to deal with these people is causing us great anxiety ... Many of these Natives who flock to the towns are young people who desert their families and get away from the control of their elders-and their contact with strange conditions has led to the breaking up of your tribal organisation, and has brought with it many social evils and if we allow this state of affairs to continue you will before very long see the complete break up of your social system, and we will have on our hands a mass of people for whom the discipline of the elders will have no force or effect. The object of the new law is to control this state of affairs, and to regulate this undesirable movement from the rural areas to the cities.

39 UG 53/ 1948 Minutes, 21/22 October 1948; NA, BTS 01, 132/5/5 v. 8, *The Round Table*, 36, 1945–46, 96; Clark 1994; Glaser 1988.

40 UG 14/1944 Social and Economic Planning Council Report 2, Social Security, Social Services and the National Income.

41 Douglas Smit Papers, Address for Ciskei, 13 September 1937 on the Native Laws Amendment Act. See, too, his Speech to the Bantu Social Club, 27 October 1944, which stresses that the move to the towns has gone just too far.

This perspective had been stated more harshly by the not so benevolent van Reenen Commission of 1935 which spoke of 'an undesirable drift of Natives to the towns [which] should be combated at the Reserves'.[42] At bottom Smit's dream was a division between an urban world for those genuinely at work in towns and a rural one for the rest under tribal control. This would eliminate the 'evils' of the migrant labour system.[43] In 1942 Smit became chair of the committee on Social, Health and Economic Conditions of Urban Areas (Posel 2005, 78). Smit was the real father of the Zwelitsha scheme for creating a textile industry based on cheap labour two miles outside King William's Town and within the location system in the Eastern Cape (Bell 1978).[44] He also effectively promoted rural development along the lines of what would later be called Betterment Schemes (Bell 1978, 108, 112).[45]

Hofmeyr, whose death followed the defeat of the United Party in the 1948 election (van der Bijl died of cancer in 1949 and Smuts died in 1950), was certainly a more liberal figure, who was considerably more open to what we could call a critique of this guiding perspective. He was in a position to understand the contradictions at play better but only a very rose-coloured liberal fantasist could imagine that Hofmeyr would succeed Smuts and preside over a rejection of segregation and a genuinely democratic political dispensation. However, it is a point worth making that those who wanted to push the envelope did have his ear. Also there were consequential people, notably men in the civil service, who genuinely wanted to see at least a partial breakdown of

42 Industrial Legislation Commission Report [van Reenen] UG 37–1935, 41.

43 For a round condemnation of labour migration and a desire to bring it to an end, see NA, UOD 2812, E296/ v.1/Social and Economic Planning Council. Social and Economic Planning Council, 17–19 September 1947, Summary of Planning Report 9 on the Reserves. Oscillating migrant labour is 'economically, socially and morally wrong' according to this report and South Africa's goal must be a 'permanent, stable labour force' (p. 14). Also NA, SEC 3, Industrial and Agricultural Requirements Commission, Reserves Report (9) 1946.

44 Here Industrial Council and wage determination rules did not apply (Glaser 1988). Anne Mager has discussed how Zwelitsha developed. In conception: 'The Zwelitsha model was developed by those in the Native Affairs Department (NAD) who espoused a segregation-developmentalist ideology. It was reinforced by the newly established Industrial Development Corporation's bid to decentralise industry.' The two state departments co-operated 'to bring factories to the workers at their homes' (48).

45 See also in this regard NA, UOD 2812, E296/ v.1/Social and Economic Planning Council, Social and Economic Planning Council, 17–19 September 1947, Summary of Planning Report 9 on the Reserves, 1947, a major summary report.

segregation. These high civil servants, often in close touch with British liberalism and with the most perceptive academics, were largely Anglophone albeit very much Smuts loyalists (Duncan 1995). Interestingly, they tended on the whole to be the free market right-wing critics of developmentalism rather than its proponents (for instance, Frankel 1947). By contrast, men such as Reitz, van der Bijl and Malherbe were really what were then called *Sappe*, loyal Afrikaner supporters of the South African Party, South Africanism and Smuts. They were the hated rivals of the Purified Afrikaner Nationalist Party that came to power in 1948. Their approach and understanding of the country has consequently been marginalised as they were pushed out of positions of power, although plenty of individuals in their ranks did adjust to the winds of Afrikaner change (notably H.J. van Eck) and move towards the conventional white perspectives of the era to come.

This chapter has tried to make the case for a developmental state trajectory pursued by the United Party government during and just after the Second World War, in tune with global intellectual tendencies. In a number of ways, South Africa fitted the model proposed in Chapter 1 but in others – the dependency on cheap coal for fuel, the limited interest in manufacturing for export and the lack of a central planning body in the government or a purpose-generated development bank – it was in fact deviant. Moreover, despite some reforms intended to mould society so as to fit intensified industrialisation, the South African racial system was not really up for criticism or even modification.

5 *The Impact of Apartheid, 1948–73*

This chapter covers effectively the generation when the South African economy knew its highest growth rate. The planning of the 1940s was now largely carried out even though the ruling United Party lost the 1948 election and was effectively cast to the winds for the remainder of its existence. Key figures in the pre-1948 policy regime, Smuts, Hofmeyr and van der Bijl, all died in short order within the first couple of years after this political shift. One theme, therefore, and thus going against the grain of most South African historiography, either champions of the newly dominant National Party or its enemies, is the reasonably high level of continuity in terms of economic policy.[1] As apartheid policies take effect, they represent at most a modification of the grand planning of the war years even though the planning process itself was not really augmented and can be said to have lost coherence.

Was South Africa therefore to be best described as a developmental state? This of course depends on how the definition is structured. Key institutions created before 1948, notably the CSIR and the IDC, continued to establish roots and become, if anything, more important.

[1] A recent book, which does justifiably query the conventional wisdom, is Koorts 2014, 362. For a shrill denunciation of Marxists who exaggerate the growth rate of the economy under apartheid, see Moll 1990. Moll is right in that there have been liberals and radicals who did indeed exaggerate. However his own figures, culled from the World Bank, show that South Africa scored well in between the figures for ten developed and twenty developing nations in the 1950s, exceeded the averages in the 1960s (5.8 per cent vs. 4.2 per cent and 5.3 per cent) and still looked quite good in the 1970s (3.9 per cent vs. 2.9 per cent and 4.3 per cent). Only after 1980, a period of low growth in most countries, does South Africa start to look bad with merely 1.0 per cent average growth for the first half of the 1980s. Of course, these figures tend to reflect demand for South African primary commodities (Moll 1990, 76). Imposing a developmental state model seems a useful way of disciplining these figures into something more coherent than test scores and more plausible than World Bank select numbers.

C.S. Richards, generally hostile to state involvement, found that state expenditure as a percentage of national income had reached on average 25.4 per cent in 1950–3, slightly higher than in Australia or the USA but actually considerably lower than post-war Britain (36.6 per cent) or France (35.8 per cent). G.W.G. Browne's figures indicate a big rise in public investment from 1949 onwards. In 1964, for instance, it was 36.6 per cent of total investment, a figure in line with those typical of Britain in the Attlee era or Australia (Browne 1965).

The parastatal sector and state economic ownership certainly became far more pronounced in importance during this period. Shortly before the end of the United Party government, ESCOM secured a buy-out of the VFTPC and became effectively a monopoly as well as a state corporation. Marquard proposes that between 1950 and 1980 its overriding concern, as a non-profit corporation, was the rapid expansion of supply, of which the crowning glory was the creation of the national grid between 1969 and 1973 (Marquard 2006, 151). During that period, Johannesburg city was forced to conclude a bulk power deal that promoted integration of electric facilities and services (Marquard 2006, 154).

ISCOR was the other main existing parastatal company whose big new plant in Vanderbijlpark on the Vaal river was in the process of developing.[2] Steel prices were initially controlled by the state (Scerri 2009). SASOL was the flagship parastatal in terms of prestige and investment of resources. It swallowed up resources and it was late in this period that it began to produce a profit (Marquard 2006). In addition, there were SAICCOR, not directly a parastatal and established with British and Italian technical assistance in 1953, and FOSKOR in 1951 (Richards 1957). SAICCOR produced cellulose from the expanding artificial forests being planted in the better-watered parts of South Africa on the east coast. There were also a number of smaller companies which will not be discussed here in detail, such as Ferrovorm, Sentrachem, da Gama and Feltex. State corporations in 1946 represented 6.2 per cent of fixed investments. This rose to 11.5 per cent by 1973 (O'Meara 1996). On the financial side, import controls were introduced in 1949.

One central figure of the 1940s, H.J. van Eck, managed not only to salvage his career but this former director of the overall planning

[2] For a brief discussion of its significance and its problems, see Meyer 1952.

operation, now head of the IDC, remained a highly influential figure. Others stepped up to the plate as well. Stephen Sparks has given us a sketch of Etienne Rousseau, the utterly dedicated, ascetic general manager of SASOL. He believed in the apartheid project as did his closest associates, but also in doing everything to make SASOL a working proposition (Sparks 2016, 715–17).

At the very end of National Party rule, Annette Seegers tried to go beyond a simple Weberian ideal type model to characterise the top people in the South African civil service, which would not be very different in character than the parastatal management. She reported that 96 per cent of the top 2,827 officials were white. Amongst these, there were few women and few English speakers. This was a male Afrikaner world. She argues that it was knit together by common cultural formation, acceptance of subordination to a clear hierarchy, loyalty to leadership but also solidarity within the ranks. An important factor was that for so many until the 1960s state employment was the key formative route into middle-class life and middle-class consumption habits (Seegers 1993).

If a decision-making elite remained in the harness, however, there are a number of key features of the South African growth model which did not fit a developmental state sort of planning. The most basic of these lay in the absence of a determined central decision-making body. Ellison Kahn pointed out in 1959 that no system had been created for structuring the relationship of the parastatals to the central government – as well as none for providing parliamentary oversight (Kahn 1959). The Economic and Social Planning Commission of van Eck, renamed the Planning Council, was dismantled in 1952 (Terreblanche 1973, 46). By 1950, Prime Minister D.F. Malan wrote to van Eck that he planned to replace it with an Economic Advisory Council entirely and consequently would fill no vacancies.[3] Indeed A.J. Norval from the Board of Trade and Industries was asked to investigate setting up such a council (*The Star* editorial, 14 September 1950). However, nothing was done through the Malan or Strijdom years.

[3] NA, SEC 2, D.D. Forsyth, secretary to Malan, 22 February 1950.

For one perspective, let us mention a quote from that same year:

> We are fortunate in South Africa that successive Governments have been willing to, down the years, indeed anxious, to consult with the private sector of the economy on all aspects of legislation and administration that affect business. (Pretorius 1982, 6)

The author of the quote was H.S. Mabin, spokesman for the Afrikaanse Handelsinstituut, Association of Chambers of Commerce (ASSOCOM), which represented largely English-speaking business in the commercial sector. His organisation promoted a complex web of consultations constantly taking place, not only with the Department of Commerce and Industries and the Board of Trade and Industries but also with the Bureau of Census and Statistics and the management of the state railways (Pretorius 1982, 3). Mabin would have defined himself as an English liberal personally and hardly a participant in a National Party created coherent network.[4] So things went in the 1950s.

Then in 1959 leading into 1960 came the Sharpeville Crisis. A demonstration of Africans protesting pass laws at a poorly planned new urban settlement outside the Vaal river town of Vereeniging led to mass shootings that stunned the world (Frankel 2001; Lodge 2011). The state took charge of the crisis with arrests, detentions, banning the ANC, etc., but it faced a severe international reaction marked by disinvestment without precedent. In response Hendrik Verwoerd, by then prime minister, did indeed create an Economic Advisory Council. The surviving minutes of this council enable us to look at the developmental state question quite concretely also because of the interest of a few academic thinkers who have discussed the council in a related way, notably Louwrens Pretorius (Pretorius 1982; 1996). It included representatives from ASSOCOM, the Confederation of Employers' Associations, the Chamber of Mines, the Federated Chamber of Industries, the South African Agricultural Union, assorted individuals and representatives of (white) labour.

[4] ASSOCOM favoured raising black wages to build the black market and stabilising African property ownership and residence in urban areas in line with the Fagan Report on which the United Party campaigned in 1948. See Economic Position of the Republic of South Africa, Confidential Memorandum of Assn. of Chambers of Commerce, June 1961, NA, TES 9007, 161/11/1 v. 1.

Pretorius believes that 'it was never meant to be a policy-making body' (Pretorius 1996, 264). Right from the start Prime Minister Verwoerd, accepted that 'the Government recognises the key role that private initiative and the profit motive can and must play in the development of our country'.[5] The state wanted to know what business thought and wanted to accommodate it, but it operated the council as the name suggested, as essentially advisory and indeed it contained a range of opinion. There is no reason to doubt what Verwoerd said in response to a *Financial Mail* editorial, which branded the Council at a later stage of its existence as a bunch of stooges:

I think that Mr Goldberg has very well explained the general sense of the meeting when, towards the end of the discussions held on the occasion of the noon meal at the first meeting of the Advisory Council (*Adviesraad*), he said that he was sure that that it would have been brought together differently, were the government to want [to assemble] a bunch of 'stooges'. Yet you are convinced additionally that we and the government can hardly expect to listen to advice that runs counter to basic government policy for which the majority of voters have put us into power.[6]

Thus Verwoerd called for democratic controls – of a sort. Indeed, however, it is possible as well to see an incipient division in the Committee between those, closer to the state and largely Afrikaner, who wanted a tighter forum and those, more the representatives of largely English language interest groups, who wanted one that was looser.[7] The Council did not have a long-term existence and after a point only met annually. By the later 1960s it had given way to the appointment of an Economic Advisor, who annually prepared a report via the Department of Planning. Econometric planning – the use of growth projections, for instance, began to take the place of structural planning that involved substantive choices and had marked the planning rage of the 1940s.[8] The strongest statement that the chief director of Economic Planning, T.A. du Plessis, could make was that 'the EDP is indicative in nature and in itself implies no prescriptions for

5 NA, TES 9007, 161/11/1 v. 1, Declaration of the Prime Minister, 26/27 July 1960.
6 Prime Minister's concept declaration, 12/13 August 1962, TES 9012, v. 7/8, 7, *my translation*.
7 Minutes of EAC, 26/17 October 1961, NA, TES 9009, 161/11/1 v.2.
8 NA, TES 9013 v. 9/10, 9, Economic Development Programme 1964–9.

public policy, but at least it should provide a useful framework for decisions in the public sector' (Browne 1971, 366).

The minutes of the Advisory Council are rich with statements of the different interest groups in the business world and their concerns. We have already noted in Chapter 3 how this world was developing by 1940. The labour representatives contributed little but business itself exhibited notable divisions. Here we can point to a striking set of declarations from the middle of 1960. Thus S.F. Viljoen called for a five-year plan that would focus on building up South African textile, chemicals and automobiles industrial sectors and expanding public corporations further. This could be backed up with encouragement of immigration of skilled workers from Europe and enhanced import controls. 'He would recommend that, as in the case of Japan, the Union should conceive its economic progress as the key to stability rather than stability as a key to progress.' Mabin of ASSOCOM, however, pointed to the reality of declining profits and the weakness of the domestic market. English speakers like Mabin, and Professor Hobart Houghton of Rhodes University elsewhere, either referred to the potentially negative effects of import controls as a kind of drug dependency that could backfire or called for a rise in African wages, if only to bolster the local market.[9] However, Philip Frame, the Natal textile czar with his German formation, liked import controls very much and based his case for industrial expansion on cheap labour and heavy protectionism.

> The textile industry is a source of mass employment, it saves foreign exchange, is easily and quickly erected, and uses raw materials which can be produced in this country in abundance, namely wool, cotton and timber. It is also closely connected with the clothing industry which is again another employer of large numbers of people.

The question of import controls continued to occupy the floor much of the time. Verwoerd himself believed in principle that they should go in time[10] but in 1968, the Department of Trade still reported that 'the maintenance of import control, on a refined and selective basis indeed, but also on a more consistent basis, is essential'.[11] They stayed in place

9 NA, ARB A153/103, Economic Advisory Council Minutes, 26/27 July 1960.

10 NA, TES 9012, v. 7/8, 7 Concept Declaration of the Prime Minister to Meeting of Economic Advisory Council, 15/16 March 1962.

11 NA, TES 9013, v. 9.10, Department of Trade: Structural Change and Import Control 1968.

and indeed Kooy and Robertson (1966, 222) argued that they were more critical than direct tariff protection in propping up South African industrial growth.

There were also continual discussions about labour. Concerns about poor whites were no longer pre-eminent but Strijdom, and even to some degree Verwoerd, honed by the struggles around the Second World War, were very concerned about filling jobs, especially those of skilled workers and management, with loyal Afrikaners. Few speakers championed the idea of enhancing skills and jobs for local whites. This was a process which was exhausting itself, although in fact Afrikaans medium technikons (polytechnics) and university courses expanded rapidly during this period. Many called for the encouragement of immigration, which did indeed take place; fears of an English take-over were fading.

More striking are the discussions about raising pay and skill levels of Africans. Nobody directly challenged this as important but there were different emphases in direction and urgency, this in a period of only short-term increase in unemployment, repression of union activity and, as the 1960s transpired, relative labour quiescence. Verwoerd himself was uninterested in building up the African market. 'A wage increase involving higher costs and prices will constitute a serious threat especially to agriculture and mining in general and to the export industries in particular.'[12] For Verwoerd, who was not uninterested in the possibility of a national minimum wage, African wage hikes had to be linked to productivity increases. He probably thought in terms of prioritising security over building markets and skills this way.[13]

For Verwoerd, de Kock and indeed others, the real issue was capital flight and the disappearance of capital for investment. Disinvestment was marked in 1960 and the negative movement of private capital only really reversed itself in 1965.[14] Thus the issue became not, as for some, targeting development targets but financial measures aimed at stanching the flow of capital and dealing with the exaggerated impact, notably since 1949 and the National Party take-over, of regular crises in the balance of

12 Prime Minister's comments, 25 April 1962, NA TES 9009, 161/11/1 v. 2.

13 NA, TES 9012, v. 7/8, Concept Declaration of Prime Minister to Meeting of Council, 15/16 March 1962.

14 See Figure 14, Houghton 1967.

payments.[15] The South African pound was devalued. This went together with the institution of exchange controls. These were again loosened in 1957 – but not for long. A crucial step that turned the situation around lay in the introduction of strict exchange controls in June 1960 aimed at preventing the outflow of stock exchange funds. These remained in place for the *longue durée* of apartheid (Lombard and Stadler 1967, 444).

This discussion virtually drowned out the frequently raised issue of exports, insufficient apart of course from the huge revenue obtained from gold. There was no consistent or coherent export strategy put forward beyond what P.J. Riekert wrote in 1960. Riekert believed that the export potential lay in direct deals with particular countries and in the further development of South African mineral exports apart from gold; this was the path South Africa would follow.[16] Within a few years, this began to happen:

> Production and exports of base metals products are being steadily built up to replace South Africa's declining foreign exchange income from the sale of gold. By 1980 South Africa will be earning R200 m. a year from the export of ferro-alloys, chiefly ferro-chrome and ferro-manganese.

Virtually all was exported (*Financial Gazette*, 27 January 1967). This substitute for a policy was first openly made a subject of debate by the Reynders Committee in 1972 but to little avail (Black 1991; Rustomjee 2012, 48).

Of course South Africa continued to have that major export: gold.[17] According to the Bretton Woods agreement, the dollar price of gold was fixed during the post-Second World War decades. It was not extraordinary profitable but it was reliable, allowing huge

[15] For instance, Report of the Economic Advisory Council to the Prime Minister, 14 November 1960, NA, TES 9007, 16/11/1 but leaning on the report of Reserve Bank director M.H. de Kock prepared for the Council. v. 1, 26/27 July 1960. De Kock, however, was equivocal. He worried about the tendency to build what he called a siege economy and rather prioritised 'exert[ing] ourselves to stop the net outflow of private foreign capital and encourage new foreign investment'. This was also not a developmental perspective.

[16] NA, TES 9007, 16/11/1, P.J. Riekert, *Enkele Aspekte van die Invloed van Uitvoere op die Volkshuishouding*; also Black 1991, 162.

[17] Padayachee points out that in 1965, as much as 2.9 per cent of all world trade did involve South Africa as a partner (Padayachee 1990, 108).

expenditures in this sector to reap long-term, predictable profits. Here tied in was in fact the country's big source of potential investment money. A steady theme in the deliberations of the Council was the dearth of capital in the country and particularly capital available to the state.[18] By contrast, in conjunction with the development of the Orange Free State goldfields, Harry Oppenheimer initiated the National Finance Corporation (NFC) in 1949, which allowed De Beers diamond money to be poured into this costly new venture. This would later become available as a valuable source of capital for private industry too and notably for the diversion of mining money into concentrated industrial concerns and other South African investments (Wallis 1953; Innes 1984, 284). In addition, it became a source of short-term lending to the state in an early form of co-operation (Rustomjee 2012, 50–1). Re-investment figures in this era were quite high, comparable to those in the USA (Lomas 1955). However, the NFC beyond its symbolic importance was in fact a minor player. The big holders of capital were according to Lombard and Stadler (1967, 6) in order, commercial banks, building societies, long-term insurers, private pension and providence funds. This inevitably put those behind these activities, largely English capital and notably often linked to Anglo-American, in a very strong position. Apart from its war chest derived from profits accruing in South Africa, Anglo-American and the mining industry also had an excellent name in the City of London, often the source of new loans.[19]

South Africa lacked a state bank or major governmental source of investment capital. Nor did the Reserve Bank counter this basic reality. It was consistently run in a conservative direction that placed its highest emphasis on the balance of payments and certainly not on the expenditure of capital for industrial investment of any sort. The construction of the heavy industry sector, impressive as it was and linked to servicing the mines, more or less left out as we have seen any significant export component. South Africa simply did not develop as a significant

[18] For instance, NA, TES 9007, 161/11/1 v. 1, 26/27 July 1960, Declaration of the Prime Minister or TES 9011, 16/11/1 v. 3, 1963 Declaration of the Prime Minister, 20/21 August 1962; Busschau 1955.

[19] On the very large requirements of gold – and uranium – mining, see NA TES 9009, 161/11/1 v. 2, Transvaal and Orange Free State Chamber of Mines Memorandum, October 1961, Fiscal Policy in Relation to the Gold Mining Industry.

Table 5.1.[20] *Selected Years: Balance of Trade (sums are in '000 £s)*

	1924	1939	1945	1948	1949	1953	1958
Imports	65,210	90,553	109,959	350,246	310,985	418,803	555,464
Exports minus gold[21]	35,149	28,834	66,326	113,619	131,256	283,395	353,661
Balance of payments minus gold exports	−30,061	−61,719	−43,633	−236,627	−179,729	−135,408	−201,803
Value of gold exported	40,199	48,069[22]	247,199[23]	242,071	108,572	98,253	221,869
Balance adjusting for gold exported	+10,138	−13,650	+203,566	+7,371	−71,157	−35,468	+23,983

20 The figures here come from the Union Yearbook of Statistics over Fifty Years, Bureau of Census and Statistics, Pretoria, 1960. For more comprehensive tables, see Feinstein 2005.

21 Ships' supplies were also subtracted.

22 This is actually the figure for 1938 as the 1939 figure was suppressed.

23 1945 and 1948 were the biggest sums in gold export value before the 1960s.

industrial exporter. The remoteness of the country from robust markets and the eventual decline of the neighbouring, initially promising but modest-sized, African markets with the coming of nationalism, consequent imperial disinvestment and the stagnation or collapse of the formerly expanding white settler market re-enforced this lack of vocation. Moreover, while the gold export total was reliable over time, Table 5.1 shows that the ups and downs of exploration and development, even in the heyday of South African gold mining, actually made for considerable annual unpredictability.

The result was habitual balance of payments crises. The more South Africa prospered, the more it imported and the Reserve Bank felt constrained to act in order to restore positive national accounts as crises, starting in 1949, took place (Mohr et al. 1989). The Bank would then impose import controls, thus giving a helping hand to local producers (Kooy and Robertson 1966, 222). M.H. de Kock, after Sharpeville and as the crisis receded, stressed the cardinal importance of blocking disinvestment and making it difficult for investors to take money out of South Africa (de Kock 1963). Padayachee and Roussouw point out that this was anything but policy aimed at development; the goal was stability (Padayachee and Rossouw 2011). De Kock struggled, eventually successfully, with Eric Louw, Strijdom's Minister of Finance, over policy and particularly stressed the need to prioritise the private sector but in the end, 'Dr Michiel de Kock was the principle [sic] architect of the economic policy of the most successful period in the history of South Africa' according to a pair of admirers (Styger and Saayman 2011, S48).

The power of the English *geldmag* [money power] leads us also to consider the question of whether the South African state's interest in business was not in good part to promote Afrikaner concerns in particular. One could potentially see the role of the Broederbond, for instance, as a context where Afrikaner power brokers could come to agree on business deals that would benefit themselves in the name of the *volk*. In fact, this was the case in that Afrikaners benefited both as skilled workers and as economic managers. The state corporations certainly hired whites even if they could not run plants only with white labour. ISCOR by the mid-1950s had 20,000 employees, almost half of them white while ESCOM had 13,000, of which two-thirds were white. SASOL with 4,000 employees resembled ISCOR in this regard (Richards 1957).

However that benefit to Afrikaners can be exaggerated, especially when the overall impact of state intervention is considered. At the end of the period covered in this chapter, Dan O'Meara estimates for 1975 that only 21 per cent of capital was held by Afrikaners (O'Meara 1996, 80) although certainly state assistance helped some companies. The big beneficiaries on the Afrikaner side, moreover, were few in number. Above all there were the finance companies tied to insurance and savings, Volkskas and especially SANLAM. SANLAM's Tienie Louw, who dreamt of becoming an Afrikaner Harry Oppenheimer, was clearly a very influential individual (O'Meara 1996, 122). Louw had a poor relationship with Verwoerd, who tended to champion small capitalists and the interior provinces. With time, it was Louw who won the upper hand. Louw's colleague, A.D. Wassenaar, will come up in our final chapter as an ardent champion of what he called 'free enterprise'. But how Afrikaner were these organisations? A study of SANLAM proposes first that by the 1960s SANLAM was losing its special vocation as a financier for Afrikaners and that in fact its wide range of financial ventures included numerous major businesses owned by non-Afrikaners such as De Beers Industrial, Tiger Oats, OK Bazaars, Dorman Long and Imperial Cold Storage (Adams 2011/12). Parallel to Albert Wessels' interest in Toyota, SANLAM became heavily involved in Nissan Motors, Nissan being, of course, a Japanese mother company.

Many firms run by non-Afrikaner businessmen were in a better position to benefit from the range of new opportunities on offer and the new levels of industrial protectionism. The increasingly obvious model was one whereby state corporations were stimuli and partners to increasingly big private firms, the majority of them owned by English speakers and many by foreigners (Rustomjee 2012, 38). Nishiura illustrates the remarkable development of interest in profitable industry by Anglo-American. In the course of the 1960s and marked by the big investment in Highveld Steel, which we shall examine in a later chapter, this investment interest went from R40 m. to R283 m. (in 1989, Nishiura 2012). Another major purchase in the machine tools sector was Scaw in 1964 (Rustomjee 2012, 138). Much of this new heavy industry clustered on the East Rand and served the mining sector indirectly if not directly (Rustomjee 2012, 55). By 1970, Rustomjee estimates that one million jobs in the mineral-energy complex, and 650,000 outside it, existed in manufacturing (Rustomjee 2012, 70–1).

Another superb example at the end of this period was the creation of the Bayside aluminium smelter at Richards Bay in Natal. This smelter involved the IDC, which agreed on feasibility and insured the project, injected equity capital and made concessionary loans available while arranging export credit. A heavy electricity user, Alusaf, was subsidised by ESCOM. The bauxite came from Australia and the aluminium was meant to boost exports. Technical and financial co-operation came from South Africa's own Anglo-American Corporation and Alusuisse, a major Swiss multi-national (Ramburuth 1997). Indeed, the most striking impact on such firms was the tendency for locally based and competitive outfits to amalgamate and merge, forming big corporations that dominated sector after sector of the economy nationally as oligopolies.

> The NP government actually promoted the transition to monopoly capitalism in a number of ways. The… Industrial Development Corporation … encouraged 'rationalisation' through amalgamation and mergers in various industries. Tariff protection and tax and fiscal policies all favoured efficient firms. The fostering of a merchant banking sector, a money market and the overall centralisation of credit and finance … and encouraged the trend towards concentration and centralisation. (O'Meara 1996, 81–2)

We have already noted the importance of mining capital, especially after the foundation of the NFC, in funding industrial and other South African ventures (Lombard and Stadler 1967, 349). Oppenheimer famously invited SANLAM and other Afrikaner firms particularly (and Louw was especially interested in gold mining) to take over a valuable chunk of Anglo-American gold mine property, which became Gencor, a remarkable turn-around. Rustomjee illustrates with the example of Samancor how the IDC gradually smoothed the intra-partnership struggles between Anglo-American and Gencor in this important state chemical venture (Rustomjee 2012, 140ff). The contrast is particularly striking with the harsh conflictual thinking of C.S. Richards, the Wits economist, close to Anglos when the United Party still had traction and a determined enemy of state intervention (Richards 1957).

It is not proposed here to repeat the detail of the business narratives in Chapter 3. However, the available literature makes it possible to get a sense for how this co-operative scene benefited a variety of industries (see also Table 5.2). Footwear, largely produced outside the biggest centres, grew and prospered behind a high tariff wall without any effort to develop exports beyond the Rhodesias (Meyer 1963). Plate glass was a key component of the glassmaking industry. Pilkington, the large British firm, failed at first to secure entry, which was given exclusively to a rival bidder; when that bid fell through, Pilkington benefited and was able to prosper (Barker 1996, 203). In telecommunications, the Post Office monopoly gave way to a small number of oligopolist competitors nurtured by the state with, once again, little interest in technological innovation or export (Kaplan 1990).

A major industrial sector came to be the manufacture of automobiles.[24] In 1964, with security a factor of continual significance, a programme was introduced to boost local content by stages. The IDC assisted in creating partnerships that would allow for rubber tyre manufacture as well as producing artificial rubber (Brayshaw n.d.). This was a heavily protected industry but beyond the struggle over the level of local content demanded, David Duncan argues that it flourished within the general growth of a largely white consumer society minus direct state involvement. It benefited from the first 1949 balance of payments crisis, which made importing parts prohibitively expensive, notably from the USA (Black 1991, 166; Duncan 1992; Duncan *c.* 1992). One major benefactor, Albert Wessels, who held the Toyota contract, was an Afrikaner. Men such as Wessels and Anton Rupert, who had a poor relationship with Verwoerd, grew into something quite different than the small town capitalist looking for government favours and they functioned within a more cosmopolitan milieu with extensive foreign links.[25] As one moved from Malan and Strijdom to Verwoerd and finally to Vorster this actually accorded relatively well, given some road bumps, with the vision of the respective

[24] Atlas began to make aircraft in 1964, Brayshaw n.d.

[25] For Rupert's outlook in this period, see Rupert 1967. Rembrandt Tobacco Corporation fortuitously opened up in 1948. This, the centrepiece of his fortune, received, for instance, government aid through its Tobacco Research Centre (Rembrandt Tobacco Company 1977). During the 1970s he was one of those who turned against excessive state involvement in the economy (Esterhuyse 1986).

Table 5.2. *Development of Manufacturing*

	1944–5	1954–5	1962–3
Number of workers in '000s	361	653	830
Value of net output in R m.	276	852[26]	1.442

Source: Houghton 1967, 120.

National Party prime ministers as well as the rise of Tienie Louw and SANLAM, while offering much to other capitalists.

The actual character of economic growth will be considered more in later chapters but the obvious trend in this period was the growth in employment and investment generally in secondary industry. Charles Feinstein bunched together manufacturing, construction, electricity, gas and water as tabulated in government statistics. These rose from 17.0 per cent of gross domestic product (GDP) (55 per cent of the size of agriculture plus mining) in 1939 to 23.3 per cent (88 per cent) in 1948 (Feinstein 2005, 129, 144), 26.6 per cent in 1960 (106 per cent) and 30.8 per cent (108 per cent) in 1970. In private employment in industry alone, the number of those employed rose from 439, 000 in 1948/49 to 1,166,000 in 1970/71 (Feinstein 2005, 185).

Pretorius views the Commission as having been cumbersome; an Economic Co-ordinating Council formed in 1964 was meant to be more efficient but he has argued that it was above all captured by Verwoerd's vision: trying to sell private capital (in corporatist language) to start investing in border industries – on the edge of the formative Bantustans (Pretorius 1982, 17–18; Pretorius 1996; Richards and Piercy 1962; Scholtz 1974). This widely held view had been perhaps less true in the wake of Sharpeville but as recovery set in, it probably was increasingly accurate.[27] Just before the crisis unfolded, the Bantu Development Corporation was established in 1959 (Kahn 1959). It followed the issue of a white paper and the report of the

[26] This and subsequent figures would have been higher if calculated the same way. Nevertheless it is interesting to note that the increase in output from the 1950s ceases to be matched by an equivalent increase in worker numbers.

[27] Kooy and Robertson (1966, 223–4) argue that the Board of Trade and Industries was also increasingly pushed in this direction from the late 1950s. The Advisory Council minutes do not indicate much discussion yet on this theme in the early 1960s.

Viljoen Commission, which promoted in particular the border industries strategy as a means of avoiding disruption of chiefly authority and minimising social change within the locations (Glaser 1988). The Border Industries policy was formally unveiled in June 1960 and a special committee was devoted to it.[28] This kind of committee arguably was more effective in Verwoerd's views than the all-purpose Economic Advisory Committee had been.

This was not a new idea, however and cannot be described as a distortion of an earlier developmental state vision. We have already seen both that the dominant view before 1948 already included a strong interest in this, discussed in the previous chapter, and particularly to be associated with then Minister of Native Affairs Douglas Smit. Philip Frame on the Economic Advisory Committee had already gone far towards creating a network of factories that fitted Verwoerd's schemes, almost entirely in Natal (Kilvington 1996).

> Frame's Waverley brand literally blanketed the country – protected from competition by the high tariff walls and the policy of import substitution, which was the apartheid state's quid for Frame's quo of locating his factories in border areas designed to keep black labour far from the white heartland. In those times, there was little talk of trade liberalisation.[29]

It was the textile and garment industry that lent itself to this thinking (Cronje 1952; Glaser 1988). Barker in 1963 pointed to a report for the Board of Trade and Industries submitted in 1950, which already suggested that an industry might thrive if it was based on cheap rural labour and had strong tariff protection (Barker 1963). Trevor Bell, somewhat after this period, suggested, at a time when many businesses were deeply angry at the government trying to force them to move to the edge of the Bantustans – notably after the passage of the Physical Planning Act of 1967 (Bell 1986; Glaser 1988, 55, 82) – that a minority were actually attracted to such a move.[30] This is probably an exaggeration, especially given that most of these businesses rapidly deserted their new quarters after 1994. An exception were the cases such as those in the vicinity of East London, Durban or Pretoria, where the new

[28] NA, TES 9014, 161/11/2, Permanent Committee for the Location of Industries and the Development of Border Areas 1966 Report.

[29] Former Democratic Alliance leader Tony Leon cited in *Business Day*, 29 May 2009.

[30] This was a considerable reversal of his position in earlier writing.

plants were in fact suburban and hardly represented a major physical shift. These were often very acceptable solutions to businesses (Glaser 1988). At a time when the state almost entirely stopped constructing black family housing in 'white' South Africa, the housing for these suburban factories could safely be built in the Bantustans. Dan Smit conceded that 'while Bell exaggerated the extent to which firms were seeking new locations, he was convincing that most of those moving out to new premises were low-skill, high labour intensity firms' (Smit 1989, 176). Daryl Glaser felt that while the state initiated this racialised decentralisation strategy, private enterprise, as Bell suggested, in the end adapted and accommodated itself to this thrust (Glaser 1988, 8).

Anne Mager has perfectly captured the strong element of continuity in the construction of the Zwelitsha Good Hope textile mill, some three miles south-east of the town of King William's Town in the eastern Cape:[31]

> The Zwelitsha model was developed by those in the Native Affairs Department (NAD) who espoused a segregation-developmentalist ideology. It was reinforced by the newly established Industrial Development Corporation's bid to decentralize industry. The two state departments cooperated '... to bring factories to the workers at their homes.' (Mager 1999, 48)

At the time of the National Party victory, Zwelitsha township was still in the planning stage. Punt Jansen, the new Minister of Native Affairs, was just as enthusiastic as Smit about this project, which might help stem the tide of black urbanisation. It was intended that the workforce consist of family men but, in fact, the initial recruits were poorly paid, single, and often very young, trainees. King William's Town Municipality refused to supply the township with a proper sewage system and Verwoerd, succeeding Jansen, closed down the industrial school intended to train skilled workers. For a time, family men did predominate but after a failed 1952 strike, they tended to be replaced by migrants for whom hostels were opened. This development made them similar in fact to the workforce we shall look at below in the parastatal towns. In the end, though, as Smit emphasises, Verwoerd's dream was too grandiose and much too expensive; only a fraction of the movement he wanted to see ever happened. It stirred up a hornet's

[31] There were less studied examples elsewhere too even at this early date such as the SAPPI paper mill at Tugela Mouth in Natal opened in 1948; Smit 1989, 94.

nest of opposition in some cases and it simply was not on a scale to shift national development substantially. The declining economic requirement for low-skill labour even when industry expanded rapidly was part of the problem, as we shall see in our final chapter.

The social part of the planning of the 1940s, superficially inclusive, surprisingly perhaps was also not brushed aside. The apartheid government generally lowered health expenditure on, and eliminated the availability of unemployment insurance to, black workers. Pensions, however, while increasingly unequal, were still distributed to elderly blacks (Seekings and Nattrass 2005). However, in two crucial areas, the ideas diffused in the 1940s were taken further. There continued to be an assumption, however grudging, that black workers would be a critical cornerstone in the industrialisation of the country. One was the increasing and unprecedented construction of black urban townships while racially mixed areas and slums were cleared away on a big scale (Smit 1989, 123). This proceeded until 1968, when its continuation was stopped as a means of curbing black urban population growth. However searing as the destruction of District Six in Cape Town or Sophiatown in Johannesburg was, it should not obscure the significance of the massive construction directly by the state of new townships at first with family housing. This put into action intentions, which had sat in the reports of liberals for decades, but were never carried out or financed. Soweto, south-west of Johannesburg, was a massive extension of pre-war state housing in this direction but there were other major equivalents in urban centres as well.

The other was the widespread diffusion of primary schools aimed at black children while the inadequate number of independent, typically mission-generated, schools, were closed down. 'The numbers of pupils in African schools rose dramatically from 800,000 in 1953 to 1,800,000 in 1963' (Hyslop 1988, 451). Hyslop also pointed out that 'the Nationalists realised that they could not wish away the existing black working class' (448) and that their policies 'were in fact capable of accommodating the needs of urban employers', at least during this era (449). Probably the third most important desideratum was health.

Smuts had summarily dismissed the idea of a national health scheme as too costly. However, under the Nats impressive if crowded hospital facilities were erected in the cities such as Baragwanath in Johannesburg, King Edward in Durban, Edendale in Pietermaritzburg and parts of Groote Schuur in Cape Town, all available to blacks on a segregated basis. The mines had their own extensive facilities. And as to the shocking nature of rural health care, for the most part this was no longer so important to the developmental project, especially once a cure for tuberculosis was developed and penicillin injections drastically reduced the incidence of venereal disease (Freund 2012).[32]

One alternative to export markets would have been to widen the domestic market. The liberals on the Economic Advisory Committee, such as the economist Hobart Houghton, made this point frequently. The very largely white middle-class, and white workers too, certainly became far more affluent (home and car owners) and widened their consumer spending enormously during this period. However, the major employers remained dependent on low-skill black labour, much of it migrant, with very poor wages, in tandem. It is difficult to tease out to what extent this was their own conception of what was possible and to what extent they were pressurised by white workers, no longer able to insist or argue for all-white workforces. A black consumer market did come about, powered by urbanisation. It is visible in the perceivable emergence of professional black-orientated sport, the emergence of a cosmetics industry specifically aimed at black people, commercial publications aimed at a black market or the efflorescence of recorded music aimed at black listeners. Yet it was poor and relatively marginal except for the basic provision of food and clothing and the businesses that catered to it were essentially large white companies.[33]

In conclusion, we can return to the question of whether it is meaningful to write about a South African developmental state. We may start with the work of Louwrens Pretorius. It is true that he does not use the term developmental state. However, based on thinking about the Economic

[32] Tuberculosis remains a serious disease and cause of death amongst poor South Africans. This is often ascribed to the failure of patients to accept a long-term course of medicine.

[33] It should be noted that one section of the non-white majority (15.4 per cent in the 1960 census), Indians and Coloured people, were considerably better treated after 1960. Their trading strata were encouraged to enter industry – they were preferred as workers and had considerably more access to higher education, especially leading to work-related qualifications. This particularly affected the two big cities of Cape Town and Durban where the majority of these 'racial' groups lived. They did not receive the vote in a common franchise, however.

Advisory Committee and its context, he has considered extensively the relationship under apartheid of the state to the business world. He rather pursued the idea that the relationship between the state and capital might be considered corporatist (Pretorius 1982; 1996). Their interrelationship was marked by extensive informal and semi-formal contacts. Joint delegations to ministers and 'summit meetings' called by them were frequent key points of contact. However, corporatist structures were not of great importance.

A further problem was the clearly distanced relation between much of English capital and the Afrikaner dominated state, politicians and bureaucrats included. The latter constituted 'a network where ideological coherence was constructed and maintained and view on policies canvassed and formed' (Pretorius 1996, 265). The notorious (to English South Africans) secret club, the Broederbond, was no doubt a key site where this network came together and it clearly always had extensive interests in business activity, albeit probably mostly in furthering the interests of an ambitious petty bourgeoisie.

Institutionally, corporatism does not really fill the bill. In the end, Pretorius believes in the continuing importance of focus on the interaction of interest groups structured in multiple ways rather than assumptions of corporatist hegemony. A valuable alternative formulation contemporary with the writing of Pretorius comes from the University of the Witwatersrand masters' thesis of Daryl Glaser. Glaser prefers to see the state (and by extension, different state agencies) and capital as being at times parallel and at times antagonistic but in general, capable of *accommodating one another* (Glaser 1988). Stephen Gelb took this issue further theoretically by considering the relationship of business to finance in comparison with the developmental state flagship of Japan (Gelb 1990). He argued that while they were inevitably close to one another in South Africa, ultimately business conglomerates were in charge of this relationship before 1990. It can further be argued that investments on the ground never strayed entirely away from the core mineral-energy complex activities that Fine and Rustomjee have insisted always remain central (Fine and Rustomjee 1996).

By contrast, in Japan the banks evolved into the dominant force pushing for diverse economic activities. Nishiura outlines the way that big, successful family firms, which he terms *Konzernen*, evolved through growing involvement in banking into giant financial houses that came to dominate the modern economy. With time, as in the West, these largely shed their links to particular families. This is a process that can also be witnessed in South Africa but at a considerably less evolved phasing and usually with the constraints imposed by the continued dominance of mining and related interests materially. He also demonstrates this dominance over manufacturing for the long-term. The state made manufacturing on a big scale profitable and desirable so oligopolies invested in it profitably but it did not evolve so as to change their character fundamentally. However, finance itself has arguably taken over any direct material links dominant in the past (Nishiura 2012). Thus financialisation itself is probably the one crucial additional element which must be added to the continued salience of the minerals-energy complex as the governing activity.

In conclusion, we could go back to the considerations in Chapter 1. The developmental state paradigm is a classic ideal type. As with feudalism or slavery or even capitalism, the real economic-social linkages on the ground show variation, relics of the past and idiosyncratic features. The ideal type only partially applied to apartheid South Africa but this may lead us to use the model as a generic testing device in a looser way that is still illustratively rich. What is still missing is a consideration of some problematic features of the South African developmental state that caused its disarray and fragmentation in the last generation of apartheid. Some of this story, but only some of it, is directly political.

6 *The Parastatals ISCOR and SASOL*

The basic factual history of the major parastatal corporations in South Africa is well-known (Houghton and Dagut 1972). This is particularly the case with ISCOR and SASOL.[1] The Iron and Steel Corporation of South Africa was founded in 1928 and began operations on a small scale in Pretoria in 1934. Under the guidance of van der Bijl from 1940, it grew tremendously and constructed a new plant on the Vaal River at the new town of Vanderbijlpark which we shall be looking at in a subsequent chapter as a subject unto itself. In the 1930s, South Africa had become the biggest foreign market for British steel production; now this dependence began to diminish as markets for South African steel would one day eventually also become problematic in the early twenty-first century elsewhere for the same reason (Cross 1994b). It is hardly necessary to make out a case, especially within the discourse of the mid-twentieth century, for the central importance of a steel industry especially for a country rich in coal and iron ore. Thus ISCOR was really a creation of Smuts, even though he originally opposed its foundation when in opposition, and it was looked on with mixed feelings to some extent by the National Party in power.

By contrast, SASOL was only formed in 1950 and, while it had a long history of experimentation and South African interest (Sparks n.d.) it was almost free of associations with the United

[1] I have benefited immensely through widening my research basis from access to unpublished thesis material in this chapter particularly. SASOL's historian is Stephen Sparks whose University of Michigan PhD, 'Apartheid Modern: South Africa's Oil-from-Coal project and the Making of a Company Town', University of Michigan 2012, has been enormously helpful, although I will leave his detailed analysis largely to his own future publications. See Sparks 2016. On ISCOR, the School of Oriental and African Studies doctorate of Nimrod Zalk entitled 'The Things We Lost in the Fire: The Political Economy of the South African Steel and Engineering Sector', has also been used extensively. I should finally mention, because this important thesis never became a book, Roderick Crompton, 'The South African Commodity Plastics Filière: History and Future Strategy Options', University of Natal, 1994 PhD.

Party era and became the much-loved economic flagship of Nationalist South Africa, into which large sums were sunk at crucial times. Initially SASOL operated out of another new town, Sasolburg, close to Vanderbijlpark but on the other side of the Vaal River in the Orange Free State. Later a far bigger plant was constructed south-east of Johannesburg at Secunda in what is today Mpumalanga Province as a response to the fears of being cut off from Middle Eastern oil supplies.

This chapter therefore really focuses on three issues that seem especially relevant to our overall theme rather than a blow-by-blow history of these two corporations. First, something will be said about skills and personnel. The racial system, which is better understood by considering as well the lives of workers outside and inside of the factory, is largely going to be left to the chapter on the parastatal new towns. Here we will look at the Afrikaner/English issue and at the difficulties of contracting skilled workers and management especially. Second, we will look at the relationship of ISCOR and SASOL to the broader economic environment and in particular the already highly developed if skewed private sector. Third, we shall consider the industrial context of the two firms and the extent to which they promoted manufacturing in South Africa, partly turning the country into a significant industrial producer.

The construction of a suitable labour force was a continued challenge to the parastatals throughout the apartheid period. Charles Feinstein has noted the dilemma as a general statement. South Africa was notorious for its cheap labour force, especially on the mines, although resolving numerous organisational issues such as recruitment for this army-size working population or feeding it was complex and costly. On the mines the white labour force was no more than 1/10 of the total although it grew in absolute terms after the Second World War. By contrast, in heavy industry the sheer proportion of white workers was far greater. If the National Party grudgingly gave up on the idea of using the mines for white employment on a huge scale, this was not true in secondary industry, and above all secondary industry controlled by the state. It was not possible, as Morris and Kaplan have shown, to run a steel mill on an all-white basis, an issue settled already before the war, but in practice the unskilled and so-called 'semi-skilled jobs', which were held by largely migrant black workers, were a far smaller percentage of the entire workforce (Kaplan and Morris 1976; Davies et al. 1976, Davies

Table 6.1. *Employment at ISCOR by Race*

	Whites	Others (natives, 1934)
1934	2,000	1,500
1954	9,000	11,500
1972	18,700	17,800

Source: NA, MES 232, H 4/12 pts ½; MPP 45, A3/10/9 part 1.

1979).[2] Feinstein has demonstrated particularly clearly the consequences: despite the cheap black labour, white workers were so relatively well-paid compared to wages at equivalent levels in other industrialised countries that the balance militated against a competitive export orientation (Feinstein 2005, 133). Thus in ISCOR in mid-1954, 9,000 whites earned £50 m. while 11,500 'Natives' earned £13 m. (see also Table 6.1).[3]

This total reached a peak of 76,000,[4] sinking to 60,700 in mid-1982 and 49,560 at the end of 1985.[5] In South African terms therefore, the issue was consequently how to train and keep on the job genuinely skilled workers, who had to be white. This was a constant struggle. The parastatals themselves ran training facilities, which were very important in producing acceptable workers.[6] Yet there was a constant labour shortage.[7] Stuart Coupe showed that for the metal and engineering trades generally, the absolute number of white workers monopolising skills hardly increased in the boom years. Capital had thus to cope generally with a diminishing proportion of skilled to unskilled workers and with questionable skill levels (Coupe 1995).[8]

2 For the recruitment of workers (and they had to be rehired each year) by ISCOR, largely in Transkei, see L.C.J. de Villiers, Personnel Manager, Report on Manpower, May 1971, NA, MPP 23. A3/10/1 pt.1.

3 NA, MES 232, H 4/12, pts ½, Annual Report 1955.

4 NA, MPP 17, A3/1/6/4/4 pt. 1, Unconfirmed Board Minutes, ISCOR, 30 January 1985.

5 NA, MPP 17, A3/1/6/4/4, ISCOR Annual Report to Minister, 31 December 1985.

6 NA, MPP 233 H/4 12 vol. 3, Memorandum from Admin. Director J. P. Coetzee to Minister of Economic Affairs O. Horwood, 10 September 1974.

7 Peter Schirmer, *Sunday Times*, 26 January 1969, NA MES 244, H4/12/3 v.2, ISCOR Annual Report 1965.

8 Coupe stresses how workers were able through their unions but also other means such as the Industrial Councils, to which only whites had representation, to block changes that might disadvantage them. However, he also indicates the means by

Table 6.2. *ISCOR Turnover Rates (1971)*

'Non-whites'	59%
Operatives	56%
Short service	100%+
Artisans	31%
Engineers	12%

From L.C.J. de Villiers, Personnel Manager, Report on Manpower, May 1971, NA MPP 23, A3/10/1 pt. 1.

Moreover, white South African workers with real skills were potentially quite mobile and the retention rates in the small town plants for ISCOR, Vanderbijlpark and Newcastle, were not good. Pretoria, with its more diverse economy, was better placed this way. However, the ISCOR plant in Pretoria lacked the space for expansion and met with increasing awareness of pollution problems, so it came to hold only a smaller share of operations.

One major answer lay in recruiting skilled workers in Europe, a policy that did not end for ISCOR until the last gasp of prosperity at the start of the 1980s.[9] To take the example of ISCOR, these workers came not only from Britain but also from Germany, Switzerland, Sweden, Norway, Italy and the Netherlands, as well as later Greece. Particularly desirable were bricklayers, electricians, fitters and turners.[10] In key periods, such workers got a free passage to South Africa and housing with rentals fixed at a maximum of 20 per cent of income. Beyond that, they were eligible for a Home Ownership Scheme and required to join a workers' club. This kind of worker was unlikely to evolve quickly into a diehard Afrikaner Nationalist but it is also true that he was also unlikely to object strongly to the racial policies which underwrote his own good wages.

which unions for workers of other races were able eventually to challenge this situation.

[9] NA, MPP 51, A3/10/9 Verslae en Notules, ISCOR Monthly Report, 30 September 1981.

[10] NA BTS no volume, 8/19/5, Facts about employment with ISCOR in Vanderbijl Park cyclostyled, for prospective employees; Secretary of Domestic Affairs to Secretary, Foreign Affairs, 29, May 1951; AES 13, AM 7/7 pt. 1; Annual Report ISCOR 1963; Secretary, Ministry of Trade and Industry to Secretary, Ministry of Foreign Affairs, 9 September 1963.

I have used the male pronoun deliberately here. Interestingly also, in the 1970s, management began to experiment with hiring women for what would have been male jobs previously.[11] This shift was obviously considered far less explosive than one fiddling with the racial ceilings.[12] The facility in Newcastle, with its large black population nearby in parts of the Zulu 'homeland' and the presence of an Indian community better primed for skilled jobs after the 1960s, also offered management some relief.[13] In the middle of the 1970s, however, the refusal to train or accept workers of colour, especially in Vanderbijlpark and Pretoria (the rules were more relaxed in Saldanha port and Newcastle where Indian and Coloured workers were present) remained increasingly salient.[14] Newcastle was less of a problem in theory but in fact this major new expanding facility in a town that did not have much appeal to white workers had its own difficulties in the form of high turnover (see also Table 6.2).

According to administrative director F.P. Coetzee,

> ISCOR has for a long period led a struggle against the use of black handymen that is so deeply rooted in the traditional way of life of the white South African. [But] this very tradition is a reason for our unfavourable comparison with overseas concerning man-hours per ton.[15]

A frustrated management then treaded a tightrope, hoping a Nippon Steel expert consultancy team would make slight improvements but not such that the white unions or the government would be unable to 'face up to', causing impossible problems.[16] However, the minister replacing Owen Horwood (who had authorised this evaluation), Chris Heunis, wrote back that the state had no objection to training blacks within Homeland structures 'but these were hardly

11 By 1971 ISCOR was trying use women to drive lorries, operate cranes and work on night shift.

12 NA, MPP 23, A3/10/1 pt. 1, L.C.J. de Villiers, Personnel Manager, ISCOR, Report on Manpower, May 1971.

13 Ibid. For a summary of the advantages and disadvantages of Newcastle, see van Eck to J.F.W. Haak, Minister of Economic Affairs, 29 May 1968, NA, AFE 30, E4/12/3, or NA, WW 289, K 12/84. Transport expenses were seen as an advantage of importance as well as the proximity of coal mines but the Bantustan border policy was also a large positive factor.

14 NA, AFE 30, E4/12/3.

15 NA, MPP 233 H/4 12 vol. 3, to Minister of Economic Affairs O.P.F. Horwood, 10 September 1974.

16 T.F. Muller, chair to O.P.F. Horwood, Minister of Economic Affairs, 12 September 1974.

available'.[17] In the short term, there was renewed effort to recruit staff overseas and indeed 27 engineers, 381 production workers and 421 foreign artisans were hired in 1975 – a banner year. In addition, the 1976 Annual Report announced that there were 979 women employed in production, mostly in Vanderbijlpark and Pretoria, and many administrative workers. However, women were still not acceptable as artisans.[18] The problem then became less acute as the industry itself fell into crisis due to economic downturn and slackening demand for workers.

However, Crompton notes that SASOL was also anxious in the 1980s about increasing numbers of black workers constituting a security breach and, as a result, white workers in some situations, became more, rather than less, numerous (Crompton 1994, 157).[19] The Managing Director of ISCOR in 1985 pointed out to his Minister that all ISCOR personnel, including management, came under systematic police and security surveillance.[20]

This is not to say that the state was unconcerned with the question of Afrikaner employment per se. In fact, ISCOR and SASOL were massive employers of Afrikaners and played a key role in endowing them with marketable urban skills. As such, they can be considered a major factor in providing skills that ultimately after 1994 allowed the lineal descendants of poor whites to manage surprisingly well without access to state patronage and state jobs. ISCOR had an excellent rate of completion of training bursaries on schedule – 65 per cent instead of the usual 20 per cent – and 45 per cent of its working artisans had been trained by the company.[21] This did not mean of course that artisans and other trained workers necessarily stayed at ISCOR or other state corporations for entire careers. Other employers paid better. However, they still entered the overall labour pool from a very improved starting point.

[17] J.P. Coetzee to Minister of Economic Affairs Chris Heunis, 9 June 1975.

[18] NA, MPP 45, 3/10/9 pt. 1, ISCOR Annual Report 1976.

[19] Crompton does note that this was more of a desideratum than a practical possibility. It contrasts with the situation which was already altering towards more black workers in other state-run chemicals operations.

[20] NA, MPP 17, A3/1/6/4/4 pt. 1, F.P. Kotzee, Mg Director, ISCOR to D.J. de Villiers, Minister of Trade and Industries, 1 April 1985, extremely secret.

[21] NA, MPP 23, A3/10/1 pt. 1, L.C.J. de Villiers, ISCOR Personnel Manager, Report on Manpower, May 1971.

In the first generation of National Party power there was much pressure on management both at the level of parliament and within the state bureaucracy (including from their own ranks) to bring to the fore patriotic Afrikaner nationalist management. One secret report noted indignantly that not only was much of top management at ISCOR of British origin but the Afrikaners in such positions tended not to be supportive of the National Party and common communications tended to be in English. This report even considered the political life of the ordinary office staff and must have created a desperate atmosphere during the research phase.[22]

ISCOR was really established in the 1930s and 1940s with engineers and managers van der Bijl poached from ESCOM, largely English speakers.[23] They did remain numerically dominant into the 1950s albeit with growing public pressure to hire Afrikaners. At the close of the 1950s, we find a note from J.G. van der Merwe of the Afrikaans Handelsinstituut (Afrikaner Institute of Commerce) to Nico Diederichs in the cabinet to recommend keeping Kallie Rood on the ISCOR board given what a good job he was doing inserting loyal Nats on the Board. The intimate nature of this elite is revealed by van der Merwe being addressed as 'kaalkop' or 'baldy' and Diederichs as a 'baie groot ou maat' or 'very big old pal'.[24] Of course, Board members were appointed by Cabinet.

At the end of the 1950s as the Verwoerd era began, ISCOR was still considered worthy of an anonymous memorandum. Rood aside, General Administrator C.M. Krueger was identified as a mole who brought in Afrikaner loyalists. However, the administration remained English-speaking (71 per cent of the top 112 posts in 1955 and all in the administration department before the arrival of Krueger were English speakers).[25] Even hiring Afrikaners at more modest levels was

22 NA, MES 232, H 4/12 pts ½, Industrial Development Corporation, Anonymous Memorandum.
23 NA, MES 232, H 4/12 pts ½, Unsigned memorandum, 'Die Afrikaner by YSKOR', 1958.
24 NA, MES 232, H 4/12 pts ½, 1 December 1959.
25 NA, MES 232, H 4/12 pts ½, Unsigned memorandum, 'Die Afrikaner by YSKOR', 1958. In response to criticism from B.J. van der Walt in parliament, management reported in 1957 that of the ninety top jobs, forty-one were held at ISCOR by Afrikaners, forty-two by English South Africans and seven by other whites. Of the next group of 750, the corresponding figures were 563, 399 and 81 others. Meyer to van Rhijn, 17 May 1957, NA, MES 235, HE/12/3/12/1.

a problem given the preference given to war veterans (not likely to be keen Nationalists) and lack of skills; this was, in the view of the author of the memorandum a situation where 'drastic steps were however decidedly necessary'.[26]

Yet competence remained important. In the next generation, it was indeed possible to find competent Afrikaner top managers loyal to the corporations and the perceived need for white solidarity and security meant that this kind of criticism faded away.[27] By this time, too, the dependence on English-linked banks such as Barclays had weakened too. This had been a major source of complaint. Minus this conclusion, the parallels between the National Party with the ANC post-apartheid government and its swingeing policy of racial affirmative action are hard to miss. However, while ISCOR felt the pressure, SASOL was seen as more Afrikaner from the start with only its distant origins to be uncovered before 1948 and in the end the question of who was a top manager was really what stuck the longest and hardest.

One might note, however, one indignant and angry memorandum from Rousseau when SASOL too was challenged in Parliament by National Party MPs.[28] In response to a question from G.F. Froneman, Rousseau wrote to Minister Diederichs that: '[w]e have here the most Afrikaans big business operation that South Africa has yet seen. Things are moving in the right direction.' There was no choice but to rely on numerous foreigners to operate SASOL while key technical posts were held by English speakers (Sparks 2016, 716).[29] He quoted a message from van der Bijl in his prime in 1945 and added: '[t]hrough ISCOR and other undertakings, he was doing more for the economic insertion of the Afrikaans speaker than what we are doing in Federale Volksbeleggings.'[30] In a speech in his honour in 1972, Rousseau called van der Bijl a 'kampvegter' (fighter on the ground) in the struggle to

[26] Unsigned Memorandum, 'Die Afrikaner by YSKOR' 1958, NA, MES 232, H 4/12 pts ½, *my translation*.

[27] Sparks evokes beautifully the enthusiastic and nationalist minded mentality of the SASOL elite gathered around Pierre Etienne Rousseau in 'An Act of Faith', n.d.

[28] NA MES 218, H 46/6 v. 1 and 46/7.

[29] Thus the Chief Chemical Engineer at SASOL was English-born William Neale-May (Bozzoli 1997, 208).

[30] NA MES 218, H 46/6 v. 1 and 46/7, *my translation*. This was effectively the investment arm of the Broederbond according to O'Meara 1983, 113ff. and others.

advance the Afrikaner (Address by P.E. Rousseau 1972, Engineers' Liaison Committee of Pretoria, Hendrik van der Bijl Lesings-Lectures, 123).

He also wrote briefly about the redoubtable Hendrik Johannes van Eck. Like van der Bijl, he had studied in Germany, in his case during the Weimar years, earning his doctorate in 1927. Van Eck's associations with the Smuts government had been so strong that he was ostracised and pushed off his children's school board, leading to them being transferred to English language schools and eventually the English language University of Natal (where, of course, E.G. Malherbe was principal). This was the reward he got, wrote Rousseau indignantly, when he left 'the Jews', which was how he described Anglo-Transvaal, the mining house,[31] and did the honourable thing, shifting to the IDC, which he headed.[32] Minister Diederichs, notorious for his pro-Nazi sentiments during the Second World War, would have perhaps been moved by this reference.

Tim Cross concludes an important article with the following:

> Finally the article has touched upon a more general issue. This concerns the interaction between white South African businessmen across the language divide. In general, the 1960s were the decade when interaction increased and traditional hostile relations declined. The result was that the politics of Afrikaner nationalism declined as an important factor determining with whom Afrikaner private and state capitalists would do business. (Cross 1994a)

However, the same material could be looked at from a different angle: the relationship of the state to the private sector in important economic settings. Typically, developmental states are going to arise where economies are weak and major capitalists scarce and deficient. South Africa had a different formation by the time that ISCOR and SASOL were born. The mining industry, global in size and clearly one of the largest in the world, had engendered a powerful and relatively capital-rich sector. To a much lesser extent, from the 1930s especially, there

31 In fact, Clive Menell of Anglo-Transvaal stood behind the early institution of SASOL!

32 Before 1948, Anglovaal took a substantial interest in the oil from coal process and was considered the most likely promoter of a relevant technology. This was the context for van Eck working there from 1936 at the time, as this was his great interest (Bozzoli 1997, 201).

was also a significant agribusiness sector with which the state had to deal.

The example of English and Afrikaner coming together has often used the example of Harry Oppenheimer's offer of mine company sales to create Gencor, a gift as it were to Afrikaner business, which thereafter could be said to have an important stake in the gold mining business. The importance of this theme is central to our analysis. Whereas Dan O'Meara wrote about how class and capital helped construct mid-twentieth-century Afrikaner nationalism, here we consider rather how nationalism helped construct capitalism as it was structured at that time (O'Meara 1983). Cross is right also to signpost this in considering a contemporary and far less well-known situation, the relationship of ISCOR to a new and surprising competitor, Anglo-American's Highveld Steel.

We have already noted the hostility of Anglos and those who spoke for it to the concept of government-produced steel. In its first years, ISCOR struggled to gain share of the market and had to be subsidised by the state (for instance, through setting cost levels) in order to service the English dominated mining sector. ISCOR steel was bound to offer the cheapest prices to South African consumers. Even the railways were set up so that they depended at first on imported steel for cost considerations. However, this changed during the Second World War.[33] Not only did production mount dramatically but ISCOR acquired experience, competitiveness and size. It then proceeded to produce for a larger and larger percentage of the South African market. A peak of 75.8 per cent of the market was attained in 1968, the last year without significant internal competition.[34]

By that time, however, a competitor had appeared. Anglos owned a property from 1959 near Witbank in what is today Mpumalanga Province, which contained the mineral vanadium. It began to be realised in the 1960s that vanadium pentoxide was an excellent material for strengthening steel and Anglos secured a contract with the Vanadium Corporation of America. This was a very rare metal and the Anglos property had more of it than any place known on earth. Suddenly in 1964, Harry Oppenheimer announced during a speech to the Witbank Rotary Club that Anglos intended to open up a big steel

[33] NA, MES 232, H 4/12 pts ½, Annual Report 1958.
[34] NA, MES 232, H 4/12 pts ½, Annual Report 1968.

plant with an investment of perhaps R100 m. This could not be justified on the strength of the vanadium export alone; there would have to be substantial penetration of the local market.[35] ISCOR management had known this for some weeks and was, despite some complimentary remarks by Oppenheimer, very worried about the loss of its near-monopoly and the potential effect on costs which were strained because of the promise to sell cheaply to domestic markets.[36]

However, Anglos was also worried about how the state would view the loss of monopoly and how prices would be set. Regulation of the industry with ISCOR now became a requirement. Vanadium would be exported, of course, but some steel needed to find an outlet in the domestic market.[37] This was in fact exactly what Minister Diederichs also had in mind.[38]

Diederichs, mindful of the power of the mining industry not to speak of Anglos' hold on capital availability through its links with the British banking world, insisted in this context on the primacy of the 'free market' and certainly of competition:

> Apart from the fact that water, import facilitation for equipment and the inflow of African labour can be refused, the government has now no legal powers to prevent Anglo-American from progressing with the erection of a steel factory or any other factory in the country. It also will not be an adequate reason to refuse to Anglo-American the right to build this facility for steel manufacture only because ISCOR is already active in this area. Anglo-American must have a much more concrete justification for such a refusal . . . [39]

This did not mean though that ISCOR would not be cut into the deal.[40] In the 1968 first annual report for a functioning Highveld, Oppenheimer specifically thanks ISCOR for its assistance.[41] This

[35] Oppenheimer speech, NA MES 135, HE/12/3/12/1.
[36] NA, AES AM 7/7 pt. 1, ISCOR board meeting, 25 March 1964.
[37] Anglo American Memorandum on Highveld, 9 December 1963.
[38] NA, MES 235, HE/12/3/12/1, Summary of meeting between Diederichs and ISCOR management, 14 May 1964.
[39] Minute oor Anglo American se Beoogde Staalprojek, 4 May 1964, NA MES 235, H4/12/v. 1 and 2; following a Note to the Minister from Ag Secretary, 4 May 1964.
[40] NA, MES 235, H4/12/v. 1 and 2 [Secret]: Notes on Highveld.
[41] NA, MES 235, H4/12/v. 1, Highveld Steel Annual Report 1968; see also van Eck to Haak, Minister of Economic Affairs, 26 June 1968. This latter reference points to the continued importance of rail supplies.

kind of approach would strengthen in the following decade. By 1974 Minister Owen Horwood was writing to the chairman of ISCOR, T.F. Muller, that ISCOR needed to sort its problems out with Highveld (in this case for planning to manufacture steel plate initially for export but potentially to cut into ISCOR's lucrative domestic market). He pointed out that the Economic Advisory Council came to see that criticism of ISCOR 'in this respect is not always unfounded'.[42]

In fact, as Cross stresses, Highveld and Anglos had another plan as well. They proposed early on to construct a steel mill in Witbank instead, bringing in ISCOR and obviating the need for the Newcastle expansion.[43] This plan never came to fruition. For this there were several reasons. One was that at least part of the government had come to see the virtues of competition. In 1968 Minister of Transport Ben Schoeman pointed out that ISCOR prices may well not have reflected the optimum for South Africa and could perhaps improve through competition with the new boy on the block.[44] Witbank, which would have been more suitable for export given its relative proximity to Delagoa Bay, was less favoured than Newcastle, so close to the heart of KwaZulu, a major Bantustan component. Cross believes a dire group of Afrikaner reactionaries also wished to keep Anglos' influence out, probably at the cost of future profits, but this is less convincing from his narrative.

It remains true that the relation between the parastatals and rival private firms continued sometimes to be uneasy if, say, the private company took up a new line of business[45] or the parastatal did.[46] SASOL faced similar issues, for instance vis-à-vis Anglos'-dominated AECI over the manufacture of fertilisers, into which both had diversified.[47] If ISCOR, for instance, purchased private companies for reasons of state security, was this not unfair violation of competition

42 NA, MES v. 234, HR/12, v. 4, 27 August 1974.

43 NA, MES v. 234, HR/12, v. 4, n.d. secret.

44 NA, MES 235, H4/12/v. 1 and 2, Schoeman to J.F.W. Haak, Minister of Economic Affairs, 4 March 1968.

45 NA, MPP 233 H/4 12, v. 3, Coetzee to Horwood, 5 November 1974 and Besprekings op 20 Maart 1975 met Dr T.F. Muller.

46 NA, HR/12/1 pt. 4, 1971–3, S. Shlagman, Pres, Transvaal Chamber of Industries to Secretary for Industries, 2 March 1973.

47 NA, AES 10, AM 7 and 7/3660, Notas van Bespreking met Mnr. Haak; NAMES 218, H 46/6 v. 1 and 46/7, Etienne Rousseau to Minister of Economic Affairs, 2 August 1960.

with private enterprise?[48] Yet ISCOR could write somewhat plaintively of the advantages, held by Anglos in particular, and why they had, on purely economic grounds, to compete very vigorously with them, for instance, as a purchaser of supplier companies.[49] A refined version of the ploy proposed by Anglos was sometimes the answer. Thus at the end of the 1970s, a joint venture between ISCOR and Anglos to share the ownership of Samancor or to create a new public-private pyramid company, which mined manganese and chrome, was debated.[50] Similarly, AECI and SASOL acted sometimes as rivals and sometimes co-operated on ventures in the chemical arena (Crompton 1994, 138–9; Sparks 2016, 719).

Tim Cross details the invention of Metkor in 1969. Metkor was a creation of ISCOR, which had only a small share of ownership but held chairmanship and half the directorships. Metkor investors also included British Steel and Anglos (Cross 1994a, 42–3). It enabled ISCOR to allow key suppliers, at the time typically British, to feel that they were in safe hands but also that ISCOR was effectively protected against possible negative ramifications of the nationalisation of British Steel. Metkor itself owned a considerable part of IPSA, the parent pyramid company.[51] This cross-fertilisation of private companies, including foreign companies with state corporations, marked the late apartheid period and actually fitted very well what one might expect from a developmental state.

It is perhaps noteworthy that this development was seen as a disaster by Afrikaner nationalists committed to the radical policies of Strijdom and especially Verwoerd. A spokesman for this school, B.M. Schoeman, could only understand it as a conspiracy engineered by the money power – *die Geldmag* – in alliance with what he considered to be Communist subversives (Schoeman 1980). The arrival in power

[48] NA, MES 236, H4/12/1 pt. 3, T.F. Muller, Director, ISCOR to Nico Diederichs, Minister of Finance, 30 March 1972, Richard Stuart, *Financial Mail,* 8 August 1977 and telex to C. Heunis, Minister of Economic Affairs, NA, MPP 31, A3/10/4.

[49] NA, MES 245, HA4/12/3/pt. 4, ISCOR Memorandum, Yskor en die Private Nywerheid in die Republiek van Suid-Afrika, 17 March 1975.

[50] NA, MPP 23, A3/10/1 pt. 1, Private and confidential memorandum, J.P. Kearney, SAMANCOR, 3 July 1979 and T.F. Muller, Chair, ISCOR to S.W. van der Merwe, Minister of Industry, Trade and Consumer Affairs, 4 July 1979.

[51] NA, MPP 23, A3/10/1 pt. 1.

of B.J. Vorster in 1966 and, even more so, the succession under P.W. Botha opened the door to this alliance advancing further now with the aid of the Ruperts, the SANLAM crowd and the rest. Schoeman pointed dramatically to the full house reception of Vorster in the Rand Club in 1968 where he spoke in English for an entire hour, and to Vorster's comfortable relationship with Harry Oppenheimer, as evidence for his perspective. Of course, the idea of Oppenheimer in league with Communists is absurd but it is quite true that, as apartheid seemed ever less able to resolve South African political problems, Anglos and other big companies were indeed prepared to do what they could to find a solution with the ANC and, if need be, its South African Communist Party allies. If Oppenheimer established a reasonable relationship with Vorster in mid-career, at the end of his life he also established a reasonable relationship with Nelson Mandela – and he took most of the capital with him (Freund 2013a). And at the end of the twentieth century, a black empowerment deal was struck that, given the relative weakness and lack of organisation on the part of black capitalists, evoked the shadow of the Gencor arrangement more than thirty years before.

The final point this chapter takes up is the broad industrial impact of the parastatal intervention. In a memorial tribute to van der Bijl, T.P. Stratten said that secondary industry in South Africa had grown 'based very largely on the impetus provided by cheap power and steel through van der Bijl's major enterprises ESCOM and ISCOR'.[52] However, even this tribute expressed anxiety that gold still played far too large a role and that industry could well experience a reversal. To what extent can it be said that an industrial base emerged in South Africa outside the direct production of steel and oil from coal, for instance, and what international purchase did it have? This goes to the heart of the developmental state issue and the answer is a mixed one. As we shall see, the products of SASOL and ISCOR did lead to an important industrial uptake but the industries that emerged failed to become major contributors to international trade by and large. There was certainly an industrial cluster created in South Africa, impressive compared to almost anywhere outside Europe and North America, but within certain limits that reflected the orientation both of private and public

[52] Address by T.P. Stratten, van der Bijl Memorial Lectures 1963, 13–14.

sectors and no doubt was partially determined by the permanent scarcity of skilled labour.

ISCOR and SASOL did start out on the right foot apparently. ISCOR's 1955 Annual Report announced that

> Plate manufacture at Vanderbijl Park, begun in 1943, has led to considerable development in the manufacture of irrigation pipes, transport and mine vehicles, tanks and numerous other items. More recently, the availability of a number of grades of hot and cold rolled uncoated sheets has led to the development of many important industries such as the manufacture of refrigerator bodies, hollow-ware, enamelware, steel furniture, shelving and drums.[53]

ISCOR had long since recovered from wartime conditions by this time and South Africa was only importing very limited specialised steel supplies from Britain. In 1958, Rousseau put forward in the SASOL Annual Report that 'I stress this point seeing that we all believe that Sasol's future role is not only to provide motor fuel and chemicals raw material from internal sources but also to offer South Africa the general advantage of becoming a centre of specialised knowledge and research'.[54] Yet the archival record is replete with references to security and to strategic considerations as coming first.[55]

In the case of ISCOR, much attention was paid from time to time to the export of steel itself. Management would, however, be brought short to be reminded that the key issue was the provision of steel (directly and indirectly to the benefit of the mining industry) to South African customers at reasonable prices set by the state. This was made very clear at the time of the rapid recovery from the Sharpeville Crisis in the early 1960s, which in fact had coincided with a major recession in global economic conditions.[56] Despite the fact that South African demand rose, and in consequence, with production having doubled in tonnage in a decade, ISCOR was exporting on quite a large scale, almost 31 per cent of it to

53 NA, MES 232, H4/12 pts ½.

54 NA, MES 218 H 46/6 v. 1 and 46/7; see also P.E. Rousseau, Co-operation with Other Companies and a Scheme for an Integrated Chemical Undertaking in SA, 14 January 1959, NA HEN 3660, 539 pts 1–3.

55 NA, HEN 3660, 539 pts 1–3. P.E. Rousseau, Considerations Regarding the Establishment of an Oil from Coal Industry in South Africa, 22 December 1951.

56 NA, MES 244, H4/12/3 v.2.

neighbouring African markets.[57] Export sales were in fact then rapidly suspended with the exception of Rhodesia.[58]

In the later 1960s, the industry was growing fast but finding it hard to meet local demand. Management was reminded that the prime objective of the company remained keeping the price of steel to a minimum in South Africa and providing for that market.[59] Once again export plans were brought short and remained at a fairly low level in the first half of the 1970s despite some plans to develop further and systematically with a sliding scale of prices at the start of the decade.[60] This evolved into a 'policy of annually supplying a limited tonnage of steel to establish foreign markets and customers'.[61] ISCOR was, however, selling substantial amounts of iron ore to Japan. This was easier to organise than steel sales in an environment of rising prices and shortages. Quickly after this, however, in 1976 crisis hit and poor market conditions made steel difficult to sell internationally. The situation was much affected by the expansion era debts that had now accrued – an 'intolerably high level of loan redemption and interest burden'.[62] The value of the Rand fell dramatically and yet South Africa was virtually obliged to grow exports quickly. Under these conditions, exports rose again from 8 per cent of steel production in 1971 and 1972 to 30 per cent suddenly in 1977 and peaked at 37 per cent in 1979, falling again to 25 per cent in 1981, while overall production steadily increased, despite poor profit figures, from 2.5 m. tons in 1971 to more than 3.5 m. in 1977 and a peak of 5.5 m. in 1980. There was equally a surprisingly high

57 NA, AES 13 AM 7/7 pt. 1, ISCOR Annual Report 1964, ISCOR Board Meetings, 22 January 1964, 27 November 1963.

58 NA, AES 13 AM 7/7 pt. 1, ISCOR Annual Report 1964, ISCOR Board Meetings, 22 January 1964, 27 November 1963, AES 13 AM 7/7 pt. 1, ISCOR Annual Report 1965.

59 NA, MES 235, HE/12/3/12/1 Memorandum from the Minister of Economic Affairs to the Cabinet, 9 October 1963. This policy remained standard for long afterwards. See report, Komitee van Ondersoek na Yskor Aangeleenthede, chair Professor C.W.I. Pistorius, created 4 July 1975. SASOL also had to be mindful of this basic idea repeatedly set forth. NA HEN 3660, 539, pts 1–3, P.E. Rousseau to D.H. Steyn Secretary of the Treasury, 16 March 1953.

60 NA, MPP 23, A3/10/1 pt. 1, Supplementary Memorandum of the Department of Industries to the Economic Advisory Board of the Prime Minister [n.d. but 1974]; AFE 29, E4/12/1 pt. 1, ISCOR Memorandum, 6 March 1973.

61 NA, MPP 44, A3/10/9 ISCOR Annual Report 1975.

62 NA, MPP 50, ISCOR Draft Annual Report 1978.

percentage of South African provision (over 75 per cent) but in a very poor international market.[63] Indeed, in 1978 there was a potential problem with dumping steel in the US market.[64] In the last short-lived boom around 1980, the roller coaster ride continued and mid-1970s conditions briefly resumed as ISCOR reached its unprecedented maximum production figure of 5.5 m. tons. However, this last fling was short-lived[65] and unrelieved crisis followed, now accompanied by rapid decline in both export and production figures, which we shall examine in our final substantive chapter.

Steel exports, however, were a different matter from the export of steel-based products more generally. The state did become heavily involved in the ownership of key steel-using companies, of considerable importance. However, these companies, almost entirely British in origin, were in fact purchased, once again with the idea of securing supplies for South Africa and ultimately for South African mining, and especially with an eye on the possibility of fending off political action aimed at the country. The possible nationalisation of the British steel industry was looked at carefully in this light. It was not only that Metkor included British Steel in order to keep it interested in South African production but it also included key companies that operated almost entirely on the Witwatersrand – Stewart & Lloyd, Baldwins and especially Dorman Long, which would form the core of Dorbyl and had long played a big role on the mines and in construction.[66] These companies were not really directed towards further conceptual planning or innovation but linked to security and mining.

Zalk demonstrates that this was more or less the same for Anglo-American, which grouped an impressive series of metal-based manufacturing companies together as AMIC (Zalk 2017, 135). This stable included Boart and Scaw. Boart used industrial diamonds to produce

63 NA, MPP 45, A3/10/9/ pt. 1, ISCOR Annual Report 1977; MPP 48, A3/10/8 Verslae en Notules, Annual Report 1980.

64 NA, MPP 50, A3/10/9, ISCOR Monthly Report, 26 April 1978.

65 NA, MPP50 Verslae en notule, ISCOR, Monthly Report, 28 October 1981.

66 NA, MES 235, HE 12/3/12/1, Ian Fleming, Ag. Chairman, British Steel, to J.F.W. Haak, Minister of Economic Affairs, 20 November 1969; Cross 1994a. Dorbyl at its peak employed some 25,000 workers. Dorman Long actually built the Vanderbijlpark works, SASOL 2 and 3, Alusaf, Highveld and Columbus steel and the big power stations. It also was important in constructing rolling stock for the railways. In 1973 it was merged with Vecor, ISCOR's long-established engineering company, to create Dorbyl (Zalk 2017, 140).

unusually hard tips for pneumatic drills although in time it shifted to tungsten oxide as a raw material. Founded by De Beers in 1936, a brilliant move given the Depression disaster in gem diamond sales, Boart had leading edge technology and important export sales (Zalk 2017, 143–4; Innes 1984). However, this reached its peak as early as the 1950s. Afterwards it was a unique profitable company that carried through a familiar technology and proved in the long run too closely linked to the particular conditions of South African gold mines once they began to decline in global importance. Of Steel and Ceiling Aluminium Works (Scaw) one could say much the same, vital to local production of gold, designed to fit the South African market in its prime, innovative and export-orientated but reaching and passing that prime already in the 1950s. It was purchased by AMIC in 1964 (Zalk 2017, 148). A variant of the theme was the key wire producer Haggie. Haggie, whose security and price were both important, was in time owned jointly amongst others by ISCOR and AMIC (Zalk 2017, 149).

Crompton argues a parallel case, that 'mining and agricultural products have dominated South African chemical markets' (Crompton 1994, 148).[67] The price structure in the industry, especially due to the price set by SASOL for ethylene, where it has been a sole producer, has been set by this huge corporation. Neither SASOL nor AECI have been crucial in setting up a diverse chemicals industry. It is possible to argue that the structure of the expensive industrial process militates against that. However, Crompton believed that from the 1980s, the massive uptake in plastics products (Crompton 1994, 154) could have led to a major and less capital-intensive diversified business with unlimited potential based on South African innovation, a road not taken by the profitable big players. Many years later, as retiring National Energy Regulator of South Africa chairperson, he continues to take this position and makes the point that structures long ago set in stone need reconsideration for new forms of economic growth to take place (Crompton 2016).

The result was a particular configuration. South Africa continues to have an important metal and chemicals production industrial sector.

[67] Sentrachem was a joint state-private sector (but heavily Afrikaner) chemical company founded in 1967. It was a leading factor together with FOSKOR for capitalist farming development.

It is hard to imagine this as taking off historically without massive state intervention. However, it is a sector that remains wedded to South Africa's mines and it has limited export traction. It is typical that when the rail line through the country was built to Saldanha Bay at enormous expenditure in the middle of the 1970s, the lucrative item of carriage was expected to be neither the metal products of the Rand nor even ISCOR steel, but the raw iron ore being mined at Sishen, aimed largely at a Japanese market at a time when the Japanese post-war developmental state was at its peak of success.[68] There were originally plans for the railway to pass through the Rand and the industrial Ruhr-like district on its east side as well as Vanderbijlpark and Newcastle, the steel-making centres ISCOR ran, but they were shelved.[69] The upshot was, however, in a period of crisis, that ISCOR had to sell the railway to the state and eventually the state took over its debt.[70]

Here we can see that the development of South African manufacturing, and here looking at its strong end, was never really liberated from the prime need to service local mines. This fits the ideas of those who see South Africa as a prime case of import substitution industrialisation but it also tends to firm up the view of manufacturing as fundamentally subordinated to a minerals-energy complex still effectively in place insofar as activity on the ground is concerned. On the energy side of things, which began to loom larger in the public eye from the 1970s, discussion is to be deferred to Chapter 8.

[68] NA, MPP 23, A3/10/1 pt. 1, ISCOR Annual Report 1974.
[69] NA, MES v. 236 sys 01 v. 5.
[70] NA, MES 245, H4/12/3 pt. 4, Meeting with Ministry, 8 October 1976.

7 *Key Institutions*

The IDC, the CSIR, the HSRC

This chapter is diffuse in content. It is unified by an idea: that institutions are a key feature in state-led development and call for description and assessment. Economic development in South Africa, in particular, industrial development, required capital so the importance of finance can hardly be overlooked. For this reason we are going to consider the IDC, founded in 1940 and still in existence.[1] We will then turn to institutions that fit the growing positive evaluation of knowledge and research based learning as a normal and irreplaceable part of the development process.

The importance of a financial institution aimed at development has already emerged in discussion above. The Land Bank played an important role in building up a capitalist agriculture, highly mechanised and capable of reaching substantial export markets. For secondary industry, however, problems remained (Rosenthal 1960, 8). As we have seen, while considerable amounts of capital were locked up in mining interests, it was those interests, not very sympathetic to an industrialisation project, that controlled the local banks primarily and also had the ties to the City of London.[2] George Kuschke, van Eck's successor, pointed out that even in 1969, whereas mining constituted 1.1 per cent of GDP in the USA and even only 4.2 per cent in Canada, in South Africa the figure was 12.2 per cent (Kuschke 1969). The independent

[1] A far more detailed and richer picture should emerge from a doctoral thesis by Nnzeni Netshitomboni, which he is researching and writing for the University of the Witwatersrand.

[2] The mining industry itself reported in 1961 that over the past fifteen years, gold and uranium mining had required investment of R740 m. of which more than half had to be raised outside the country, as well as another R470 m. for capital purposes. NA, TES 9009, 161/11/1 v. 2, Transvaal and Orange Free State Chamber of Mines Memorandum, October 1961, Fiscal Policy in Relation to the Gold Mining Industry.

Reserve Bank, with its focus on stabilisation, was also not going to play this role.

The IDC filled an important gap, although more indirectly than directly, therefore. By 1970, it had given out R850 m. to 1,250 odd projects. It held R378 m. for further investment with R40.5 m. in reserve money (Cartwright 1971). The first loan was given out to a small town Eastern Cape business, Ouma, the rusk maker (Cartwright 1971, 13–14). While the IDC did help many small businesses of this kind with loans of R50,000 and less on application, most of them incidentally owned by English speaking whites (Brayshaw n.d.), its true vocation lay somewhat elsewhere.

The key figure was H.J. van Eck as managing director (van der Bijl was the first chairman), whose prominence has already been signalled in Chapters 4 and 6. Van Eck was the chair of Smuts' wartime planning commission and a love of planning guiding him throughout his career up to his death in 1970. He saw his work during the war as 'the first attempt in South Africa at planning on a rational basis in a democracy by the simple method of submitting factual reports which had to be published' (van Eck 1961, 56). In the early years, while contributing to the war effort, the IDC focused on overall planning, on how to activate the commission desiderata put forward (Brayshaw n.d., van Eck 1951). Jan Hofmeyr, a somewhat equivocal developer, had in fact wanted some government body to oversee the development of the parastatals and that was what the IDC was set to do more than any other institution (Cartwright 1971, 18).

In two fatal ways, van Eck also pursued developmental goals distinctively. One was the dependence on cheap coal for energy 'the basis of confidence in the future of industry in South Africa and will be the outstanding instrument for building up the standard of living of the peoples of the Union'. The other was the disinterest in conquering foreign markets:

> The present industrial development in South Africa is designed largely to satisfy our requirements. While there may be opportunities in certain selected lines for export to other parts of Africa, I feel that our industry in South Africa should be devoted largely towards the satisfaction of the wants of its own people. (van Eck 1951, 20)

In his 1951 speech to the Institute of Race Relations, still thinking of the reforms of the 1940s, he pointed to the institution of black housing

1. Source: NA, MES 244, H4/12/3 v. 2, ESCOM to Minister of Economic Affairs, 5 August 1964. Bank loan of 50 m. francs from **Switzerland**
2. Source: NA, MES 244, H4/12/3 v. 2, ISCOR Board Meeting, Minutes, 23 July 1969. Public issue on the European capital market of DM150 m.
3. Source: NA, MPP 44, A3/10/9, ISCOR Board Meeting, 30 June 1976 Small loan obtained from **Canadian** Export Dev Corp and Bank of Nova Scotia.
   Source: NA, MPP 44, A3/10/9, J.P. Coetzee, General Manager, ISCOR, to S.L. Mueller, Minister of Economic Affairs, 15 February 1971. Loan issue via Westdeutsche Landbank approved and loan via Algemene Bank **Nederland** is being made as private placement.
4. Source: NA, MPP 44, A3/10/9, ISCOR Board Meeting, 23 February 1972. Loan arrangements to be renewed with Union Bank of **Switzerland**.
5. Source: NA, NIPP 44, A3/10/9, ISCOR Board Meeting, 26 July 1972, Loan in process from Kredietbank SA **Luxembourgeoise**.
6. Source: NA, IviES 236, H4/12/1 pt. 3; This file discusses various loan agreements: credit arrangement with Commerzbank Aktiengesellschaft Frankfurt as well as Westdeutsche Landesbank as of 1971 guaranteed by the South African government for DM 100 m.; revolving agreement with **Kredietbank NV Brussel** for US $25 m. 1972 loan for 60 m. florins from the **Algemeen Bank Nederland**; 1973 loan from Euro-Credit **Panama** of $200 m., 1972 loan from consortium of **German** banks aimed at the construction of the ISCOR Newcastle plant.
7. Source: NA, MPP 233 H/4 12 v. 3. Also aimed at Newcastle, ISCOR loan from **International Bank of Settlements**, Basel.
8. Source: NA, MPP 29, A3/10/4 vols 5/6. It is a German bank that led the consortium to loan the money for Newcastle and a Belgian bank that provided the money as leader to construct the port at Saldanha. Reference also to an ESCOM loan from the **First National City Bank, USA,** 1974. 1973 loan from **Japan** (Mitsubishi). By contrast a $10 m. loan from Volkskas is small.
9. Source: NA, MPP 45, A3/10/9 pt 1, ISCOR Annual Report 1977. ISCOR borrows money from **Crocker National Bank (USA)** and Standard Bank Import and Export.
10. Source: NA, MPP 31, A3/10/4. Loans in the late 1970s: Trade Development Bank,. **Switzerland**, Swiss francs 18 m., **Bayerische Vereinsbank,** DM 20 m., **Union Bank of Switzerland**, Swiss francs 30m., **Commerzbank (Frankfurt)** DM 20 m., **Société Bancaire Barclays**, Swiss francs 30 m.

Figure 7.1. Archival Notes about Foreign Loans

programmes, the beginnings of pensions and disability rights accruing to black people and saw what was on offer as demonstrating 'respect for human rights and human dignity'. Van Eck, despite the close links to Smuts, became a fairly enthusiastic collaborator with the National

Party government, with whom he shared industrial dreams and he had no problems with the growing need for defending the regime militarily and in other ways (van Eck 1967). To begin with, he defended the importance of the Good Hope textile plant outside King William's Town as a model for building up homeland economies that would also flow into betterment scheme success as well as reduce the influx of Africans into cities. Indeed by 1950 more than R15 m. had been invested in textiles (Brayshaw, n.d.). In 1967 he proposed that textiles 'offered opportunities both for the extensive employment of non-white labour, well adapted to repetitive manual operations' and located where jobs were needed.

> The IDC had irrevocably set its imprimatur on the desirability of decentralization and the practicality of the application of this general principle to industrial development where it could be justified in the long term on economic grounds. (van Eck 1967, 46)

He had been equally emphatic when speaking to the South Africa Club at the Savoy Hotel in London in 1966 in tribute to Verwoerd shortly after his assassination (van Eck 1966). What was desirable and practicable became possible with separate development.[3] In his last years, he focused on the construction of the Cabora Bassa dam on the Zambesi in Mozambique.

It could be said that the IDC went through two distinct phases if one wishes to characterise its activities up to the 1970s (see also Table 7.1). One was the emphasis on assisting SASOL and the chemical industry more generally (Brayshaw, n.d.). Here van Eck had some expertise and interest going back to his youth. He wrote with great enthusiasm about visiting Ludwigshafen in 1929 with van der Bijl during the Weimar years in Germany where, in violation of the Versailles Treaty, he experienced the thrill of going to a secret IG Farben experimental operation where hydrogenation was being used as a process to transform coal into oil (van Eck 1967, 47). This sector was estimated to swallow almost 40 per cent of direct IDC spending up to the early 1980s (de Waal 1982).

Other investments, often in chemicals-linked operations, were also significant. Thus the IDC helped nurture the SAPPI plant opened at Tugela to produce newsprint, calcium cyanide manufacture at

[3] His successor, George Kuschke, was equally committed to separate development. Address by George Kuschke 1971, Engineers' Liaison Committee of Pretoria. 7th Hendrik van der Bijl Lesings-Lectures 1963–72.

Table 7.1. *IDC Investments up to 1965*

Chemicals, drugs, petrol products	145 m. Rand
Textiles and clothing	19 m.
Metal, engineering, machinery	12 m.
Construction and property	4 m.
Agricultural and pastoral processing	4 m.
Wood	3 m.
Financial institutions	7 m.
Transport and miscellaneous	15 m.
TOTAL	214 m.[*sic*]

Source: Brayshaw n.d.

Klipspruit made from methane (1955), sheet glass by the British firm of Pilkingtons at Springs (1952), abrasives at Isando and petrol refining at Wentworth, Durban (van Eck 1961).

> No post-war picture would be complete without reference to the phenomenal growth of our fishing industry, the development of plastics and paints, and the recent growth of electronics (van Eck 1961, 60)

As we have noted in Chapter 6, emphasis on building up the Bantustans took up more and more thought and determination as time went on (South Africa Department of Information n.d.).[4] This second thrust took over much of the developmental impetus of the IDC (Cartwright 1971, 18) and about 25 per cent of loans in quantity up to the early 1980s (de Waal 1982).

Afrikanerisation was also an important factor (Cartwright 1971, 45). Tienie Louw joined the Board of Directors in 1949 (Rosenthal 1960, 14) and two other Afrikaner business figures joined the following year. In the late 1950s, while always a mix, it included A.J. Visser of the Afrikaanse Handelsinstituut and F.J. de Villiers, organising director for industrial development in the Department of Native Affairs. There was also a protectionist bias. Safmarine was backed as a South African entry competing with an American shipbuilding company. Foreign firms gradually were given particular special deals at times where effectively technology could be sold but there was little

[4] Eventually the Development Bank of South Africa would be founded and prove to be a more efficient agent for this side of things.

desire to promote real joint ventures (Rosenthal 1960). This was less true in the later apartheid years, however, particularly if a strategic technology were at stake and the joint venture tended to make the technology transfer safer.[5]

The constitutional constraints that governed the IDC's budget and relation to the state prevented it from becoming a massive source of industrial support finance itself. One way the IDC could help finance South African firms was through creating a national discount house in 1961 at the end of the first major crisis in international credibility and then establishing relations with British discount banks (Brayshaw n.d.). However, before this it had already acquired considerable efficacy. No doubt nurtured by van Eck, it held growing capacity to establish the linkages for key concerns with those that could play this role.[6] In the 1950s, the rise of ISCOR, ESCOM and SASOL impressed foreigners, as did the determination of the South African state to take them further.[7] The 1949 balance of payments crisis created real difficulty in securing loans, especially on the London market; even then, Americans and Swiss financiers were largely the ones who came through. Chase Manhattan Bank was the icebreaker in the USA. Yet Britain too became more interested as long as loans could be repaid in gold. As the 1950s proceeded, London ceased to be an obstacle for South African borrowing.[8]

This made loans to the parastatals and eventually other important industrial firms feasible. The IDC provided the research, the contacts, notably with governments, and negotiated the financial deals. However, Shan Ramburuth in his University of the Witwatersrand masters' dissertation captured the IDC's central role as a creator of linkages, especially in his case in regard to the formation of Richards Bay and its aluminium smelter. He argues that it was critical as the source of information on technical and financial feasibility, on the means of insurance, on the injection of equity capital and then of concessionary loans and export credit facilities (Ramburuth 1997, 3).

[5] IDC, Correspondence with Sandock-Austral Ltd, Boksburg 1979.
[6] NA, TES 9009, 161/11/1 v. 2.
[7] See the favourable assessment from the USA: NA, HKE 139, H7/54 v. 2 and H7/55, US Department of Commerce. World Trade Information Service. Economic Reports I, 58–78, Industrial Developments in the Union of South Africa, 1958. At this point, foreign liabilities were still some 60 per cent held by Britain, showing the weight of the mining interest.
[8] NA, BTS 28/8/1.

Figure 7.1 gives the reader some idea of the foreign loan system expedited by the IDC, mainly for ISCOR up into the 1970s. SASOL received more direct state assistance, including IDC money.

Loans are noted coming from Germany, Switzerland (particularly important), the Netherlands, Belgium, Luxembourg, Japan, Canada and the USA. In addition, note the role of the International Bank of Settlements and a presumably deutschmark or florin denominated Panamanian bank. Money also did flow in on a smaller scale from local sources starting with the successful launch of the Industrial Selections Corporation in 1962, intended to gather up South African capital.

I was given the opportunity to inspect the correspondence from 1979 between the IDC and the Sandock-Austral Ltd Company of Boksburg on the East Rand. This was itself owned by Genmin, formerly Gencor, the SANLAM dominated company created by the 1964 deal with Harry Oppenheimer to bring Afrikaner business into mining. Sandock-Austral was a company that produced 'alternative transmission in this high volume market segment ... in the interests of the South African truck manufacturers'. In 1973 Gencor had bought this firm from Paramount, a monopoly producer, specifically so that military vehicles could be accommodated. It had a precedent:

> Following the ADE engine project, in terms of which a range of Mercedes-Benz and Perkins engines will be manufactured in SA ... and although the manufacturer would be South African, the axles are a joint MAN-Daimler Benz project.

These were top German companies.

This deal was considered as especially desirable by IDC planners and technical experts. On the one hand, it fitted the desire to build up the motor and motor parts industries in South Africa. It also had to be compatible with the new diesel engines that would be constructed by the state at Atlantis, a very costly project. There was a key security link and that was the other hand. It was also assumed that Germans were not very likely to interest themselves in the sanctions campaign that was gaining ground elsewhere, for instance in the USA during the Jimmy Carter presidency. Sandock-Austral was involved in manufacture of Ratels and Eland armoured cars. They made the gearboxes and rear axles but not, from the military angle, profitably, so the use in commercial vehicles was also important.

There was a counter-proposal for manufacture at Isithebe in Natal by Fuller, but Minister Heunis believed the project had too much at stake in terms of border warfare to be appropriate for homeland manufacture even though that kind of factory might have been more profitable as it was more suitable for purely commercial vehicles. Moreover, Sandock-Austral was part of an empire associated with Afrikaner capital. De Villiers linked up closely, not only to the Minister of Economic Affairs and the Minister of Trade and Industry (arranging a favourable tariff plan) but also to Armscor (Krygkor), increasingly important in the economy producing military goods for the state, and NAAMSA, the arm of the auto industry. The Atlantis project also itself had security implications. Zahnradfabrik (ZF) in Friedrichshafen (Germany) proposed manufacturing in Boksburg perhaps 15,000 axles per annum, of which two-thirds would be for normal civilian use but with the understanding that the military consumer was the most important one. This would be governed by exclusive rights as a monopoly firm and the cost estimated at R40 m.[9]

Eventually the following memorandum was issued having been sent for approval to de Villiers on 7 July 1979:

> The General Mining and Finance Corporation Ltd announce that they have decided to embark on a major project to expand their existing facilities to manufacture gear boxes, axles and steering boxes for commercial vehicles ... a new subsidiary company of General Mining is to be formed in joint venture with overseas know-how partners. The IDC has been invited to participate in the project to ensure the closest co-operation with Atlantis Diesel Engines so that complementary product ranges will be available to local vehicle manufacturers[10] ... The range of gear boxes to be manufactured will cater for commercial vehicles from 2 250 kilogram g.v.m. and upwards. Expansion of manufacturing activities will commence shortly and it is envisaged that 100 per cent local content will be achieved by the end of 1983. Capital requirements for this phase are estimated at R40 m. License agreements concluded with overseas companies ensure complete technical support for the locally manufactured products.

The military part was well catered for.

> Gears for the Ratel and Eland are manufactured according to German technology with 80% local content. The most important imported parts

[9] Sandock-Austral director, 7 August 1979 to A.J. van den Berg of the IDC.
[10] For Atlantis, see also IDC Special Survey, *Finance Week*, 22–8 June 1980.

are bearings and seals. The Germans maintain that their quality is as good as what can be found overseas ... Special ... gears for helicopters and fighter planes are manufactured for Atlas Aircraft. A core of specially skilled personnel has already been raised and the site is well supplied.

ZF was effectively chosen by the South African Defence Force. While Fuller hoped to reach a maximum of 50 per cent local content, ZF could attain 88 per cent: 'There were advantages in the support of Mercedes for this project' (Senior technical staff know German and have close ties to Mercedes and to ZF personnel).

The Fuller project is really limited to assembly and much more dependent on unskilled labour. Austral can pay 50–60% of capital costs ... The thought is to establish the Fuller premises in a homeland. The Army will not be happy with this and it is undesirable for strategic reasons.[11]

This complex deal with its tariff and financial implications, its link to the military and the total defence strategy in place nationally, was in large part put together by the IDC. Thus it could be said to have achieved its purpose, even though this particular project also shows how the entire developmental project gets effectively slanted in the final decade of the regime towards homeland industry and apartheid (in this case an unsuccessful contender for prioritisation) as well as to military requirements and self-sufficiency, the themes that will take over towards the end of this book.

Although chance was more of a factor, it might also be noted that the IDC itself generated financial power and financialisation. In 1977 a group of Stellenbosch University graduates, largely Afrikaners, got a small loan to form Rand Consolidated Investments. Its first profitable venture was financing transformers purchased by the West Rand municipality of Krugersdorp. Reasonably successful, in 1984 they were effectively merged with the Ruperts' Rand Merchant Bank. This was a key part of the tactics of Johann Rupert, the second-generation heir, moving into finance and luxury goods (and internationalising) and out of tobacco and liquor in South Africa. By 2014, RMB/FNB had become 'Africa's largest bank for savings and market value' (*Financial Mail*, 17 October 2014) with the key leg-up from the most successful Afrikaner-run enterprise in the country. This fitted so well the drift of

[11] *My translation*, see also Memorandum of 25 July 1979.

the macro-economy of South Africa during the late twentieth and early twenty-first centuries.

The CSIR was formed in 1945 as the Second World War ended (Kingwill 1990, 13–14). The University of Pretoria contributed 100 acres of land to the CSIR for a campus. It was headed by a geophysicist with an international reputation, Basil Schonland, Smuts' influential scientific advisor, while van Eck was the first chair of council. The brief was to further university research, centralise library/technological information, create national science laboratories, notably in physics, chemistry and building sciences, pursue tax rebates to reward innovative firms and to create research institutes serving particular industries. Smuts' idea was above all to find uses for natural products found in South Africa such as asbestos, uranium and timber. In the next years, institutes were indeed founded to promote Physical Sciences, Chemistry, Building Sciences, Telecommunications and Personnel Research. A Sugar Milling Research Institute was established, linked to the University of Natal, in 1949. To some extent, mining was left out apart from mining equipment, as the Chamber of Mines had its own substantial research facilities and perhaps preferred a high level of research autonomy.[12] The Atomic Energy Control Board was quickly established as a related but quite separate institution and became entirely autonomous in 1959 (Kingwill 1990, 17).[13] Three years later a Defence Research Council was created. Still centralisation was not entirely effective and the CSIR was not always happy with the autonomy of specific research units. It was relieved of the embarrassment of direct military research initiatives standing out, however.

Assessing the CSIR is not easy and difficult to make objective. Science is too manifold and too dependent on individual trajectories for precise evaluation. It needs, and comprised in fact, a wide range of specific and distinct units. Inevitably, much research went on in universities, which was very much Schonland's preference. It can be said that science budgeting rose and was not poor, that university departments of science were sometimes very creditable, notably in natural science

[12] The National Mechanical Engineering Research Institute, an instance of co-operation with the Chamber, was an exception (Kingwill 1990, 27).

[13] We shall examine atomic energy in South Africa in Chapter 9 as a subject on its own.

relating to the South African environment and university science had considerable blue sky autonomy from government directives. There were, however, relatively too few South Africans qualified in science degrees in the population at large, even in the white population. A study published in 1967 suggested that Research and Development (R&D) expenditure per annum remained at the modest figure of 0.6 per cent per annum (van Wyk 1967).

Schonland himself resigned in 1950 and in 1954 emigrated to Britain. There have so far been five scientists awarded Nobel Prizes in their fields born in South Africa. Formed in South Africa, it cannot have been an accident that all of them have had the most critical years of their career in other countries also. Contact with Britain was very important at first, with France and Germany growing in significance over time, but the evidence after a point is that the USA became the Mecca of young achievers. Yet this is not necessarily a condemnation of South African science given the extent to which scientific research at the top level is now largely confined to a dozen countries or so. It just does indicate that the outlet for real talent lies in emigration, despite good training at a lower level. Science is also a very international concern and the threat of sanctions and isolation loomed large for the talented. Following Smuts' ideas about South Africa's need to present itself as leader in Africa, early co-operation focused on the Scientific Council for Africa South of the Sahara, which involved the colonial governments in their later reform phase (Kingwill 1990, 29). In the later years, links to Taiwan and to Israel (with a treaty here signed in 1976) were significant safe alternatives (Kingwill 1990, 38).

The relationship to government needs and to industrial desiderata is also hard to determine. The Council was shifted to the aegis of the Ministry of Economic Affairs early on although the government continued to have scientific advisors. 'This move inevitably diminished the status of the CSIR as a co-ordinating and advisory body to the Government on all matters affecting scientific and industrial research' (Kingwill 1990, 19). Verwoerd created a Scientific Advisory Council in 1962. Meiring Naude, successor to Schonland, had to steer a path between attending to government service which guaranteed funding and independence, which the best scientists normally wanted. He had the reputation of helping to train and promote young physicists who would be encouraged to get doctorates overseas. Yet Chris Brink, who in turn succeeded Naude in 1971, was a University of the Orange Free

State chemist who had also worked in the laboratories of ISCOR and was attuned to industrial initiatives.

The CSIR had a division of industrial research. From the 1960s the growing centrality of military and defence research was a source of tension (Kingwill 1990, 25). A strengthening group tried to steer towards more independence, especially from state policy (Kingwill 1990, 41). This was more easily accomplished in the name of veering towards servicing the private sector. The scientific field changed in the 1970s. Beyond the shifts involved in separating out controversial military research, a new sense of the economy was met with the formation of an Environmental Sciences Programme, later renamed the National Programme for Ecosystem Research and in 1978 a National Programme for Energy Research, which excluded atomic energy, was formed, areas which will take on more importance in the remaining chapters of this book (Kingwill 1990, 79). A major shake-up encouraged scientists to compete, first and foremost, for research funding pushing them towards direct relations with the private sector. Staffing was halved and scientists were increasingly forced to depend on consultancies. Funding virtually took the place of results as the measure of prestige to the detriment of scientific research, some might argue. In 1992, Garrett and Clark advocated rewarding scientists according to productivity, i.e. how much research money their tenders and proposals brought in. This controversial re-orientation to servicing business from 1986, such a powerful current by then, was itself critiqued, and to some extent reversed, after the end of the old government in 1994 (Garrett and Clark 1992; Walwyn and Scholes 2006).[14]

In summary, the CSIR assisted in the establishment of a respectable scientific community with a fairly constant R&D record, modest but not disastrous, characterised by a large amount of emigration and distinct, sometimes tense, divisions between those who wished to serve the state, the business world or were committed simply to advancing science and its uses as they saw it. Its role in activities that enemies of apartheid would consider nefarious was mostly masked or hived off. It has been an important resource if initial expectations were naive and not fully realised. Scientific development was not negligible from the

[14] For a thoroughgoing critique of the logic and practice of privatisation, see Walwyn 2013.

perspective of evaluating the existence of a developmental state but it was also far from determinant.[15]

The last section of this chapter considers what might be termed the parallel to the CSIR in the social sciences, the Human Sciences Research Council (HSRC). If a judgement as an institution on the CSIR would have to be a measured one, the signal failure of the HSRC is part of the story of why, in human, social and political terms, the South African developmental state was unable to deliver a better life for the majority of South Africans.

The real inspiration of state-sponsored social science research in South Africa was E.G. Malherbe. American-educated and taken by the potential of statistical research to understand people better (in both these respects just like Hendrik Verwoerd). However, his initial background was in education studies. In 1929, he set up the Bureau for Education Research under D.F. Malan as Minister. He shared Malan's interest in poor whites, thus linking up to the Carnegie Commission, which supported the Bureau financially, and researching them. He also was an enthusiast for measuring IQs (Fleisch 1995, 357). 'Research was strongly oriented towards contemporary thinking in the United States on measurement and evaluation as the basis for allegedly rational approaches to educational planning' (Chisholm and Morrow 2007). For a time before the war, Malherbe had been director of the Bureau of the Census (Fleisch 1995, 366). His wartime opinion polls of soldiers were considered important and innovative. During this phase, as has been mentioned earlier, there was a considerable debate about whether it was possible to educate black South Africans to the same level as whites. Here Malherbe took the liberal side of the argument. His concerns about the growing radicalism in Afrikaner nationalism made him champion the cause of bilingual education rather than education in one's home language alone; here he was distinctively a Smuts, not a Hertzog, man.

It took a long time after the war for this stepchild of the developmental state to be reborn and emerge as a new structure. The Bureau was effectively reopened as the National Bureau for Educational and Social Research (Chisholm and Morrow 2007) in 1946, which devised tests, mostly with the enrolled divided by race, for schoolchildren. But

[15] I am very grateful for discussion of CSIR history with David Walwyn.

this was on a small scale. It gave way eventually to the HSRC in 1969. The first head, P.M. Robbertse, was closely linked to the Vorster government. Robbertse, like Vorster, was influenced by Geoff Cronje, who had admired fascism, exactly unlike Malherbe, during the 1930s.

At the same time as the National Bureau was established in 1945 however, the CSIR sponsored a new institute, the National Bureau of Personnel Research, of which the leading light was a liberal psychologist, Simon Biesheuvel. It was tied in both to Malherbe's love of statistics and to the formation of the new profession of personnel manager (Webster 1981). The Institute took off on the idea of black educability and did interesting research. However, it shared with its more conservative contemporaries the assumption that populations, in order to be measured, had at first to be divided by race, sex and language group. The core idea was comparative study with these foundations although it was possible to make comparisons with liberal-minded ends. Moreover, Biesheuvel was reluctant ever to challenge big business, which shaped the workplace. Eventually Biesheuvel found it too conflictual to work in an institute linked to the state. He quit to work for South African Breweries in 1962 and, a decade later, for the University of the Witwatersrand and thus in a liberal setting (Coupe 1996). With his departure, the Institute lost its cutting edge. It is debatable whether Biesheuvel's approach actually affected industrial development in South Africa.

Robbertse's Bureau had a very modest budget at first that tended to grow in time. It was R1.6 m. in 1969–70, and reached R6.7 m. in 1978–9. Most striking was its failure to develop links to university and to active outside research. Only a small part of its budget went to university grants (White 1992). Instead it focused on its own establishment and maintained a growing army of permanent researchers. By the end of the 1980s, it employed over 800 people. (Interview, Ralf Stumpf 2014; Chisholm and Morrow 2007)

Perusing HSRC research from the Robbertse years can well bring laughter rather than tears – it was so remote from international interests and standards. The Institute for Educational Research sponsored titles in, for instance, effective planning and utilisation for school grounds to be used for extramural activities and consideration of possible leisure activity for children during holiday time. D.J. van Berg, EdD perorated on whether the 'black man' could comprehend mathematics since he 'is unfamiliar with objective time and therefore does not attach much value to clock time and absolute punctuality [in his traditional cultural milieu]'. Black problems with maths are thus due to his '[sic] culture'. N. Snyman in 1976 pondered why it was that some personalities were inexplicably drawn to scandal and vice in the media (how could this be controlled?) as South Africa finally began the institution of television broadcasting. At the same time K. Prinsloo considered how to use Afrikaans as a second language teaching medium just as Soweto was about to go up in flames over this very issue. The historical reports section concentrated on Afrikaner family genealogies. In fact, most social science problems were carefully confined to white subjects in these self-published research papers of arcane interest.

In 1979, Robbertse was replaced by Johan Garbers and a reform era, not unconnected to the arrival of Chair of Council Piet de Lange, commenced. The de Lange report of 1981 spelt reform. Garbers was interested in moving the HSRC some distance from the state, or at least its politicians, but as an intellectual, his training as yet another educationist absorbed with statistics was certainly limiting. His successor, the geographer Philip Smit taking charge in 1985, was also a reformer (Interview, Ralf Stumpf 2014). When examined today, some of the research from the 1980s, for instance J.A. Jakobsz on how blacks in the Pretoria-Witwatersrand-Vaal Triangle area perceived the idea of the free market, Johanna Labuschagne's figures on Coloured graduates by sex or W.J. Schurink on the life experiences of lesbian women, can still be read with some interest.

However, the new leadership had little success in convincing English speakers to join the HSRC (apart from the Natal based Lawrence Schlemmer, who also thrived on surveys and numbers) and in effect failed to connect with the very different social science culture emerging in the universities (Webster 1981; Cloete et al. 1986, 37). The National Institute of Personnel Research passed into HSRC hands in 1985 but its perspectives, with the old racial categories, seemed outdated and unable to serve as an engine of transformation. In the English language universities, younger academics, often schooled abroad, were inspired by anti-apartheid political and social ideals and created a literature with unprecedented international influence and appeal on a completely different wavelength. This was a critical social science, not a positivist one. To put it mildly, 'there was little sense of identification with the

HSRC on the part of the English language or historically black universities' (Chisholm and Morrow 2007, 50).

Moreover, the structure of the HSRC was in the way. It continued to be dominated by in-house research, now modified by the growing demand for commercial contracts just as with the contemporary CSIR.

> The overwhelming majority of public funds for human scientific research in this country is directly controlled by in-house committees not accountable to open academic screening procedures. The brief from the Cabinet is clear: it is to be directed towards socio-economic and political problems. (Cloete et al. 1986, 40)

Indeed the detachment from academic research led the CSIR to sponsor the creation of the National Research Foundation as a way for university researchers to access funding, really a rival project to the convoluted HSRC.

Social science research was an extremely weak area within the research state of pre-1990 South Africa. The responsible parties were afraid to part from a pseudo-scientific total dependence on statistical research and, even in the case of liberals, the starting point of racial and sex categories. This reflected all too clearly the separation and exclusion politics that went with the developmental state's economic initiatives.

The material in this chapter has hopefully illuminated the situation of potentially important institutions in the half-century before the abolition of apartheid. The IDC was clearly of central significance and generally very active but one has again to note the limitations that it did not actually formulate plans and it had to establish other connections in order to arrange for big financial demands. As an agency that made the crucial connections on orders from the political bosses, it can be judged quite successful. As we shall see, these orders lose developmental coherence in time and give way especially to strategic and military concerns. The CSIR retained considerable independence from the state although further research would probably yield information on important services rendered by some units and breakaway organisations parallel to the IDC. The inherent failure of apartheid to understand and promote the potential of the whole South African population was mirrored in the tardy and drastically inappropriate HSRC organisation. The competing social science world in the English language universities by contrast offered an almost entirely critical perspective to the intentions of the state. The three looked at together provide a sharp sense of the developmental character of the South African state over this period and its increasingly substantial limitations and contradictions.

8 *The Company Towns of the Vaal Triangle*

Introduction: Inequality in a Developmental State

This chapter focuses on space and on social inequality, two frequently discussed and fundamental parts of apartheid thinking.[1] Instead of reiterating these very well-known general perspectives, it hones in on relatively ignored company towns created in the 1940s and 1950s to accommodate the needs of the parastatals. This book is not primarily a work in social history but voices from below will rumble in it. Two spectacular events on the edge of the company towns, the Sharpeville Massacre of 1960 and the Vaal Uprising of 1984, are obviously events that emerge from what was happening on the ground and at initiatives far removed from state operatives.

At the same time, the principal actors of previous chapters will continue to be on hand. Thus the social setting and the spatial setting will now be linked to the set of dominant social relations which were accepted and pursued by the major developmental state actors. Here at a local level one can discern a system meant to square the contradictions from the social point of view, to find a means of developing a modern and industrialised country while retaining the racial social order desired by the overwhelming majority of the electorate. The black majority of the population found their labour power massively in demand as rural household viability collapsed further

1 This chapter is indebted to the ideas and material made available to me of Alan Mabin, Victor Munnik, Mark Oranje and Stephen Sparks. This is true also for later material relevant to the history of these towns in a later chapter. Much of the literature on South African black urban society under apartheid has been written based on voices of the victims and sources such as newspapers. This study has emphasised by contrast still largely unused if more traditional, sources in the South African national archives, now available for the apartheid period. Amongst the writings of planners and geographers trying to make sense of the totality, see Beavon 2004; Smit and Mabin 1997; Parnell and Mabin 1995; Smit 1989, 72.

but with little opportunity to establish a basis through skills, organisation and work organisation for social mobility and the construction of a viable new way of life.

Apartheid ideology proposed trying increasingly forcefully to limit black urbanisation and to encourage economic development in the rural locations, now dubbed homelands. Hendrik Verwoerd as Minister of Native Affairs and later prime minister, tried to move things around in a direction that would push black energies into homeland economies and to cut off black aspirations to citizenship in the South African heartland. Yet this chapter concerns itself with a region far from the homelands, as far as one could get apart from the Western Cape, the so-called 'Vaal Triangle'. One corner of the triangle was the city of Vereeniging, a small urban centre that already before 1940 had attracted some industry, for instance the pioneer steel company, USCO.[2] Its development had much to do with the entrepreneurial activities of South Africa's early industrialist, Sammy Marks (Mendelsohn 1991; Munnik 2012, 137). It was the site of the treaty than ended the Anglo-Boer War in 1902.

Vanderbijlpark, the site of a huge ISCOR plant and the apple of H.J. van der Bijl's eye, constructed in the 1940s, and Sasolburg, built some years later, where the oil-from-coal project had its headquarters, were new model towns created from scratch in the mid-twentieth century. There is much continuity between the two communities, both designed by relatively liberal urban planners. There were other model towns as well, notably the string of six important urban communities that serviced the new Anglo-American developed Orange Free State goldfields from Welkom south.[3] These were much less successful in attracting economic activity apart from mining itself.[4]

[2] USCO was to become part of the ISCOR stable. Chaskalson 1986, identifies Vereeniging as a United Party controlled town extremely eager to promote industry with slack environmental and pass control systems. The population was counted as 40,490 in 1946 and 78,845 in 1960 censuses.

[3] Natural Resources Development Council, *A Regional Survey of the Orange Free State Goldfield* 1954, Government Printer, Pretoria. William Backhouse was the planner for Anglo-American. Wits Archives.

[4] T.J.D. Fair and B.G. Boaden, *Sasol II-The Regional Setting: Population Growth and Shopping Structure,* Urban and Regional Research Unit, 1975, University of the Witwatersrand. Prinsloo notes for Vanderbijlpark the opening of VICOR (1945), Dorman Long (1947), Acrow (1949), Metal Box (1952) and later a couple of gas companies, Acoustical Products Ltd, Slagment (building cement) and Resinite (plastic packaging) amongst others (P.J.J. Prinsloo 1993). SASOL

Why were Vanderbijlpark and Sasolburg so critical? They were near coal mines, the Vaal River provided a good water supply, Pretoria but especially Johannesburg, as well as much of the mining industry, were not far away and there were already lines of rail crossing the area which was largely flat terrain. Sasolburg was virtually on the main Johannesburg-Cape Town line. In strictly material terms, this led to a striking form of economic development. Measured in 1959–60, the percentage contribution of industry, construction, electricity, gas and water to local GDP in Vereeniging, Vanderbijlpark and Sasolburg taken together was respectively 63.3 per cent, 80.0 per cent and 70.6 per cent. This was far in excess of Johannesburg (32.1 per cent), Cape Town (32.7 per cent), Durban, (40.0 per cent) or even the East Rand industrial belt (Boksburg 50.4 per cent, Benoni 49.6 per cent, Germiston 46.5 per cent). The 137 Vaal Triangle factories in 1963–4 were valued as highly as the 408 in Port Elizabeth or the 1,080 in Cape Town and thus treated as a unit ranked third in value nationally after the Johannesburg and Durban magisterial districts.[5]

Moreover, both chemicals and iron and steel, while certainly employing large number of black workers, had ratios of white to black (and presumably skilled to unskilled) that favoured the former compared to consumer goods industries. In 1959–60 this ratio was twice that in the country as a whole for Vanderbijlpark and notably higher in Sasolburg, which was very dominated by SASOL as an employer. Vereeniging with its diversified industrial base was different, in fact with more African (referred to as Bantus) to white workers than the national average. These ratios did not alter radically through most of the apartheid years (see Table 8.1).[6] Even in 1990 a very large part of the workforce was white.

The Group Areas Act of 1950 followed from a long history of legislation about racial segregation. The Urban Areas Act of 1923 provided for sections of cities to be 'proclaimed' off-limits for African residence albeit with the proviso that blacks needed to be accommodated elsewhere in that case (Beavon 2004, 98). In the 1930s, as industrialisation in South

today still embodies major government economic interests and is the country's biggest tax generator while Sasolburg still gets designated new activities. ISCOR, as planned before the political turn of 1993, has been privatised and is part of the giant international Mittal stable.

5 NA, GMO 1836, 28 pt. 1, Sosiografie van die Vaaldriehoek.

6 NA, GMO 1836, 28 pt. 1, Sosiografie van die Vaaldriehoek, Die ekonomiese struktuur van Vereeniging, Vanderbijlpark en Sasolburg met spesiale verwysing na nywerheidspesialisasie en die indiensnemingspatroon in die nywerheid.

Table 8.1. *Vaal Triangle Towns: Officially Registered White and Black Population Totals Compared*

	Whites	'Bantus'
1959–60		
Vereeniging	6,120	14,061
Vanderbijlpark	6,303	6,409
Sasolburg	2,003	1,730
1965–66		
Vereeniging	6,341	15,947
Vanderbijlpark	9,607	9,189
Sasolburg	3,808	5,488

Africa grew apace, an urban planning system was created which allowed for the 'proclamation' of space to be used for particular purposes only, purposes which included racial exclusion and definition (Smit and Mabin 1997). The Transvaal Township and Town Planning Ordinance of 1931 was a key stepping stone (Kirchhofer 1958). It was imitated in the other provinces in subsequent years (Smit 1989). Both towns contained inbuilt inequalities, not merely between black and white but to a lesser extent within both population groups. This was inherent even in their layout and construction.

The evolution of policy vis-à-vis race and inequality particularly and its consequences will be traced for the Vaal Triangle towns under the apartheid system. I argue for three stages which are, however, not entirely distinct. First of all, there was much emphasis on securing the right sort of management, dealing with the problem of dependence on immigrants and trying to secure Afrikaner cultural and manpower dominance which, of course, tied the parastatals to the questions exercising the state apparatus. This was the company town phase. Second, the Verwoerdian phase emphasised turning race into class compression, particularly at the level of ideology, within race groups (Morris and Hindson 1992). In this period, new township construction, dependence on migrant labour resident in hostels and an endless war against anomalies, were hallmarks. This was a period of rapid growth, considerable prosperity and white demographic expansion. The third stage was a response to the crisis of the 1970s. White population expansion almost halted and forms of anti-social behaviour grew or intensified. The state reconsidered compression and tried instead to foster a black elite in the townships as its junior partners. Living conditions improved substantially – for a minority. The popular response to the second wave of inequality in part was (partially and) infamously the Sharpeville Massacre of 1960. The popular response to the third wave was the Vaal Rising of September 1984, after which the South African state found itself unable to restore order in the country substantially and reform was taken further into, and superseded by, the negotiations process with the ANC in 1990. However, one might at least also mention the Boipatong Killings of 1992, where hostel dwellers set upon local residents in the old township near the ISCOR factory as part of the open social wounds that were manifest in the transition of power years. The later phases are discussed in succeeding chapters rather than here, however.

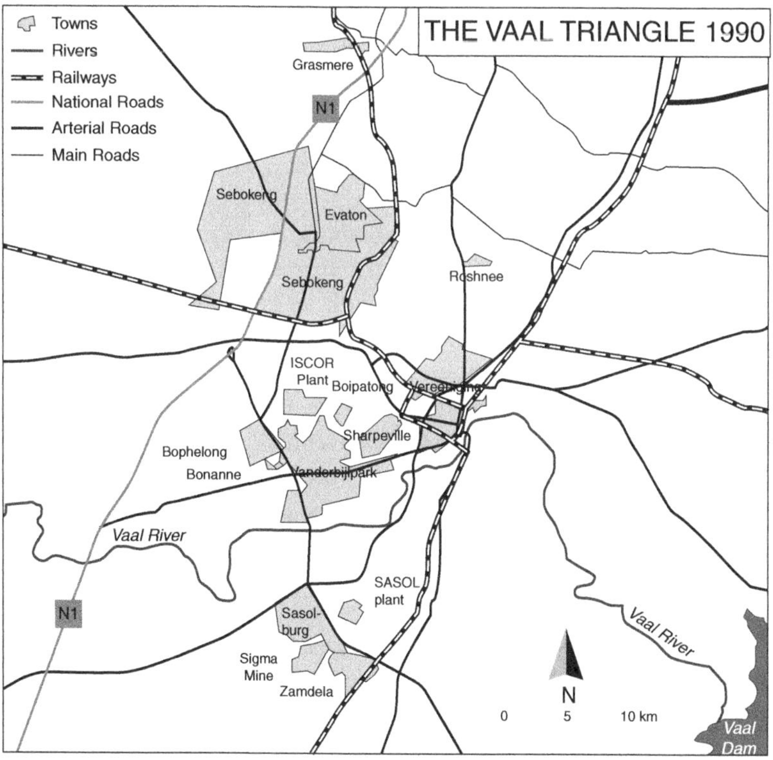

Map 8.1. The Vaal Triangle

Utopias on the Vaal

Vanderbijlpark was laid out in 1941 on 25,000 acres purchased by ISCOR, including five miles of Vaal River frontage amounting to forty square miles in all. For H.J. van der Bijl, who was then directing the South African economic war effort, Vanderbijlpark was a prize project that encapsulated his sense of the good life.

> I visualised a town with people living in surroundings and under conditions which will be conducive to a healthy, happy and productive life. For this reason I was determined to make ample provision for parks, playing grounds, health clinics, hospitals and schools. A town, like a flower or a tree, should at each stage of its growth possess symmetry and completeness and the effect of growth should never be to destroy that unity but to give it greater purpose, not to mar that symmetry, which at all stages makes it a comprehensive whole.[7]

He also tried with some success to make space for other businesses so that Vanderbijlpark would not simply be a company town. The 'roads [were] named after postal districts or scientists, engineers, musicians, medical men and the like' to give the town an elevated character (Ibid. 5). Van der Bijl had a fine house built on Beethoven Street.

Great emphasis was laid on tree planting (Ibid. 6). The wealthiest neighbourhood around Beethoven Street still passes today, like the affluent northern suburbs of Johannesburg, as an urban forest. While the town was to have a business centre with some apartment buildings, the dominant mode was suburban with an emphasis on green space and recreation and supposed isolation from industries, which were themselves to be relatively clean. No building was to exceed six stories.[8] Most houses were built by the planning arm created for ISCOR, VESCO, although some were eventually constructed privately according to company planning rules (Prinsloo 1993, 132). The Vanderbijl Park Estate Company was created to produce houses

[7] P.R. Nell, compiler, *An Historical Review of the Town of Vanderbijl Park for the Period 1941 to December 1951*, Van Riebeeck Festival Committee, Vanderbijl Park, 3. Wits Archives.

[8] *Vanderbijl Park, The Planned Industrial City,* Vanderbijl Park Estate Company, 1948. Wits Archives.

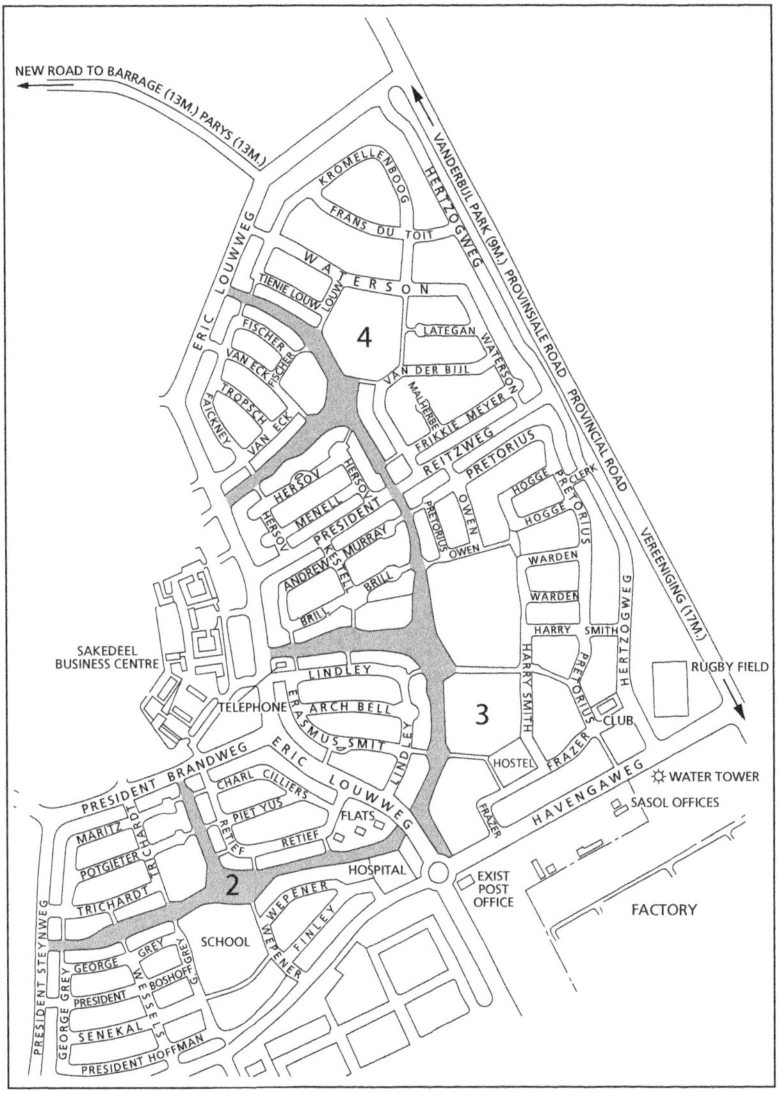

Map 8.2. Blueprint for White Sasolburg

on a 'mass scale' efficiently and quickly. The goal of a new house finished every day was often realised (*Vanderbijl Park; The Planned Industrial City* 1948). All of this was well-developed before planning for the 'Natives' began – except on blueprint.

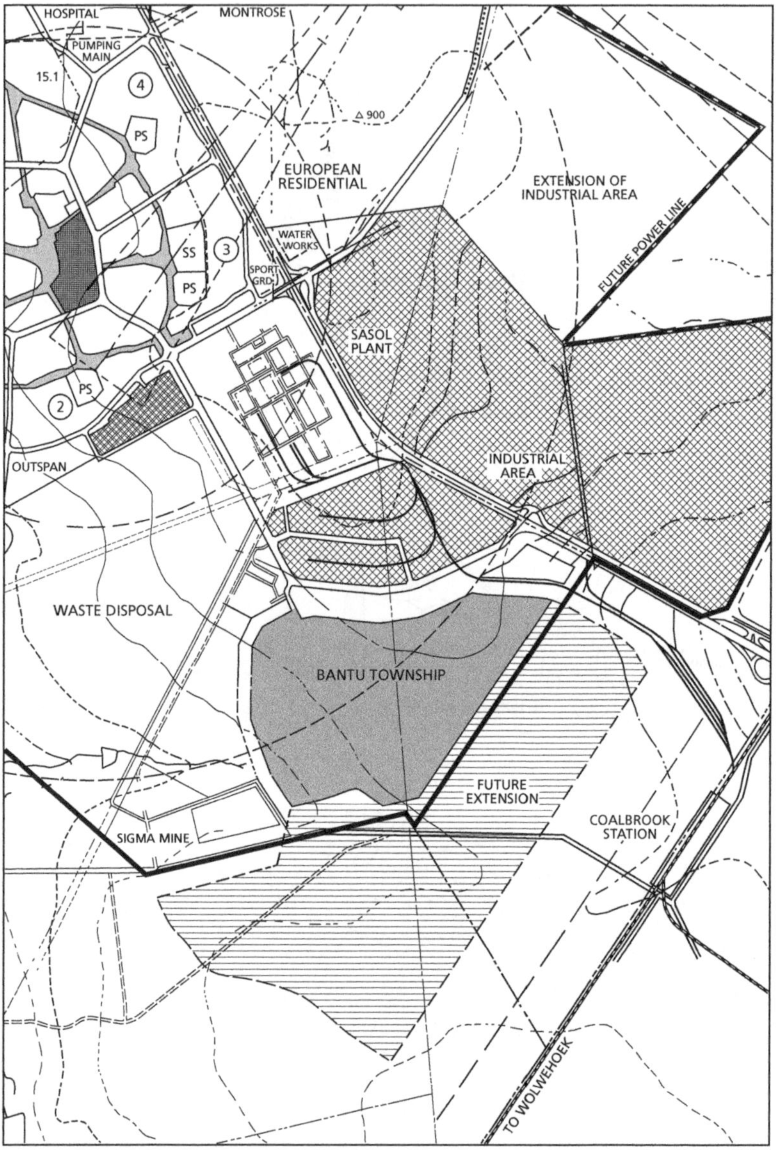

Map 8.3. Blueprint for Sasolburg Town
Source: National Archives

The designer was Roy Kantorowich, a student of Carl Feiss at Columbia University, known for his enmity to the grand urban renewal plans of Robert Moses in New York City (Alan Mabin interview 1991). Kantorowich would later go on to design Ashkelon in the new state of Israel in the wake of the expulsion from, or desertion of, the town by Palestinians, a job which he thought was disastrous, and then would become Professor of Planning at the University of Manchester whose department today is housed in a building named after him. P.R. Anderson, the town engineer who planned Vanderbijlpark and whom he admired, went on to be a key member of the team that redesigned late colonial Nairobi (Ibid.).

Kantorowich was also implicated in the construction of the much-excoriated corporate/administrative high rises on the reclaimed Cape Town Foreshore. Vanderbijlpark and the Foreshore evoked the two ideal forms in modernist thinking in architecture at the time: the green belt suburb with curving streets and easy avoidance of the growing menace of automotive traffic and the imposing dense use high-rise for the city centre. It could be said that Kantorowich was one of a number of South African architects and planners eager to bring these ideas from the metropolitan high culture to South Africa: his greatest pride with regard to Vanderbijlpark was its contour road plan (Ibid.). In the judicious words of Dan Herwitz:

> Their buildings were of apartheid in the sense of having been built with the economy that kept its politics going. They were of apartheid in the sense of conforming by law to its rules of use. However they were, in fact, about a kind of architectural indifference to the political system, an indifference [with] which, it must be said, Corbu [le Corbusier] and Mies [Ludwig Mies van der Rohe], would have probably felt comfortable. (Herwitz 2003, 161)

Alan Mabin takes a sterner view: he has pointed out that the greatest common view of the time amongst the rising stars of urban planning was their hatred for messy, unsightly slums, their dislike of laissez-faire in urban development and their faith in what planning could do. He asks the question: 'Does this urge to control disorder and create separations characterise all modern planning?' Perhaps baldly put, South Africa witnessed a 'marriage of modernity and racism'.[9]

[9] Mabin 2000, 560. The distaste for laissez-faire and mixed-use development, the hatred for unsightly slums, are virtually exemplified in Kantorowich's writing.

Sasolburg, just south of the Vaal and inside the Orange Free State, proclaimed a white urban area in 1955, and grew very rapidly until the economic crisis of the 1970s manifested itself. As with Vanderbijlpark, the plans, over which the architect-planners for a long time continued to hold control, saw Sasolburg in relative isolation, a world unto itself which was not really integrated into the farm and mining environment around the valley of the Vaal.[10] Here, with the planning situated in the early apartheid period, streets were typically named for Afrikaner, or at least South African, political figures and national heroes.

Sasolburg was created under the direction of Max Kirchhofer, a Swiss immigrant who believed strongly in the green belt and was profoundly concerned with the issue of school location. He, too, believed that 'a town is an entity, a whole living organism' and that planners needed to focus on the 'self-contained residential precinct', a model easily adaptable to racial segregation.[11] As with Edwin Mallows, the British-born 'doyen of South African planning' at the University of the Witwatersrand, who worked closely with him on the site, the question of separation of automobile traffic from pedestrian usage was perhaps his biggest concern.[12] The chief menace facing the South African town was 'the nerve-racking and dangerous intermixing of pedestrians and motor cars' (Kirchhofer 1958, 26). The cornerstone of a neighbourhood was to be the primary school to which resident children could walk safely without crossing busy roads (Ibid.). The principal environmental idea in both places, apart from functional separation, was the massive planting of trees, including in the black

He would have preferred Vanderbijlpark, however, to have had far less detached housing. He liked le Corbusier style radial or circular planning. Kantorowich 1958. For a sustained analysis along lines similar to Mabin, see Smit 1989 and for a global scale comparison, Zipp 2010.

10 Max Kirchhofer, Preliminary Report on Sasolburg, 31 January 1951.

11 For Kirchhofer's vision, see Kirchhofer 1958. An unpublished source is his Notes on the Planning of Sasolburg, 1957, SASOL Papers.

12 Max Kirchhofer to D.P. de Villiers, 3 August 1957, SASOL Papers. Mallows felt that Sasolburg would set a new standard for urban planning in South Africa, Mallows to Kirchhofer, 7 December 1951. As occasionally appears in correspondence, Kirchhofer's largest anxiety, insofar as the Plan was adhered to, was the inevitable proximity of white suburbia to a giant chemical plant. He believed that Sasolburg was too hemmed in and would be prey to the chemical plant's 'smoke and smell'. However he also thought that tree planting would solve the problem. In fact, he had far less space with which to work than did Kantorowich at Vanderbijlpark.

locations. This forest effect is noticeable to the present day when it incurs worry as shrubbery hides criminals and pathways become littered or unkempt. Kirchhofer was inspired by the New Towns being constructed in post-war Britain beyond ideas that came from his native Switzerland about urban citizenship and urban tidiness. He would have identified himself as a liberal and liked to consider that potentially as much thought was given to black housing in Sasolburg as to white. Among the factors that he took as professionally important, the black population had the same needs as the white and these were accordingly accommodated, or so he was convinced.[13] Yet 'organisms' could display gross inequalities.

Creating a Racial Order in Industrial Urban Life

Beyond white suburbia, the plans for both towns began with indicative plans implying an urban socialisation of black South Africans but appropriate to their low wages. Austere male hostels played a big part from the beginning and, as Beavon shows for Johannesburg, only became more important with time. Black housing began with a big basic hostel for men in 1942 in Vanderbijlpark (as Vanderbijl Park began to be spelt). Within a decade it housed 2,570 men described as 'inmates' (Nell 1952, 8). Hostel space continued to be constantly in demand and necessarily catered for. A manager for Non-European Affairs was appointed in 1948. This was accompanied by the construction of 'hutments' for building workers. In 1949, space was 'proclaimed' for African habitation; apart from domestic workers and some resident employees, all other Africans were to be obliged to live there (Ibid. 16). Only in 1951 was a beginning made on small family units which were rented out.[14] Even then, the largest number of inhabitants were hostel dwellers, 4,560 counted in 1954. In 1953 a suitable 'group area' was proclaimed.

[13] Beavon records for Johannesburg also apparently benign plans to suit garden cities both for Orlando before the Second World War and Dube afterwards in considering the origins of Soweto. Such plans were trimmed down dramatically in reality and the Vaal Triangle would also display this truncated planners' vision when it came to African inhabitants' neighbourhoods (Beavon 2004 121–30).

[14] NA ARG v. 163 VK 132/1/14, 1 Verwysings van Beplanningskomitee, verslae: Town Council of Vanderbijl Park, Memorandum on the Proclamation of Group Areas 1953.

Townships (Bophelong, and then Boipatong, created in 1960, served Vanderbijlpark) were designed in such a way as to allow easy foot access to work. The town clerk reported in 1953 for Vanderbijlpark as 'happily true' that Africans would not need to pass through any white residential area to get to work.[15] Their erection was part of a huge thrust of residential housing construction for which legislation allowing cheap black labour to perform most construction work and the allocation of national funds along with building levies from employers that typified the 1950s.[16] Indeed moneys for construction were borrowed from profit-making Soweto.

However, they were also originally supposed to go with the proffering of lessons in civilised family living. Bophelong, built with finance from the National Housing Funds in early apartheid times was surveyed so that the two-bedroom brick houses constructed were considered to be of an appropriate size. They were supplied with garden space, electricity, water points inside, water-borne sewage, refuse removal and tarred roads (Nell 1952, 15; Prinsloo 1993, 136). However, there were features, or a lack of features, that would have been completely unacceptable in white Vanderbijlpark even for the poorest families. No electric or water connections were provided in the kitchen and no bath recesses provided in the bathrooms.[17] No hospital served the residents for quite some time (P.R. Nell to Native Commissioner, Vereeniging, 12 November 1954, NA, BA0 6947 P 114/1709/2). The core of Bophelong took the form of an imitation traditional kraal settlement (Munnik 2012, 140). The black locations were secluded in such a way that the ideal could be observed that black and white would meet only in the factory and perhaps a business centre. The 'buffer zone' demarcating them was to be marked by trees to make it invisible from outside.[18]

The vision of the Smuts era, paternalist, segregated and extremely unequal, was strikingly on display in Vanderbijlpark. The hope was for loyal parastatal employees, whose residence would be tied effectively to employment, and which would remain a home for a lifetime. A 1948 brochure laid out the vision very clearly:

[15] NA, ARG v. 163 VK 132/1/14 p. 1 Verwysings van Beplanningskomitee, verslae: Town Council of Vanderbijl Park, 1953 Memorandum on the Proclamation of Group Areas.

[16] P.S. Reinecke, *Site Planning for Low-Cost Housing*, 1963. Wits Archives.

[17] NA, NTS 7064, 404/322 Memorandum on Proposed NE2 Housing Scheme approved by Health Committee, 26/2/52.

[18] NA, BAO 6947 P 114/1709/2. P.R. Nell, Town Clerk, Vanderbijlpark to Secretary, Native Affairs, 1 June 1953.

> Provision has been made for the establishment of five non-European residential districts from which industries at Vanderbijl Park will draw their native labour. These native residential districts are in all cases contiguous or in close proximity to the various industrial areas. The advantages of this arrangement are obvious. In the planning of these districts, the welfare of the native, as in the case of the European resident, has been given primary consideration. Special attention has been paid to the housing of the natives with a view to creating optimum living conditions which will be conducive to good health, a contented frame of mind and productive labour. While there will be parks and open spaces in these areas, the inhabitants will also be encouraged to establish their own gardens. Apart from the clinics which will be established, the health of the inhabitants will be safeguarded by the fact that any possibility of overcrowding has been eliminated by the layout of districts, while water-borne sewerage, water and electricity will be provided throughout all the districts . . . The care and forethought devoted to the living requirements of the non-European will therefore not only ensure his welfare but also that a stable labour force is at all times available to industrialists. (*Vanderbijlpark; The Planned Industrial City* 1948, 27)

Thus the Natives would be at the disposal of management.

A further refinement already early in the apartheid era was to create ethnically defined sections of these locations, in other words internal differentiation not by class but by ethnic identity. Already in 1954 there was the intention to separate Bophelong between Sotho and Nguni speakers (the 2:1 ratio) with 'complete Ethnic grouping' also as ISCOR policy in the hostels. For family units, this did partly jibe with the intention of creating primary schools functioning in Bantu languages but this could hardly be said to be the case for the hostels.[19]

The situation was not very different as Sasolburg's planning got underway. Despite Kirchhofer's claims of relative equality in planning white and black residential areas, black lots in the township were half to a third the size of white lots and in fact, approximately one-tenth of the early lots in white Sasolburg were double size; these were the furthest away from the location.[20] This was the obvious spatial measure of inequality. A meeting of SASOL management and Kirchhofer with the Minister

[19] NA, NTS 609/313 N2, Vanderbijlpark Town Clerk P.R. Nell to Secretary, Native Affairs, 2 November 1954; NTS 7065, 404/322, Memorandum on Proposed NE2 Housing Scheme, 12 November 1954.

[20] NA, NTS 10089, 519/4082.

and his team carefully went over the question of buffer zones and black access routes that did not cross white leisure or residential space.[21] Furthermore in Sasolburg, typical of many South African towns of the day, a curfew for Africans operated by decree after 9 p.m.[22]

SASOL, arch-paternalist, handed out free beer, food to its workers gratis twice a week and housing was at first free.[23] In other words, much of the wage goods were determined by management in kind. In 1954–5, SASOL and various officials fought over the extent to which SASOL would be able to have power over the workers outside the workplace as opposed to the municipality, as was usual in South Africa. As an executive pointed out, the need for black population concentrations hardly meant that SASOL was interested in harbouring an uncontrolled 'black spot'. Management wanted a security system with a substantial fence around the location and permanent policing of the entry in part to deal with the need for workers to come and go in shifts. 'It is thus desirable that our compound administrator has strong direct control over our Natives.'[24] The plan envisioned a secured 'native village' with a resident location superintendent. It then was decided in 1958 that SASOL would name the administrator but that he would eventually be transferred to the municipal payroll.[25]

Given that a small coal mine, Sigma, adjoined Sasolburg, providing fuel to the oil-from-coal process, SASOL actually wanted the area where Africans resided entirely to be classified as a mine which would give it more power over workers. Some of the struggle about control was fought over the Sigma mine. Here management made an unusually clear exposition of its understanding of the situation as it existed in the 1950s; they wanted 40 per cent of their workers to have family housing and they preferred literate miners. The view was that such workers, even though largely from the British protectorate of Basutoland, were more stable (and thus dependent), less likely to

21 NA, NTS 6134, 481/313N, D.P. de Villiers, SASOL to G.I. Nel, Secretary, Native Affairs, 17 September 1952.

22 NA, ULU 3257, 1719 pt. 1.

23 NA, NTS 5846, 481, 313/M, Bantu Affairs Memorandum 1955.

24 *My translation.* NA NTS 5846, 481/313/M, J.J.S. van der Spuy, secretary, SASOL to Secretary, Department of Native Affairs, 29 August 1954; A. Brink to Max Kirchhofer, 22 November 1952, SASOL Papers.

25 NA NTS 5846, 481/313/M, Memorandum, Secretary, Administration of Native Affairs, 4 April 1957 with further letter 29 April 1957 and record of meeting, 27 March 1958.

spend money on prostitutes or turn to violence. Domiciling them at Sigma, tying the family to the mine, was then considered ideal. Decreeing this, management argued, would become more difficult once Sasolburg was proclaimed a municipality and began to have elected officials who would vie for control.[26] Harry Oppenheimer of Anglo-American and also then a member of parliament, got wind of the story and was very annoyed that Sigma was in fact permitted to have one-third of its workforce in married housing whereas Anglo-American miners at best were allotted one-tenth (a figure rarely attained in practice).[27]

The Vanderbijlpark town clerk opined in 1952 that 'it is the Committee's policy to endeavour to keep the natives out of the European areas as far as possible. For this reason steps have been taken to provide shops, recreation and social centres and a clinic at Bopelong' (Nell 1952, 15). Not only did these small townships have little planned business districts, there was even a hope that they develop craft centres and reach the ideal that blacks would rarely have to be spotted in the white town. At first, the town possessed monopoly rights for trading in clothing, groceries and ran a cafe in Bophelong; the motive generally was to discourage Africans from going out into commercial centres.[28] This was unsurprisingly bitterly resented as expressed by the Native Advisory Council, which called a tense meeting with the Town Clerk in 1951. The Vanderbijlpark Council was forced to change by the middle 1950s and, given that the licences were too costly for most aspirant shopkeepers, select businesses were actually getting loans from the Vanderbijlpark authorities.[29]

Company paternalism took on a personalised character in the early history of the townships. Examining records of the Bantu Advisory Board for Bophelong and Boipatong, we find that the manager exhorted black parents to get involved and take charge of children who appeared potentially or actually delinquent. A widower-

[26] NA, NTS 5846, 481/313/M, Steyn van der Spuy, SASOL to Aveling, Secretary, Native Affairs, 21 November 1955.

[27] NA NTS 5846,481/313/M, telegram, Harry Oppenheimer to *Herald*, 17 February 1955.

[28] NA, NTS 5375, 609/313F, P.R. Nell, Health Committee, to Native Commissioner, Vereeniging, 5 December 1951.

[29] NA, NTS 5375, 609/313F, P.R. Nell to Native Commissioner, Vereeniging, 7 November 1956, BAO 1995, A20/1709, Bantu Advisory Board, Bophelong and Boipatong, 22 September 1966.

householder named Ephraim Peete was permitted to stay in his household because he had a daughter to care for his younger children, he had an excellent record in paying his rent and he was hopeful that he would remarry. Widows were generally forced to leave if they were left without a resident employee who had Section Ten rights in a house but board members were informed that this was not done unfeelingly and that they were certainly given time to find another domicile.[30] However, the Bantu Advisory Boards, whose members were elected by certified rent payers,[31] based on proof of rental payment, protested against the material issues that most affected them and might be remediable: the problems of house dwellers before 1960 to access beer or make it at home, the difficulties made in housing lodgers, the restrictions on movement. The Zamdela council complained that the Sasolburg town council insisted on making all announcements, undercutting any sense of local self-government.[32]

A major factor that motivated the state was the considerable revenue potential in municipal beer halls and beer provision although claims that these revenues could solve the problems of African housing were very exaggerated.[33] Beer halls subject to controls and used as a form of revenue were the main form of entertainment – in Vanderbijlpark legal beer purchase only developed after 1960. ISCOR provided its black men with free beer but after some time, the beer hall was introduced as an alternative to the illegal local taverns. Hostel dwellers (3,000 in 1967) still got their beer from ISCOR in the late 1960s but at this point they were purchasing it.[34] Legally the Health Committee was given the 'exclusive right to manufacture, sell and supply' beer, which at first meant free distribution and linked to an eating house franchise.[35]

[30] NA, BAO 1995, A20/1709, Bantu Advisory Board, Bophelong and Boipatong, 22 September 1966. Section 10 exempted Africans with a long record of work for a single urban employer from the need to leave a township once they were no longer employed. There were grey areas around qualification.

[31] NA, NTS 5751, 481/313 K, Proclamation of a Native Advisory Board, Orange Free State Official Gazette, 14 June 1957.

[32] NA,. NTS 5437, 481/313G, Kaffir Beer Regulations; Bantu Affairs Advisory Council meeting, 9 January 1959, Minutes.

[33] For Johannesburg, see Beavon 2004, 116.

[34] NA, BAO 9160, A1/1709 pt. 1, J.H de Plessis to Bantu Affairs Commissioner, Vereeniging, 18 August 1967.

[35] NA, NTS 7064, 404/322, R.L. Eaton for Native Commissioner, Vereeniging to Director of Native Labour, Johannesburg, 15 October 1948.

In Sasolburg, the idea at first was to prevent any beer brewing in the township, an especially current view within the police. It was considered desirable for beer to be available only at the beer hall or the hostel although management considered, as at ISCOR, that beer was an inevitable basic cultural and material requirement for workingmen.[36] It was also doled out free in the Sasolburg hostel at first.[37] This, of course, did not satisfy the needs of the 400 African families in Sasolkor, the future Zamdela, township. By 1954 transferring beer sale from SASOL to the town council of Sasolburg was considered necessary.[38] Finally in 1960 a beer hall was opened.[39]

The regulation of beer was a major bureaucratic concern.[40] It became increasingly difficult to block the sale of grain that could be used by customers for beer brewing; it was not difficult for the thirsty to buy supplies from the Indian shops outside the township. A further step was the purchase of beer directly from this source.[41] Moreover, as the Native Advisory Board pointed out, grain was also a necessity for the manufacture of other foodstuffs and non-alcoholic drink.[42] There was the question of whether to allow women into beer halls and whether the halls could be open on Sundays and, if so, even in the morning at the time of church services.[43] While the community halls did show films,[44] in general the planned locations were boring and lifeless. Black people unsurprisingly spent time in the general

36 NA NTS 5437, 481/313G, Kaffir Beer Regulations, W.H.S. Sharp, Village Administration to Native Commissioner, Vereeniging, Sasolburg, 1/3/57

37 NTS 5846, 481/313/M, Memorandum, Secretary, Administration of Native Affairs, 4 April 1957.

38 NA NTS 5437, 481/313G, Kaffir Beer Regulations, 27 March 1954. Meeting between representatives of government and town management of Sasolburg.

39 NA, NTS 6237, 48/313O, G. White, Secretary, Native Affairs to Secretary, Village Board, Sasolburg 5/6/57.

40 NA, NTS 5440, 609/313G, *passim.*

41 NA, NTS 5440, 609/313G, Health Committee to Secretary, Native Affairs, 11 August 1948, P.R. Nell, to Native Commissioner, Vereeniging, 16 March 1955.

42 NA, NTS 5440, 609/313G, Extract from Minutes, Native Advisory Board, 27/9/50.

43 NA, NTS 5440, 609/313G, Colin Harris, Secretary, Health Committee to Minister Native Affairs, 7 December 1948; M.G. Green for Town Clerk to Native Commissioner, Vereeniging, 7 March 1951; P.R. Nell to Native Commissioner, Vereeniging, 7 May 1952.

44 NA, BAO 1995, A20/1709, Bantu Advisory Board, Bophelong and Boipatong, 22 September 1966.

town centres and indeed liked to go into the old business district of Vereeniging from the whole region (Prinsloo 1993; Frankel 2001). Indeed they often preferred to buy their liquor there once it was sold legally to them.[45] A signal reform after the 1960–1 political crisis that led to the banning of the ANC was the legalisation of standard Western-style beer purchase for Africans (Mager 2010).

Probably Sasolburg was created with the desideratum that domestic workers be forced to live in the location rather than 'accommodating them on the European premises' – something that proved impossible ever to enforce.[46] Kirchhofer fended off any responsibility for this later.[47] 'All squatting was to be prohibited.'[48] However, before permanent dwellings were available, where were the workers to stay? From the beginning, squatting was hard to control.[49] The female domestic workers who were permitted to live on premises inevitably had male visitors and, more furtively, resident lovers or husbands whose residence promoted the availability of workers to the employer. It could not possibly be illegitimate for these women to go to church and worship God but that required inevitably large black crowds walking through white Sasolburg, for instance, on a Sunday. Another anomaly in the system, critical in the phase where black labour was in heavy demand, was the apparent right of potential workers to spend the first 72 hours in a proclaimed white area without an endorsed pass while looking for work. Finally there was the problem of legitimate workers for whom there was no legitimate space in the townships. A fascinating memorandum from 1958 points to the large presence in Sasolburg of men and children in servant's quarters; the domestic workers were successful in agitating that there would be no work for the white household if these were expelled with nowhere to go.[50] Such households were obviously tempted to wink at

45 NA, BAO 1995, A20/1709, Bantu Advisory Board, Bophelong and Boipatong, 22 September 1966.

46 Kirchhofer, Interview with Director, Native Labour, 23 July 1951, SASOL Papers.

47 Max Kirchhofer to Cecil Hersch, architect, 18 September 1965, SASOL Papers.

48 Kirchhofer, Interview with Director, Native Labour, 23 July 1951, SASOL Papers.

49 NA, NTS 6134, 481/313N, P.E. Rousseau to Verwoerd, 26 August 1952.

50 NA, BA9268, A15/1603. Regulations for Management of Bantu Residents, Sasolburg; W.H.S. Sharp, Secretary-Treasurer, Village Administration of Sasolburg to Native Commissioner, Vereeniging, 15 January 1958.

regulations vis-à-vis SASOL workers if they had a satisfactory arrangement with their employees.

Moreover, for any other transactions involving sex and other relations between men and women, marijuana, gambling opportunities or, above all, beer, there was the uncontrolled or perhaps more accurately put, difficult to control, world of peripheral peri-urban properties.[51] In the Verwoerd era, trawling the peri-urban sea was an important but unending task for mariner policemen.[52] Here it was possible to find ramshackle businesses of all sorts. Owners might be absent; in a few cases, they were themselves not white and here transgression could occur. Thus in 1954 officialdom discovered that a whole row of Indian-owned shops and houses could be found at the southern border of Vanderbijlpark on the property of a Coloured woman, Susan Wessels, married to an Indian man described as a general dealer named Kajee Omar. Some of these shops, however, appeared to be rented from white men in Vereeniging. This typical anomaly was shut down but would reappear in new guises.[53] In 1961, state agents once again found the row of Indian shops on the south end of Bophelong rented from white women in Vereeniging, this time full of white shoppers who preferred this to the carefully planned town centre. This zone included Chinese businesses that bore the traces of gambling for the day's horse races.[54] From Zamdela, the Sasolburg township, while it was true that it was rather easy for black residents to walk to the SASOL entrance, the reality was one of littered, unsanitary and potentially even dangerous footpaths by the dozen. Moreover, Sasolburg had attracted AECI and other employers, creating more complicated commuting trajectories that could hardly be stopped.[55] This

[51] For an impressive look at the life of urban Africans understood as cultural history in Sharpeville, a Vaal Triangle township near to Vereeniging but not far from Vanderbijlpark, see Jeffrey 1991.

[52] NA, BAO 9575, B23/5/1603, C.P. Barnaard, official entrusted with the carrying out of Chapter 4 regulations to First Administrative Official, Squatter Management, 11/10/62. This official suggested setting up a Labour Tenants Control Board to this end.

[53] NA, BEP 228, G7/170/7, Enclosure in P.R. Nell, Town Clerk to Land Tenure Advisory Board, 24 May 1954.

[54] NA, BEP 228, G7/170, Groepsgebiede te Vanderbijlpark, 2 October 1962, Gemeenteskaapreport.

[55] M. C. Tisdall, Manager, Production of Co-ordination and Despatch, to General Manager, SBD, SASOL, 16 July 1976.

irregularity had already irritated the planners twenty years earlier in Vanderbijlpark.[56]

The paternalist regime of SASOL and ISCOR and the industrial hegemony that underpinned all the early planning, based as it was on extreme inequality, was acceptable more from constraint than accord.[57] Pay was drastically unequal. In its first twenty years, for instance, ISCOR reported that it had paid out Ł50 m. to 'Europeans' and Ł13 m. to 'Natives'. The latter outnumbered the former in mid-1954 by 11,500 to 9,000![58] Victor Munnik recorded the views of veteran ISCOR workers recently. 'Blacks were like tools. Where there was hard work, blacks were always taken ... We were the first people to be the machines of ISCOR. We were the people who were doing the work of the machines of today' (Munnik 2012, 133–4).

There was also humiliation from the naked medical examinations and the corporal punishment sometimes administered just as in the mines. At work, black overseers at ISCOR came equipped with sjamboks and white security guards and supervisors carried guns (Hlatshwayo 2003, 66). The regime was particularly stark for hostel dwellers, who had to wear special bracelets different from the house residents outside the hostel perimeter, and could be confined to a detention room provided in the hostel (Ibid., 70, 85, 90, 95). Interviewed hostel dwellers were largely recruited from rural sites in the Homelands often with the assistance of chiefs, although ISCOR employees went out on recruitment drives, and typically had been previously employed on the mines, to whose system they were inured (Ibid., 71–2). Their lives included considerable episodes of violence, occasionally aimed at white supervisors (against whom they were never

[56] NA NTS 7064, 404/322, P. Nell, Town Clerk to Native Commissioner, Vereeniging, 25 March 1954.

[57] See the National Archives, for an official account of a big 1964 strike of black SASOL workers, possibly to be associated with the South African Congress of Trade Unions (SACTU) but very similar in form to the famous Durban strikes of 1972, and conducted with no reference to politics. The refusal to name leaders and the insistence on wage demands as the core issue are very reminiscent of the many accounts of those strikes (NA ARB 1226, 1042/11/952, letters from February 1964). Webster (1985) looks at the heavy metal sector of industry from the perspective of the labour process and the conjuncture of Taylorism and South African racial divisions. He paid attention to the general situation of black labour migrants and did some research in the Vanderbijlpark firm of VECOR.

[58] NA, MES 232. H 4/12 pts 1, 2, ISCOR Annual Report 1955. This included all ISCOR operations including Pretoria.

allowed to testify in disciplinary proceedings), drunken and squalid sessions where they were able to sit, dream and talk about life at home, notably about their herds of cattle and opportunities to pilfer mine equipment that made up a little for the limited pay (Ibid., 84, 89). Guards would beat up drinkers they perceived as unruly or out of control. The beer was supplemented from illegal shebeens in the hostels as well as drinking possibilities outside (Ibid., 99). ISCOR had a credit regime which allowed purchase of extra food (a major source of disputation) and other services and goods providing the employer with some extended control. Worker relations with black 'bossboys' in particular were complex, including systematic bribes for latitude and favour (Ibid., 94). This went as well for the headmen who dominated living quarters and were usually defined in terms of tribe.[59]

And there was no mobility (Frankel 2001). In 1967, ISCOR, which dominated the economy of Vanderbijlpark, opened up a training facility for black workers. The training consisted of (a) an induction course, (b) instruction in the bastard work language of Fanakalo, (c) pre-school education, (d) safety instructions, (e) training of instructors and (f) training of operators. That was it.[60] Workers themselves remember training as being only to a limited extent about performing tasks and focusing mostly on the need to work hard and obey all whites. Fanakalo was in fact not much used on this account. Instead, workers were obliged to understand Afrikaans, which they resented acutely (Hlatshwayo 2003, 69, 72ff, 83). Accident risk was discussed but in practice accidents were always defined as the fault of the worker.

The compound dwellers especially were trained to see the world and did so with racialised lenses but without of course the inherent racial assumptions of those responsible for the system. At least one popular work song summed it up: *Qubula zasha, Abalungu ngodem* ('Lift up, damn the whites') (Hlatshwayo 2003, 91). There is good reason to think that a tribalised perspective took hold as well (Ibid., 93).

However, as the discussion above suggests, the apparently neat, if complex, world of controls established in the Vaal Triangle towns had inherent contradictions and met with a whole range of insubordinate

[59] For instance, Hlatshwayo 2003, uses the example of the Hlubi, a Zulu speaking lineage group who were not part of the political Bantustan division, as a defined group in an ISCOR hostel, 67.

[60] NA, BAO 3/2035, A6/S2/V4, D.C.U. Conradie, Personnel Manager, ISCOR to Bantu Affairs Commissioner, Vereeniging, 9 June 1967.

and tacitly resistant behaviour in terms of the drive for pure segregation. There are interesting parallels amongst the beneficiaries of the system, the large white population attracted to expanding employment opportunities.

Whites in an Industrial Social Order

The core towns built for whites lay at the apex of the planning exercises. These are therefore classic suburban towns built according to plans in which particular areas reflected closely the cost and appropriate status in the parastatal world that went with positions at work even though an increasing number of residents worked for firms other than the parastatals, albeit with parallel hierarchies. The oldest modest parts of white Vanderbijlpark had no garages although this altered in the 1950s. In Sasolburg, all houses that were sold off had garages but in an early phase, others which were rented were only provided with carports. In response to an indignant resident who felt demeaned by this, Minister of Economic Affairs Nico Diederichs felt obliged to respond that this was a gesture intended to benefit those who would struggle to pay higher rentals.[61] This meant that particular blocks were all of a muchness in terms of size and amenity.

However, what is perhaps more striking than the tiered layers of demarcation created by housing is the extent to which the white town in both cases was intended to civilise the paler skinned natives. White louts unused to urban living were to be made accustomed to a regime of suburban neatness and order and hopefully rendered suitable for further social and material mobility while foreigners unused to the 'South African way of life' had to be domesticated. Club membership for immigrant ISCOR employees was a requirement. The system of amenities, much of it sporting, also had a socialising effect, it was hoped. In time, VESCO actually introduced large African fauna to Vanderbijlpark (which abutted the Vaal river) as a symbol of desirable elevating appreciation of the natural environment.[62] Sasolburg was equipped with a botanical

[61] Diederichs to Mev. C.F. Cilliers, 28 July 1959, NA, MES 218, H 46/6 v. 1 and 46/7.

[62] The game park near the river housed at peak four rhinoceroses, two lions, fifty-seven springbok and twenty-nine impala. However, the lions were overly confined and the rhinoceroses ate up the bush excessively. Most of the game died

garden and a bird sanctuary.[63] Those numerous men hired who were not married were placed in controlled situations – specially designed hostels with appropriate recreational facilities nearby. Residential areas were placed separately from business premises. Churches were located far from spots where men might take to drinking. Neat lawns were supposed to stay clear of rusting old cars and other working class or farm boy appurtenances. An apocryphal bit of Sasolburg urban legend was the monthly encounter at the SASOL factory gate between husband and wife. The wife took the money required for household necessities immediately on payment and the husband then went off with his mates for a major weekend drinking bout, marking an incomplete, if perhaps predictable social transition from the point of view of the planners.

In a correspondence over what was termed 'backyard development', the Swiss Kirchhofer considered that untidy backyards were a throwback to rural living that needed to be eliminated through strict regulation according to his big plan. They were due to the fact that

> living in towns is a new experience for a large portion of the white population of this country. It is understandable that the backvelder when he moves into the closely knit urban pattern will bring with him a mode of life conditioned by the vast open spaces ... A certain amount of guidance would be helpful and strict application of the laws should do the rest.[64]

This, he argued was better than the official idea of concentrating on hiding views of the backyards.

Class differences in the white population were considerable. Many white workers making £2-3 per month or less in the 1950s received subsidy payments from the Department of Social Welfare. These bottom wages improved but apprentices continued to be a special category at the bottom of the wage ladder. Much as the state hoped to turn 'poor whites' and those on the fringe of being 'poor white', so typical of the Highveld countryside, into respectable working class families, the skill

out. Yet the goal remained 'quality outdoor recreation'. Mallows et al., 1973, SASOL Papers.

63 NA, GMO v. 1/7234, Max Kirchhofer, Guide Plan for Sasolburg, November 1975, Notes. In effect Max Kirchhofer was really concerned with the aesthetic and did not come to grips with the basic environmental issues. For early environmental issues that were surfacing in Sasolburg from 1960, see NA, ARB 1226, 1042/11/952.

64 Max Kirchhofer to D.P. de Villiers, 3/8/57.

requisites were such as to require much outside assistance. The poorer paid workers and hostel dwellers were largely Afrikaners[65] but significantly the parastatals advertised for immigrants to come out to the Vaal Triangle from Europe as noted in Chapter 6 and integrating these foreigners was defined as a major task for the social services and schools (Nell 1952). On arrival, single workers were placed in hostels and then later assigned to housing. Rents were levied at a maximum of 20 per cent of income. A home ownership scheme was instituted and the socialising influence of club membership compulsory.[66]

For a long time in both towns, authorities attempted to enforce planning regulations that fitted the original plans of the architects approved by the state.[67] It was claimed in 1949 by ISCOR that 'the Company will not permit any alterations or additions to the existing buildings, which will tend to destroy the character of the buildings in terms of the Establishment designed for use as a dwelling for a single family'.[68] The Archives are replete with detailed correspondence about proposed alterations through the 1970s. However, this and other aspects of enforcing the model town order, was a never-ending struggle.

It gradually became more expensive and difficult to recruit from overseas. However, the pool of skilled workers in South Africa that ISCOR was prepared to hire was too small through the years of economic growth. ISCOR had an apprentice and bursary programme and most of its recruits at bottom level came through there. However, the monotonous life in Vanderbijlpark was not such as to reduce the high turnover rates so long as jobs for white South Africans were plentiful.[69] Life in a regulated small industrial city was less attractive to a workforce than was imagined in the dreams of van der Bijl and the city planners. It is not entirely by chance that the most famous Afrikaner anti-establishment rock 'n' roller, Johannes Kerkorrel, came from a modest home in Sasolburg.

Whites exhibited both a loyalty critical in some respects to the whole parastatal-governmental authority but in some respects they sought to

[65] NA, VWN 1493 pt. 1, pt. 2, 1955–66.
[66] Ibid., Facts about Employment with ISCOR, cyclostyled.
[67] SASOL Papers B.1, *passim.*
[68] NA, TAD 4/8 PB 4/2/2 1358 Deel 2–1359 v.1.
[69] NA, MPP 23, A3/10/1 pt. 1, L.C.J. de Villiers, Personnel Manager, Report on Manpower, May 1971.

carve out space that did not always fit what the authority desired or even opposed, and regimentation bred rebelliousness. Resident whites may have been keen on racism and racial laws but they also sometimes profited from illegal activities and sponsored them themselves. Like the black residents, they often preferred to shop in the multi-use Vereeniging centre rather than the planned precincts of the new towns (Prinsloo 1993). Whites did not really like the planned racial separation favoured by authorities but they wanted to interact with blacks on their own terms.

Whites who did not like the controlling regime of the company towns also turned to the countryside where they could lead an unregulated or much less regulated existence. This also involved business possibilities, illegal or unregulated. On a little property, a man could keep a few cows and grow some maize as well as tinker at rusty machinery and fix cars. In time, many white families, for example, settled in what became known as Greater Steel Valley, close to the ISCOR factory, on some 600 smallholdings. This was originally defined as a waste disposal area but got settled anyway.[70] Here ISCOR employees engaged in multi-tasked, multi-income lives on land that was disastrously seriously polluted well outside the regulated world of the town.

As was true generally in the Vaal Triangle region, smallholdings housed not only white individuals and families but workers and other black residents in time-honoured fashion. In 1967, a survey by the Vanderbijlpark Council found 4,555 Africans in the surrounding area. Some were ISCOR temporary construction workers. Only 353 were farmworkers legally employed but the largest number were domestic workers, employees doing other than agricultural work and minors.[71] In the official records, bureaucrats were plagued with complaints by white residents about supposedly illegal black activities and presence, generally found to be more or less legal in fact.

Whites occasionally exploded outside the confines of the company controls. In Vanderbijlpark, a resident who worked for Metal Box recalled that in the early days, 'there was one pub and it saw fights

[70] See map, NA, BAO 1561, A18/1709 pt. 1.

[71] NA, BAO 8005, 164/1708, pt. 1, Head Commissioner, Bantu Affairs to Secretary, Bantu Affairs, 9/6/67. This was also true south of the Vaal around Sasolburg albeit less densely. NA, NTS 5846, 481/313/M, Memorandum, Secretary, Administration of Native Affairs, 4 April 1957 with further letter, 29 April 1957 and record of meeting, 27 March 1958.

every night' (Prinsloo 1993, 166). This in turn meant that white civil society required not merely the intervention of the churches but of welfare and charitable organisations with a mission to intervene in acute social problems. The Red Cross, Noodhulpliga, Kindersorg, Family and Marriage Society of South Africa, the Cancer Union, Kreupelsorg and the South African National Council for Alcoholism had no problem keeping busy on the Vaal (Ibid., 167). This was a kind of insubordinate behaviour in contradistinction to the controlling power of the planned town. Only after the end of the apartheid government, did residents feel empowered to engage in protest against the big employer, which apart from employing the majority, was also sometimes the provider of credit (Prinsloo 1993; Munnik 2012, 118). Until apartheid broke, ISCOR 'people tend to work for ISCOR for their whole lives and you step into a culture of how people do things' (Munnik 2012, 274). Moreover, even the white smallholders were bound to ISCOR by the accepted dictates of security in a beleaguered white South Africa; many were members of an ISCOR Command.

The Vaal Triangle towns were very largely a black and white world. Only in Vereeniging were there an established community of Indian traders and workers and a small settled population of mixed race. Neither Indian nor Coloured was officially welcome in Vanderbijlpark or Sasolburg.[72] Sasolburg was in fact located south of the river in the Orange Free State where Indian residence was illegal. The small Coloured presence in Vanderbijlpark, and even smaller in Sasolburg, was a source of ongoing if low-key official anxiety as there was no 'group area' to house the handful employed there.[73] Finally, an attempt was made to move all the Coloured people in the Triangle to Grasmere outside Vereeniging.[74] However, apart from the misery it

[72] NA, ARG v. 163 VK 132/1/14 p. 1, Verwysings van Beplanningskomitee, verslae: Town Council of Vanderbijl Park, 1953 Memorandum on the Proclamation of Group Areas. NA GMO v. 1/7234, Sosiografie. The 1960 census counted no Asians and 110 Coloured persons in Sasolburg, largely domestic workers.

[73] NA, NTS 7064, 404/322, P. Nell, Town Clerk to Native Commissioner, Vereeniging, 18 March 1956; BEP 506, G7/550 1 and 2, W.H.S. Sharp, Secretary, Village Board of Management to Provincial Secretary, Bloemfontein, 8 August 1960.

[74] NA, BAO 1561, A18/1709/pt. 1, J.S. Campbell, Ag. Town Clerk to Secretary, BAD, 6/7/1962.

caused, this was quite impractical and led to Coloured people living illegally on peri-urban properties or elsewhere.[75]

Apartheid: Class Suborned to Race and Ethnicity

The ascendancy of Hendrik Verwoerd politically was accompanied by an attempt to clear up anomalies, scotch resistance and get the economically vital Vaal Triangle into a box that fitted a broader vision. Verwoerd personally as Minister of Native Affairs scoured the countryside to familiarise himself with local situations all over South Africa. He busied himself with every detail about racial buffer zones as they were called, byways, basic school and health facilities and everything that touched on the segregationist ideal.[76]

With reference to Sasolburg and, while acknowledging the regional character of some basic infrastructural issues, Kirchhofer wrote still in 1975 that 'at the present juncture it is important that the new town be allowed to pursue its organic pattern of growth and that it be protected from the damaging effects of premature development of adjoining areas'.[77] However, from Verwoerd's perspective, developing Sasolburg and Vanderbijlpark as discrete inward-looking company towns in isolation was not a realistic or desirable approach precisely as these towns grew and thrived. Key 1953 regional planning legislation would allow a different kind of planning paradigm to take root (Kantorowich 1958). Vanderbijlpark administration was drawn into a larger planning perspective and in the 1970s, a growing Sasolburg, albeit in a different province[78] was also included, pointing towards the creation of an Orange-Vaal regional authority that would make the planning decisions of the 1980s. Moreover, the growth of Vereeniging, a town still controlled early in the 1950s by the political opposition, was also a problem: there was need for the various black townships to grow approaching one another as part of a black block.[79] Verwoerd

[75] NA, BAO 1747, A19/1603 v. 1, W.H.S. Sharp, Town Clerk, Sasolburg to Secretary, Department of Planning, 22 May 1969.

[76] NA, NTS 6134, 481/313N, Meeting between Verwoerd, SASOL Secretary de Villiers and Kirchhofer, 2/9/52.

[77] NA, GMO v. 1/ 7234, Max Kirchhofer, Guide Plan for Sasolburg, November 1975, Notes.

[78] Ibid.; NA, GMO v. 1/ 7234, W.H.S Sharp, Town Clerk, Sasolburg to Secretary, Planning and Environment, 19 December 1975.

[79] NA, BEP 228 G7/170/7 extract from the *Vereeniging News,* 15 May 1954.

worried about the distance between black and white, securing road and rail access to prevent any unnecessary black access.[80] Thus following from this perspective,

> The policy of the Department [of Native Affairs] in regard to the access roads of locations is that generally only one such road should be provided and the course should be the most direct between the town and the location. It should not link up with main arterial roads leading from the town as it must serve the location only.[81]

Nor did Verwoerd like the entrenchment of black family settlements, however linked to employers, in the heart of white South Africa. There was also the issue with much lobbying from farm interests that industry should not be poaching labour from badly paying agriculture.[82] Consequently, he wanted to see the black labour force more and more concentrated in migrant hostels, typically with residents coming from Basutoland, which in 1966 would become independent Lesotho, and deprived of any unnecessary luxuries that might 'spoil' the natives. Migrants were now increasingly viewed as safer and more controllable generally in 'white South Africa' (Frankel 2001). In Sasolburg, already at the end of the 1950s, half the 5,500 Zamdela residents were single men staying in hostels.[83] Migrants comprised two-thirds of the SASOL workforce by 1965.[84] Kirchhofer admitted that while his idea had been for black family residence based on 'criteria similar to those employed in white residential areas', dependence on single male hostels had become dominant.[85] The picture in Vanderbijlpark was similar. By 1980, some 70 per cent of black ISCOR workers at Vanderbijlpark were migrants from the Transkei, Lesotho and elsewhere. Many of these could be relied on to return to the plant in successive contracts so the problem posed by black worker turnover

[80] Interview with Officers of Urban Areas Branch, Department of Native Affairs, 30 July 1951, D.F. de Villiers to Max Kirchhofer, 18 December 1951, SASOL Papers.

[81] G. White, Secretary to Native Commissioner, Vereeniging, 25/2/54, BAO 6947, P114/1709/2.

[82] NTS 5846, 81/313/M, Landdrost of Sasolburg to Secretary, Bantu Administration, 5 July 1962.

[83] NA, NTS 5437, 481/313G.

[84] NA, NTS 5846, 481/313/M, Town Council, Sasolburg to G.P. Froneman, MP, 3 May 1965.

[85] NA, GMO v. 1/7234, Max Kirchhofer, Guide Plan for Sasolburg, November 1975, Notes.

had greatly lessened.[86] However, this was not the end of the story even in the most intense phase of apartheid. It was still expected that white families would require black women as domestic workers. Where could these come from except surrounding farms where they were poorly paid if at all? And with the women came men, few of whom had bona fide Section Ten rights. The result was an endless surveillance struggle over passes and illegal residence on white-owned property.[87]

The second aspect of the new policy, following from the report of the Mentz Commission of 1953, was to create a large concentrated black township where blacks would reside having minimum contact with whites. This was a sharp contrast to earlier policy which tended to favour small locations at a distance from one another.[88] Sebokeng was intended as a kind of giant southern Soweto along the new lines. The idea was to force all blacks in the Triangle to move to Sebokeng in time, which would in turn stretch east to Sharpeville. In the middle 1950s Verwoerd saw this as a black city with 200,000 houses; existing townships would be extended and then extinguished and small numbers of inconvenient whites (in Residensia on the site of the future Sebokeng) compensated and moved out.[89] The emergence and extension of Sebokeng was a massive planning exercise that required the removal of white landowners and the relocation of access roads. It was just one aspect of a project that is laid bare in archival records with literally hundreds and hundreds of maps, surveying exercises and plan-making, just as the previous paternalist company town projections.[90]

By the mid 1960s, there were 7,000 hostel dwellers in Sebokeng, many being shifted from Sharpeville where lodgers were the next to be

[86] NA, MPP 42, A3/10/6, ISCOR Direction to Piet Koornhof, Minister, Department of Co-operation and Development, 3/6/81, MPP 23, A3/10/1 pt. 1, L.C.J. de Villiers, Personnel Manager, Report on Manpower, May 1971. Another major advantage of using hostel workers was their disposability for shift work, Hlatshwayo 2003, 81.

[87] NA, NTS 5846, Town Council of Sasolburg to G.P. Froneman, MP, 3 May 1965.

[88] NA, RNH 54, NH 4/7/17 pt. 1, W.W.M. Eiselen, Secretary, Native Affairs to Secretary, Orange Free State Townships Board, 22 September 1951.

[89] In fact, by 1980 Sebokeng was estimated to have a population of 274, 666. (NA BAO 7/1862 E12/3/3/516 v. 4 and v. 5 etc.). NA BEP 228, G7/170/7, cut outs from the *Transvaler*, 8/6/55; *Rand Daily Mail*, 21 June 1957; Frankel 2001.

[90] NA, BAO 7/1861, E12/3/3/S16.

moved out, and the state began to push Boipatong and Bophelong residents to start moving there.[91] ISCOR completed building a big hostel there in 1973, following in the wake of Anglo-American owned AECI. These hostels were built by the big companies and then sold over time to the state.[92] Beyond Sharpeville lay the freehold settlement of Evaton and here the state had to proceed slowly because expropriation was no longer legal so freeholds (owned by people of all races) had to be bought out and thus paid for although large-scale removals of tenants took place. A new incentive lay in the construction of the Golden Highway, intended to function as a white traffic artery from the Rand to the Vaal river. Sebokeng, north of the highway, was the obvious place to remove those to its south or in its path.[93]

In 1960, one bit of the Triangle exploded. Sharpeville was a township on the edge of Vereeniging where people had been removed from Top Location, the home of much of the older town's black labour force but considered too close to the centre of town. Vereeniging was a town controlled by the political opposition and its whites prided themselves on its paternalistic racial culture. Initial removals to Sharpeville were fairly well timed in terms of the creation of amenities and the quality of houses. However, with the Verwoerdian impetus in place, movement halted as the future of Sharpeville became unclear, at a time when so-called 'Russians', Basotho gangsters, were prevalent, unemployed black youth were beginning to be a factor and circles of Pan-African Congress and ANC militants in Vereeniging plants were starting to form (Jeffrey 1991; Chaskalson 1986; Frankel 2001).[94] Rents were raised and began to be collected more systematically just as an international economic slow-down dampened growth (Jeffrey 1991; Chaskalson 1986; Frankel 2001). Municipal controls were slack.

91 NA, BAO 1995, A20/1709, Bantu Advisory Board, Bophelong and Boipatong 22/9/66; BAO 9276, A15/1709 pt. 2, P.G. Gray, Chief Commissioner for Bantu Affairs, Johannesburg to Secretary, Bantu Administration and Development, 12 February 1973.

92 NA, BAO 3/3264, A6/6/2/S8, J.C. Knoetze, Chief Director, Bantu Affairs Administration Board, Vaal Triangle, to Head, Bantu Affairs Chief Commissioner, 17 April 1974.

93 NA, BAO 1269 A16/1709 pt. 1, P.A. Grey, secretary, Bantu Affairs to Secretary, Community Construction, 29 August 1961.

94 For a resident's view see Tom 1985.

This was the site of the massacre of people fleeing an anti-pass law demonstration that created headlines around the world and marked the very public rejection of apartheid planning by African residents. Even at this time, the company town residential logic of urban planning in the Triangle had been breached. Many Sharpeville residents actually worked elsewhere and buses were regularly running to Vanderbijlpark; ISCOR was shut down effectively for a time after the massacre.

However, the records also reveal under the surface a significant shift starting in the early 1970s. A revealing set of notes from a meeting then showed that many locally based officials were inclined to question the removal obsession. So did the representatives from SEIFSA, the steel employers' federation, which pushed for upgrading instead as well as to expand the scale of family housing being constructed in Sebokeng. This would, however, inevitably require higher rentals and costs for residents.[95]

True, there remained much reactionary back-stepping within the bureaucracy. Thus, secretary E.A. Johns of Bantu Administration and Development wrote in 1974 about a 'better type' of housing for 'Bantus' being planned: 'Planning housing standards must not exhibit inappropriate luxury. As a norm, the goal should be to build as effectively, not as luxuriously, as possible.'[96] AECI, in constructing one hundred houses it had permission to build in Zamdela, also chimed in to note that these would definitely be 'not too luxurious'.[97] Even in 1978, another official stressed that the clinic, now authorised to be constructed in Zamdela, should not be 'luxurious'.[98] A mean-spirited letter insisted

[95] NA, BAO 3/2395, A6/6/2/V4, report of meeting between various stakeholders, representatives of the Bantu Administration Board of the Vaal Triangle and Minister M.C. Botha, 12 November 1976; Regional Representative, Department of Community Development to Chief Director, Vaal Triangle Bantu Affairs Administration Council, Vanderbijlpark, 19 May 1978. For other improvements in the area see Planning Co-ordination Meeting of the Oranje-Vaal Administration with Co-operation and Development, 26 May 1980. NA, BAO 7/1862, E12/3/3/516 v. 4 and v. 5 etc.

[96] NA, BAO 3/3264, A6/6/2/S8, to Chief Commissioner, Bantu Affairs, 7 April 1974. *My translation.*

[97] NA, BAO 3/1148, A5/1/3/1/S10, Secretary, Community Development to N.B.C. Korsman, Secretary, Bantu Administration and Development, 18 November 1975.

[98] NA, BAO 3/2365, A 20/1603/8, J.C. Knoetze, Chief Director, Administration Board, Vaal Triangle to Chief Commissioner L.S. Geldenhuys, 4 December 1978.

that Zamdela did not require the services of Dr Tsolo, an African medical practitioner already in the area on a locum, who would be better placed moving to a Homeland.[99] Such decisions were going to be reversed within a couple of years as apartheid evolved into a new phase that intensified some old problems and evoked new ones.

99 NA, BAO 3/2940, A7/6/2/S10, Bantu Affairs Administration Board, Vaal Triangle, Executive Committee minutes, 9 October 1974.

9 *Energy and the Natural Environment*

The development model thus far in use has exposed the role of extant capital, new capital, the state and key agencies intended to take South African industrialisation much further. It has also considered a small elite group at the core of a developmental state project that had some success and its political and historical context. However, international literature of the past generation has made it clear that this in itself is insufficient. In this chapter, we will look at two further developmental dimensions.[1] First is the question of energy. What enabled mining and heavy industry to function economically and materially? What were the costs? We shall conclude that these were so substantial and the choices so complicated, that they were a factor in shrinking the developmental state back very significantly to its minerals foundation: the minerals/energy complex indeed. This takes us inevitably to a second related question: what did this do to the remarkable natural environment of South Africa? No doubt virtually all human activity leaves a footprint but the impact of major chemical and metal-making sections of the economy and the by-products of these industries are inevitably enormous. Here we will start to look at the industrial economy of South Africa in the final decades of apartheid when the nascent developmental state struggled to find answers to mounting problems and huge contradictions. One window into this side of things involves looking at environmental outcomes in the Vaal River Triangle towns that we have already examined with a sociological eye. This is a very incomplete picture, of course, but it hopefully is indicative and a spur to further research.

[1] For a gendered perspective, yet another dimension, see Annecke 2003 and 2009.

Uranium and Nuclear Power

When Jan Smuts discovered that uranium was a fairly commonplace by-product of gold mining in South Africa, he was delighted and amazed.[2] Uranium throughout this era cast a very large shadow but it actually proved to be (and still is) economically relatively intractable, some would say for better rather than worse given the dangers that have never been entirely overcome by the nuclear energy industry.

The story of South African uranium is tantalising and possession of this potentially astonishing source of power has transfixed its rulers, who continue to long for its further development as a source of prestige and ultimate success. Not only Smuts was keen on uranium, his successor Malan was also very pleased (as would be Verwoerd) and South Africa was at first the main supplier of uranium exported to Britain and the USA after the Second World War (Fig 2005, 41).[3] Smuts created a Uranium Research Committee autonomous from the CSIR and just under his own jurisdiction; this became the Atomic Energy Board (Fig 2005, 39). It was Malan who found a loyal National Party scientist, A.J. LeRoux, to initiate a research programme and inaugurate the first processing plant in 1952 (Fig 1998). Van Eck was a keen supporter although there was scepticism in some quarters, notably from ESCOM, which in the end was eager to embrace atomic power within its growing empire rather than have it remain outside. Under Verwoerd the Atomic Energy Board was formed in 1959 and LeRoux moved his research centre to Pelindaba near Pretoria with his dream of a reactor (Fig 2005, 41). South Africans went to America to study this new field of science in terms of negotiated agreements and learn in particular how to enrich the uranium, a far more complex process than mining the metal. Moreover, even though this co-operative environment existed, enriched uranium was not for sale outside the nuclear powers. However, South Africa was able to acquire a research reactor (Polakow-Suransky 2010, 40). The new field of atomic energy therefore had an institutional home with a high degree of autonomy and special political linkage at the top. Nevertheless in the 1950s it was primarily a question of uranium as a valued raw material export.

[2] The footnotes perhaps do not do justice to my dependence on the popular writing of David Fig on this subject and the brilliant unpublished University of Cape Town thesis written by Andrew Marquard, the best guide to energy policy in twentieth-century South Africa.

[3] Another convenient narrative by David Fig can be found in Fig 2009.

The real change came some time into the National Party years of supremacy. In 1970, B.J. Vorster began to take this new kind of precious metal very seriously and plans for a post-experimental enrichment plant were underway with the foundation of the new Uranium Enrichment Corporation (Fig 1998; Edwards and Hecht n.d., 15). This probably marked the high-water point in thinking about nuclear power as a major source of energy in South Africa; there was certainly a nuclear fantasy, that atomic energy – as in France – could provide most of South Africa's electricity (Hecht 2009). Here there were two crucial elements. First, a scientific establishment in South Africa sought to learn how to activate uranium in order to use this source of energy as part of, or perhaps better put a complement to, the power grid that was being completed. This involved a complicated learning process and imports of numerous complex and expensive parts. In effect, it was possible to generate electricity this way but not very economically (Fig 1998, 169). The agreement linked to uranium sales with the USA and Britain lapsed in 1964–70 as they found other sources for a mineral actually needed only in small quantities. South Africa turned to Germany for assistance (Fig 1998, 167; 2005, 54–5) where Franz Josef Strauss, the Bavarian Christian Social Party leader, a government ally there, was also a close friend of the government in South Africa. However, while the German firm of STEAG was first prepared to be a key associate in this regard, Germany also moved out of the picture after Willy Brandt became Chancellor in 1969 and in 1976 a key contract was instead signed with France, on which a bit more below (Fig 1998, 168).[4]

In the wake of the oil price hike that followed the Yom Kippur War of 1973, it seemed marginally possible to justify a decision to establish a nuclear power generator to serve the Cape Town area, the part of South Africa where coal mines were most distant. Its construction was delayed by sabotage on the part of anti-apartheid activists (Fig 2005, 56) and this was not the only headache that slowed construction. Koeberg was finally opened in 1984–5 but it has not been a roaring success, confirming the doubts of some of the relevant scientific personnel who were less attached to the apartheid project and less fascinated with a national development dream.[5]

[4] In discussing these deals, Fig effectively shows how private and public mesh in the forging of key economic policy in a major European country, France.

[5] Fig notes that the Forsyth Commission in 1961 already knew enough to show considerable scepticism (Fig 2005, 55).

By the time the power station opened, prices were squeezing in such a way as to obviate any possibility of profitability. Electric usage in South Africa was stagnating while prices were rising. Only 4 per cent of power in the country (as of 2009) comes out of Koeberg and the uranium used is actually not local (Winkler 2009, 92). It is supplied from outside the country – in order to save money! The huge expense involved in building and maintaining Koeberg owes little to the price of uranium, which is actually only needed in quite small quantities and is not, as seemed to be the case before 1960, in short supply in the world. The problem was rather the very expensive processes from the point of view of energy use and money that allowed the power station to be built.[6] ESCOM did finally take charge of Koeberg and had to pay for its big deficits (Marquard 2006, 160, 213, 216). Moreover, nuclear power never was properly integrated into energy planning as a whole (Marquard 2006, 99, 126). In the final decade of apartheid, under the auspices of P.W. Botha as State President, who saw Koeberg essentially as an icon of South African technological sophistication, the reluctant atomic midwife ESCOM was largely shunted aside in favour of the growing military complex around Armscor (Fig 2005, 48). The dream of electrifying South Africa with nuclear power has remained that.

The expensive and complex processes involved in enriching uranium must have played a role in its separate structural existence. Yet at least in part this is best explained by the potential other application of uranium – the manufacture of highly destructive bombs. The so-called 'Y plant' constructed in 1971 allowed for this kind of development as well but this too had to be subsidised by ESCOM (Marquard 2006, 200ff). Fig notes that it was probably already aiming from the start at possible nuclear weapons construction (Fig 2005, 45). Vorster certainly became more interested in the deterrent value of a nuclear bomb on African nationalists. In 1976, South Africa was kicked off the International Energy Association Board of Governors, a notable marker in the growing desire in the West to remove South Africa off the table of demonstrable and respectable allies until the apartheid albatross was removed from its neck.

[6] Marquard argues that it absorbed Rand 31 billion in costs up to 2000, 196.

Thus, by the middle 1970s despite initial and usual good intentions declared, the Vorster regime was increasingly determined to use the Pelindaba, and especially the Valindaba, plant to move into secret weapons production (Marquard 2006, 221–2). This in fact took place between 1978 and 1980 (Fig 1998, 168). By 1979, South Africa was able to produce enriched uranium (Marquard 2006, 220). It was now France which did supply key technology and learning assistance based on a contract signed in the eventful year of 1976 (Fig 2005, 56). It was French credit too that made this possible financially.

In 1976 Vorster went to Israel and signed an important document that initiated substantial military co-operation. Well before this South Africa had sold Israel the uranium illegally under international law which it used in order to build up its own nuclear capability (Polakow-Suransky 2010, 120). There is good reason to assume that the Israelis, who have their own semi-secret nuclear bombs, were critical in providing necessary training and know-how and were particularly important in the testing phase (Fig 1998, 171, 174). By 1980 there was a South African bomb. To this end, much time and expense were involved in developing such a bomb, of which several existed, and at least one tested over the South Atlantic, before this programme was put to an end by F.W. de Klerk (Polakow-Suransky 2010, especially 140–1).[7] The former Y plant would be shut down entirely in 1993. This initiative may indeed have had some impact on potential enemies of the regime.

David Fig has written that the enthusiasm of government supporting the work of technicians and scientists was critical in solving various technical problems that arose; South African technology cannot be fairly seen as backward. However, it is not clear that the acquisition of this knowledge in either electric power provision or weapons construction has led to any further economic development of real importance. There is little reason to think that the ANC government has any interest in a nuclear bomb (on whom could one drop it?) but important figures in the government since 1994, and especially under President Jacob Zuma's leadership since 1994, have clearly remained very smitten with the idea of building more nuclear power stations at immense expense. So far, however, this has remained in the domain of private and

[7] Marquard believes that P.W. Botha actually stopped further development of bomb construction in 1985 as pointless; Marquard 2006, 200. It was essentially there to frighten opponents of apartheid, especially those supporting military resistance from across the borders, 222ff.

inconclusive negotiations (notably, but not only, with Russia) and speculative talk although potential properties have been bought up and identified by the state.

The presence of uranium on South African soil was very real but it functioned as a kind of chimera. This is a test case of a thrust which began with a developmental ethos and perspective but became in part a very expensive white elephant – Koeberg – and in part was diverted to narrowly military ends. It must be understood, however, not as having led to an extension of the developmental state that could function effectively in the global economy but as a temptation that led in exactly the wrong direction, towards dependence on export of a raw material. There was no concrete success in formulating technology that would make South Africa a valued trading partner, rather than just a customer for very expensive materiel. Marquard suggests that at its peak of popularity, nuclear power might well have become the very heart of the minerals-energy complex had it been more economic, but it certainly was in no sense a departure from the defining core complex itself (Marquard 2006, 210).

Coal

As Harald Winkler says '[a]t the point of use, electricity is a clean energy carrier but upstream there are significant local environmental impacts' (Winkler 2009, 15). After considering the potential use of uranium in this regard, we now turn to coal. By contrast to uranium, coal in the here and now has been of incalculable importance in industrial life. The coal reserves, the coal mines and the huge power stations, usually close to coal mines, are as central to modern economic life in South Africa as gold. Electrification itself was always fundamental to the big state planning of post-Second World War South Africa. The provision of cheap coal was really axiomatic in the heavy industry strategy in addition to mining pursued in late twentieth-century South Africa.

Coal is a mineral which South Africa has in abundance albeit with 'high ash, low sulphur and low caloric value' (Winkler 2009, 59). The industry has its origins in the nineteenth century, was strongest at first in inland Natal where rail connections linked mines to Durban and to the Rand. Initially coal was most important in fuelling trains and ships. Perhaps one-third to one-sixth of this coal was exported but the proportion tended to decline. However, it is more than just another mined product; it is also overwhelmingly the source of electric power in the country. At the same time, coal mining itself, as with the other mining operations, consumes considerable energy as well. Jaglin and Dubresson report that electric power fed by coal accounted for fully 32 per cent of gold mining costs as of 2011 (Jaglin and Dubresson 2015, 18).

Electrification has in particular remained tied to the gigantic needs of deep-level mining. On the eve of the disappearance of the Victoria Falls and Transvaal Power Company in 1948, the gold mines consumed some 59 per cent of electricity produced in South Africa (Jaglin and Dubresson 2015, 22). Soon after, a plan was devised to construct ten coal-based electricity power plants in the South African interior (Jaglin and Dubresson 2015, 26). Those constructed, according to Jaglin and Dubresson, were considered amongst the most powerful and modern in the world at the time (Jaglin and Dubresson 2015, 27). Within a decade, capacity had doubled. Marquard has characterised this era as one where the level of productivity in coal mining remained largely stagnant with the growing demand from ESCOM for use in power stations the one area of growth. It was characterised by low levels of beneficiation, cheap and plentiful local labour, poor levels of mechanisation and a low level of product differentiation (Marquard 2006, 76).

Internationally cheap oil was replacing coal in its traditional areas of strength; coal looked inwards for a market. Regulation had been mainly about differential pricing for external and internal use and a licence was required for any export of coal. In fact exports brought in most of the profits but the dominant view until the end of the 1960s had been the crucial importance of coal supply available for consumption in South Africa. The price set for domestic use was set by the state and intended not to make a profit, part of the ESCOM charter (Marquard 2006, 76). The state had tried to control the dual demand situation by setting different prices for internal and external customers.

> Thus by the end of the 1960s, coal policy within a narrow framework focused conceptually on the domestic market and institutionally based in the Department of Commerce and Industry, which regulated the domestic price, promoted industrialisation based on cheap coal and controlled coal exports. (Marquard 2006, 93)

The situation would change dramatically in the 1970s. In this decade, electric power was in huge demand locally as electric use expanded significantly. As the price of oil shot up after 1973, coal was now wanted again to replace it. The gold mines' interest in set prices for coal purchase diminished (Marquard 2006, 81). They too wanted to own coal mines and sell coal instead. The result was massive government investment in this basic minerals-energy complex component based in good part on foreign loans, now legally possible for ESCOM, coupled with a declining capacity to regulate volumes and prices. During this decade, coal capitalisation rose from around R175 m. to R2 billion; coal was the hottest item on the stock exchange. It was a sector that offered possibilities to Afrikaner business following the Gencor deal with Anglos, after which they tended to be favoured for power contracts (Marquard 2006, 160). Output doubled in the 1970s (and doubled again by the end of the century) as new, ever bigger, power stations came onto the now national grid (Marquard 2006, 151). Municipalities were more or less forced on to the grid, including a notably reluctant Johannesburg, with advantages in avoiding duplication of equipment and costs in general. The state too lost its interest in price fixing for domestic use. This had been based on long-term contractual arrangements but these began to run out (Marquard 2006, 91). The whole price fixing scheme was terminated by stages with the Coal Resource Act of 1985.

Consequently, there was an equivalent pressure to boost exports which had almost disappeared as a factor. Already in 1969, a small-scale deal with Japan was signed (Marquard 2006, 109). There was ever more interest in making money through this new surge in export. By 1980 the two greatest gold mining houses also owned two-thirds of the coal mines in the country. It was crucial for instance for the vast coal resources of the eastern Transvaal (now Mpumalanga Province) to get to Richards Bay, a new port created for this purpose on the Zululand coast facing east towards Asia. In 1975 there were actual coal shortages in South Africa and the pressure was all on increasing supply in a technologically rather backward industry.

As a result, and starting with the Petrick Commission, which met between 1970 and 1975, clearly spurred on in the middle after the 1973 Yom Kippur War in the Middle East, there was a growing awareness of the need for a new form of regulation.[8] Marquard points specifically to

[8] See, for example, T.P. Muller, chairman, ISCOR to Chris Heunis, who suggests the need for a Coal Council that could include Anglos, the organisation of

the role of Dirk Neethling, a key figure in the Department of Mines and later in the Department of Mines and Industry and then the National Energy Commission, as a key individual in the setting of changing policy with a vision of the entire energy sector (Marquard 2006, 98).

The decade of the 1980s was different again with yet rougher winds blowing. Marquard's views is that this led to a more structured way of dealing with energy, advanced by the creation of a Ministry of Minerals and Energy (which still exists) in 1980 and culminating in the National Energy Commission, which existed from 1987 to 1991. The dominant tone was one of deregulation. Domestically, electricity demand, together with economic growth generally, stagnated at best. In particular, profits were falling at last in gold mining. Electric consumption increasingly shifted to the parastatals, ESCOM, SASOL and ISCOR.

Financially the state was squeezed badly given the huge investments made when the going was good. At the same time, the demand for coal, especially in East Asia, continued to be reasonable if profits were less spectacular. Access to South African coal could be made contingent on recognition of South African international legitimacy. Coal mines were bought up by new foreign entities, often created out of oil money, and also became a point of entry for Afrikaner capitalists. Even gold mining houses created distinctive and separate coal consortia (Marquard 2006, 82). Expensive and technically difficult as it was, the coal transport across the Drakensberg to Richards Bay was in order and of growing importance (Marquard 2006, 107). Eventually Richards Bay surpassed Durban in cargo volume. In 1970, domestic consumption had added up to 90 per cent of coal consumption; fifteen years later that would be down to 38 per cent (Marquard 2006, 78). The deregulation era also worked, however, in terms of supply; the domestic supply problems of the 1970s were completely forgotten (Marquard 2006, 106).

The old structural forces that had lain behind key energy decisions but perhaps without much co-ordination were now being challenged by new elements that made it possible still to speak of a small elite that, despite internal struggles, co-ordinated key national policies, but were

Transvaal based coal companies and Gencor, as well as ISCOR and the state. These parties did meet on 2 June 1976 but attempts at co-ordination on the issues of price and availability were not entirely successful. NA, MPP 23, A3/10/1 pt. 1, 28 May 1976.

not comfortable with the old partners. In particular, Marquard cites the growing autonomy of ESCOM to expand internationally, raise or lower prices and function as a law unto itself. He refers to its modus operandi as 'hermetic' by the middle 1980s (Marquard 2006, 168). P.W. Botha had to appreciate its large capacities and the necessity of working with it but increasingly wanted to tame it in the interest of a more systematic and less conflictual energy policy. Here he had some but far from complete success, especially in depriving ESCOM of the right to set prices as it chose. The 1970s boom had brought about significant inflationary pressures; it was only the stagnation of the domestic economy in the 1980s that reduced them. A stakeholder conception of the world of energy provision now began to loom, even before the end of the old regime (Marquard 2006, 342).

It might be useful in summing up to consider the objectives listed by the new Department of Minerals and Energy in 1980 for their first annual report:

1) an uninterrupted energy supply at reasonable cost levels
2) continuously decreasing reliance on imports of crude oil within the boundaries of strategic and economic considerations.
3) optimal extraction of coal
4) exports of especially coal and uranium to earn foreign exchange
5) active pursuit of conservation of energy
6) R&D to be pursued to reach these goals
7) continued search for oil source in SA
8) continued further development of synfuels preferable in private sector
9) long-term planning looking at alternative energy resources (Marquard 2006, 366–7).

In considering this impressive set of objectives, however, Marquard, reports on the rise of figures like CEO Johann Maree whose strength lay on the financial side. He adds that 'energy planning was consistently advocated as the basic solution to energy policy problems during the apartheid era. But ironically not much of it actually took place, due to lack of both capacity and data' (363). The planners met but the plan never happened.

Coal also is tied to the story of the great oil-from-coal parastatal SASOL – 'synfuels' – which in recent years has been a user of 30 per cent of coal production in South Africa (Marquard 2006, 249). SASOL actually was turned into a private corporation in 1970 so that it could go out and finance major expansion. SASOL 2 and 3 are themselves huge consumers of electric power and thus coal. It has at times been successful under a system of regulated prices that makes petrol relatively expensive in providing fuel for trucks and cars (Marquard 2006, 254).[9] However, it also remains, as it was originally intended to be, an important player in synthetic chemicals manufacture.

Marquard's unusually rich analysis contains more thoughts on energy and energy policy but to conclude this section, it seems more significant for our purposes to make the point on which we shall build the subsequent chapter. The expensiveness of energy and the problems involved in sorting out energy policy and conflicting needs greatly reduced the potential of South Africa's developmental state. Providing energy for the minerals-energy complex to continue functioning profitably with security issues increasingly in mind became paramount in state thinking. The capacity for planning diminished, the players perhaps became too numerous and it became increasingly impossible for the laying out of a complex, profitable industrial sector with great prospects for further growth. The state and business found themselves rather tied in to the confines of the minerals-energy complex boundaries: the export of raw materials and the provision of energy supply to the large-scale operations that beneficiated these raw materials but did not lead to an internationally competitive tertiary economy.

> The proposed plant was thus premised on the same kind of economic linkages which had characterised most South African industrial development in the 1960s and 1970s, raw material from the gold-coal complex (uranium and electricity) and the product partly exported and partly supporting the fuel supply and thus boosting electricity demand ... (Marquard 2006, 222–3 and with reference to the transition of the 1970s)

> The visionaries were sidelined. The political leadership and establishment was confined to a narrow set of strategic goals, which could not be sustained in an environment driven almost entirely by strategic imperatives. (Marquard 2006, 242)

This big shift can be dated to the Yom Kippur War in 1973 or to a series of events in 1976 or even to 1980 when the last great gold boom came to an end. The issue by then was not merely export vs. industrial use.

[9] However, dependence on SASOL for fuel at the pump was as low as 6 per cent in 1955 and 3 per cent in 1973 according to Marquard. A maximum would have been something like 50 per cent at perhaps the end of the apartheid era.

Increasingly, security played a growing role, fears of sanctions and sabotage were paramount. Van Eck for instance, came to believe in the need for South Africa to stock two years' worth of fuel at all times (Marquard 2006, 288). However, exploring this period will be the subject of Chapter 10, the last substantial chapter in this book.

Collateral Damage: The Vaal Triangle's Environmental Problems

The character of the developmental state in South Africa presented a very heavy footprint indeed on the natural environment of South Africa. The harbours that loom large in this narrative, Durban, Richards Bay, Saldanha, all bear witness to damage to plants, animals and humans.[10] To bring out the kind of problems that emerged with the world of the parastatals, some material has been put together on the Vaal Triangle where the first SASOL and second ISCOR plants were constructed. What are the interactions between steel-making, chemical production and human habitation? The costs from this side of developmentalism cannot be added up definitively but they have been massive and they continue in terms of the needs to patch up the worst plans. Environmental impact was simply given short shrift in the planning stage and for long after.

At the time when Vanderbijlpark and Sasolburg were planned, conceptualisation of the environment was skewed towards aesthetic interpretations of what residents, overwhelmingly the white residents, needed. Prolific presence of trees, with much concern about their indigenousness, and the introduction of nature in the form of a miniature game park replete with rhinoceroses were considered proof of a healthy situation in the former town. However, the realities of the great industries generated provided threats to health especially in three areas which must remain today of intense concern, the actual layout and organisation of the industrial plants, the quality of water and the quality of air.

Within the great factories, health issues clearly affected workers. This kind of work contained dangers. Stephen Sparks describes some perilous episodes in the pioneer history of SASOL. Black workers had

[10] Hallowes 2011 provides an excellent environmentalist approach and, in Hallowes 2010, the Vaal Triangle figures prominently.

little opportunity to complain but a post-apartheid set of interviews with ISCOR hostel dwellers by one researcher discussed a litany of them: headaches, breathing problems, seeing and hearing difficulties, kidney and liver failure and psychological depression (Hlatshwayo 2003, 78). Vanderbijlpark blast furnace workers showed a strong tendency towards the acquisition of serious respiratory problems, including cancers (Sitas et al. 1989).[11] The problems hardly stopped at the factory door. In the planning of the new industrial towns, it might be thought that concerns for pollution and the problems the population would experience inside the plant, but also on the outside, would be paramount.[12] However, there was a very limited understanding in mid-century of what these problems might be and a surprisingly superficial grasp of dealing with them. Added to this was the patronising contempt the authorities felt for the wayward ideas of ordinary people, black or white.

Steel mills are now known to increase the incidence of cancer, certainly without suitable precautions taken, both through air pollution as well as through the experience of work near the furnaces (Munnik 2012, 93).[13] The top limits the factory chimneys were, according to statute, supposed to reach were imposed but are now understood to have been inadequate (Munnik 2012, 160). The Scorgie Report on air quality in the whole Triangle of 2004 reported particularly on sulphur dioxide, nitrogen oxides and particulate matter, which was modelled as bringing about various breathing orientated health problems and some premature deaths, particularly in downwind locations (Hallowes 2010, 73ff).

Max Kirchhofer thought about these matters in terms of 'the *nuisance* [italics mine] of smoke and smell' which could be countered with the suffusion of tree cover in emergent Sasolburg. Thus the nuisance in his view was 'less of a problem than expected'.[14] Some tree

[11] I am very grateful to Eddie Webster for directing me to this article and also pointing out that the workers discussed were employed at ISCOR Vanderbijlpark.

[12] For a brief reference to the conditions workers experienced in the ISCOR plant, see Munnik 2012, 144. On p. 99, the general picture of parastatal pollution is proposed.

[13] For the possible dangers from steel mills, see Munnik 2012 160ff. I benefited not only from reading this dissertation but from an interview with its author. Much that follows also benefits from an interview with activist leader Samson Mokoena.

[14] Max Kirchhofer, Notes on the Planning of Sasolburg, February 1957, SASOL Papers, B4. This story is repeated in Kirchhofer 1958. And for a late perspective

planting was all-important even in black townships but, conveniently, especially in defining the borders between black and white. Bopelong was in fact in the right direction to avoid the worst air pollution, close as it was to the ISCOR plant, but that was not true of Boipatong (Munnik 2012, 140) nor of Zamdela (Ibid.),[15] the Sasolburg township, which suffered from the probably more serious depredations of SASOL operations.[16] At first the Coalbrook site proposed by Kirchhofer was described as 'comparatively sheltered from winds' but this was not so true of the eventual location of the township.[17] The statutory limit of four kilometres' distance between residences and the source of noxious odours continued for decades to be considered if anything as too great.[18] When Sasolburg planned a location extension, it ran into problems due to the proximity of the Sigma coal mine. The danger of subsidence and aesthetic issues were raised but there was little realisation of the need to take other environmental issues in concern as well.[19]

Yet this was hardly sufficient, as a rare incident that surfaced in the official records, shows. Thus in 1961 it was the Bantu Advisory Committee in Zamdela that complained about the noxious conditions due to the opening of a crucial state-backed chemicals business linked to SASOL, Fisons Fertilizer. Flowers that residents planted started to die. Fisons and SASOL insisted that no harm at all could come to humans in connection with the questionable smell. Yet whites in the vicinity also began to complain about the impact on their noses and throats and their breathing due to the fluorine used in the factory. Indeed a government inspector finally did attest to the sight of scorched

that is not fundamentally altered, NA GMO v. 1/7234, Guide Plan for Sasolburg, Notes, November 1975.

15 However white Sasolburg was also very vulnerable to air pollution.

16 Although SASOL had on the whole a better record of controls than ISCOR, Interview with Victor Munnik.

17 SASOL Papers, B1, Preliminary Report by Kirchhofer, 31/1/51, 7.

18 SASOL Papers, K1. SASOL/Secunda, The Need and Desirability for the Twp Secunda Extension 6 for SASOL, Motivation Report by L.J. Oakenfull for Mallows etc. and Max Kirchhofer.

19 NA, RNH 68, NH 4/11/17 pt. 1, F.W.C. Aveling for the Secretary, Native Affairs to the Secretary, Mining Affairs, 10 April 1958 in Beplanningshulpkomitee vir Beheerde Gebied No. 1, Ontwikkeling in die Gebied Sasolburg. Subsidence is an old story in South Africa, no doubt because it affected property rights.

and damaged trees and vegetation.[20] The former location superintendent, Gieseke, himself was affected. He noted the high percentage of fluorine due to the Fisons process, which burnt the maize township people were growing. He remarked that when the wind blew in from Fisons, its smoke covered Zamdela; the cause was only too obvious. His wife was herself deeply troubled by the effect on her health.[21]

International stories gradually penetrated as expertise in this area slowly had some effect. It is notable that when SASOL expanded following the oil crisis of the 1970s with a huge new operation at Secunda in what is today Mpumalanga, environmental issues came more to the fore, residents raised serious issues that bothered them and a new regulatory regime began to come in place. Thus in official correspondence, it is tighter regulations but also hostile reaction that arose in discourse. A woman from Evander described SASOL's careless 'disregard for anti-pollution laws' while another new Secunda inhabitant referred to 'a sulphur-type odour emitted from the nearby SASOL Two and Three plants which billow flames and fumes and loom over the town like an industrial Godfather'.[22] The disenchantment with modernist magic was starting.

However, it was the political change that opened the gates to a more critical understanding by the people actually living in what is unkindly called the 'Foul Triangle' at times.[23] Almost all the following material on current conditions pertains to Vanderbijlpark but there is no reason

[20] Prof Douw Stein to Dr P.W. Vorster, Secretary, Department of Agricultural Technical Services, 6 February 1962. Steyn insistently pointed out the potential dangers of fluorine to plant life, air and water without adequate controls that were typical internationally, NA, MES 21, H46/v. 1 and H47.

[21] NA, BAO 1747, A19/1603 v. 1, F.H. Cronje, Chief Bantu Commissioner, Witwatersrand to Local Director, Bloemfontein, State Health Services, 14 December 1961; Badenhorst, Town Area Commissioner, Vereeniging to Chief Bantu Affairs Commissioner, Witwatersrand, 12 February 1962.

[22] *Star 23.9.77, 18.3.80, Sunday Express, 2.8.81*. Not coincidentally the two correspondents cited were both women, not company employees. For the official view that problems had all been solved see SASOL Papers, K1. SASOL/Secunda, The Need and Desirability for the Twp Secunda Extension 6 for SASOL, Motivation Report by L.J. Oakenfull for Mallows etc. and Max Kirchhofer.

[23] For some interesting parallels in another of the four South African designated environmental hot spots, the South Basin area of Durban, see Freund 2001. The other hot spots are the Platinum Belt and the Witwatersrand. This designation received official recognition in 2004 in the Air Quality Act. Interview, Samson Mokoena.

to think that Sasolburg is exempt from these problems.[24] Before 1990, especially for whites (and it was not easy for blacks to complain), a sense of belonging to the company, the source of jobs, a more comfortable life and availability of credit, was very strong (Prinsloo 1993; Munnik 2012, 118).[25]

Only after the end of the apartheid government, did residents feel empowered to engage in protest against the big state-controlled employer. A post-1990 environmental critic stressed that in Vanderbijlpark, ISCOR 'people tend to work for ISCOR for their whole lives and you step into a culture of how people do things' (Munnik 2012, 274). However, with restructuring under Mittal control, while the industry was restored after years to profitability, the size of the workforce was drastically reduced. Bophelong, the oldest Vanderbijlpark township in walking distance of the steel mill, was only saved from destruction and removal at the very end of the apartheid years as the reform Nationalists became stronger. The old houses are the legacy of the van der Bijl era, but today the largest number of employed men in Vanderbijlpark are workers in construction, not steel (Interview, Samson Mokoena).

Moreover resistance to company regulation could itself involve serious infringements of environmental good sense. Here the issue of water pollution comes to the fore (Hallowes 2010). The industrial use of the Vaal River polluted the Vaal 'intensely' especially below the Vaal Dam (Munnik 2012, 129, 157). Flooding and spill-over into the Vaal in 2006–7 were especially noteworthy (Hallowes 2010, 78–9). In Victor Munnik's view, the need to clean up the Vaal was a key factor in the massively expensive construction of the Lesotho Highlands scheme dams from the late 1980s. Near Sasolburg and Vanderbijlpark it was hardly advisable to jump in the water on a hot day.

River water pollution was just one aspect of the problem. Around the ISCOR plant, the area initially marked for polluted water drainage became Greater Steel Valley. Here ISCOR employees engaged in multi-tasked, multi-income lives on land that was disastrously seriously polluted, located well outside the regulated world of the town. This

24 Thus SASOL in general has just withdrawn a legal suit to prevent new legislation on air pollution, having been given an extensive extension to clean up its act. *Business Day,* 30 April 2015. See references in Hallowes 2010.

25 I found this also in my Durban research, Freund 2001.

was a form of resistance to company control in a sense – but one that took a terrible turn. A recent University of the Witwatersrand thesis captures powerfully the severity of the subsequent environmental problems, especially the highly toxic water flows, which led finally to the almost complete extrusion of the Steel Valley population by ISCOR's successor firm, Arcelor (now after a further international merger Arcelor Mittal), early in the ANC era (Munnik 2012; Cock 2004; Bezuidenhout and Cock 2007).

It was white inhabitants of the Valley, particularly individuals represented on the Western Services Council, who took the offensive with regard to the questionable quality of the water, which proved to be suffering from leakages out of the ISCOR plant. The effluent had never been properly packaged and the water table on the site was high (Interview, Samson Mokoena). In the first post-apartheid period and under the watch of Kader Asmal as Minister of the Environment, the new government was sympathetic and the matter went to court. A judge ruled that Mittal had to settle with the plaintiffs on pain of closing down. These were the so-called 'front plots' nearer the plant.

However the back plots were also obviously problematic for residents. Here the hand of the law was less sympathetic in a second court case and the landowners were unable to collect any compensation at all and indeed had to pay legal costs in 2000. A sad part of the story is that they included quite a few black individuals who had bought land after 1994, professional people and long-time ISCOR workers cashing in their pensions eager to escape the confined townships. Only a very few were amongst the beneficiaries of the first court case; they were too reluctant to sign up and to accept that, finally being able to own land legally, the land was poisoned (Interview, Samson Mokoena). NUMSA, the workers' union, was moreover also constrained for fear of job losses if the factory closed; here the older logic continued to hold. In fact Solidarity, which organises largely white and more skilled workers with more options, played a bolder role (Bezuidenhout and Cock 2007).

Almost nobody is left now in Steel Valley. However, the continuing inclination of squatter settlement inhabitants to use the surrounding land with its high water table generally to grow vegetables comes up against the problems of pollution and also loss of wetlands and thus environmental degradation. Mittal was held to a long leash: they were required to see the problem cleaned up by 2010. However, the master plan for dealing with it was kept a secret apart from a short summary statement. From 2011, the activists in the Vanderbijlpark Environmental Justice Alliance went to court to obtain a copy. This became a lengthy legal battle that engaged the support of environmental non-governmental organisations (NGOs) and finally resulted in victory in the Supreme Court of Appeals in 2014. At time of writing, however, an assessment was not yet available.

A new regulatory regime, especially given the intense need for acceptably paid employment, is unlikely by itself to solve all problems. In 1956 a beginning was made with the passing of the Water Act. In 1961, ISCOR created a committee to liaise with the Department of Water Affairs on these matters. However, the parastatals could often secure exemptions given national priorities, an outcome which still is used. This inevitably continues to affect the impact of regulation. Munnik characterises the late apartheid years as ones whereby 'a pattern of lax regulations, exceedances [sic] and breaking of permit conditions' dominated the regime (Munnik 2012, 159, 195). This pattern continues albeit in complex form.[26] One suspects that for Arcelor Mittal, a global company with headquarters in Europe and an Indian magnate at its head, the entire Vaal environmental damage question is so large as to make it desirable for a private company to evade comprehensive solutions.[27] In areas such as union recognition and scholarships for workers' children, which do not entail complicated and costly solutions of this sort, it has been a good employer according to worker testimony, at least when business is profitable.

In 2007 a Green Scorpions report revealed that Arcelor Mittal was dumping waste illegally and causing serious water pollution problems. This report showed major contravention of the National Environmental Management Act of 1998 and led to the requirement of the company response that is still not available as a plan for the public to see (Bezuidenhout and Cock 2007, based on a story in *The Star*, 26 July 2007). That all is still not well emerges with regard

[26] In fact it has a long history in South Africa. Chaskalson indicates that in the older unplanned Vaal Triangle city of Vereeniging, with a Council long keen on encouraging industrial investment, legislation was long ago countered by official exemptions that allowed pollution against the rules, actions that were not permitted in Johannesburg, already observable by the 1940s (Chaskalson 1986, 3).

[27] For a good general discussion of Arcelor Mittal, the world's top steelmaker, and its strategic vision of steel-making in South Africa, one operation amongst many, see Bezuidenhout and Cock 2007.

to Arcelor Mittal at a recent shareholder's meeting. Here the chief executive, Nonkululeko Nyembezi-Heita, acknowledged that there had been numerous environmental incidents during the 2012 financial year. During the year, community members in the Vaal region around the group's regional premises marched to the company's offices in Vereeniging to hand over a list of demands to management. The list dealt with 'misleading information regarding environmental impacts, air quality, medical issues and compensation for occupation-related illnesses'. In addition, the Gauteng Department of Agriculture and Rural Development issued a compliance notice ordering the company to cease certain operations due to non-compliance with conditions in its atmospheric emission licence.

Air quality remains contentious (Hallowes 2010).[28] In the opinion of Vaal Environmental Justice Alliance leader Samson Mokoena, some facets have improved and some have not. Carbon dioxide emissions remain a problem and new legislation is intended to bring up to date the old legislation on what is permissible. Still constant monitoring from outside is and will be necessary on all issues which are not resolved straightforwardly by the passage of protectionist legislation. Enforcement is needed in order to bring results. Thus quite recently Arcelor Mittal was apparently found by a Scorpions police unit dumping polluted waste in a disused site near the Vaal in Vereeniging illegally through a chance sighting (Interview, S. Mokoena). This matter is still *sub judice*.

The Vaal Environmental Justice Alliance has a growing record of activism on the environmental front. It concerns itself with air and water issues, climate change and waste disposal (Interview, S. Mokoena).[29] As this implies, there are now serious environmental problems related to sewage and waste that emanate from the townships, especially in the giant Soweto of the south, Sebokeng, the township city which was intended by Verwoerd to serve the entire Vaal region. These are no different than equivalent situations in residential

[28] Ann Crotty in *Business Day,* 30 May 2013. For a more upbeat appraisal, see the letter by Philip Lloyd of the Energy Institute, Cape Peninsula University of Technology, 23 March 2014, in response to a critique: 'Industry in the Vaal Triangle used to be appalling, but efforts over the past few decades have made the area habitable! . . . '. Of course this admits the previous situation with regard to air pollution was poor.

[29] For a perceptive review of the Environmental Justice movement and of environmental activism in South Africa more generally, see Cock 2004.

areas all over the country, of course. Thus the South African Waste Pickers' Organisation has ambitious plans to clean up Sebokeng through systematic clean-up campaigns, recycling and creation of valuable fertiliser to enhance gardening possibilities under safer if less spacious conditions than those in Steel Valley (Interview, S. Mokoena). VEJA co-operates to some extent with other environmental groups that effectively emanate from the white community. These are less interested in township issues and more conservation orientated. An environment assessment is bound to qualify the extent to which lives improved due to the most determined and successful elements of the South African developmental state.

In Conclusion

This chapter has begun the process of taking the reader into the period of growing complexity but also of growing challenges to the developmental state project that emerged from the middle 1970s. In a deeper sense, these challenges are certainly environmental given the heavy lifting that has been expected for development from the extraction of natural resources. The costs and choices involved in energy policy have been more immediately apparent. High winds started to blow the economy this way and that after the long, rarely interrupted period of satisfactory growth and profitability for capital. It became more and more difficult to discern the workings of a developmental state even if the state and business continued to make large-scale plans to counter growing problems.

10 *Developmentalism Dismantled*

It would not be far wrong to take 1976 as a date for when the developmental state impetus starts to become so difficult to discern that this paradigm really ceases to work as a plausible way of grasping state and capital together in South Africa even with qualifications.[1] Perturbations develop both on the side of the state and of capital. In 1950–60, according to the rather sceptical Terence Moll, South Africa averaged 4.1 per cent economic growth per annum rising to 5.8 per cent in 1960–70, one of the higher figures internationally. In 1970–80 the same World Bank figures report a fall to 3.9 per cent, still well above many countries as this partly reflected global conditions and then fell dramatically to 1.0 per cent per annum in 1980–5 (Moll 1990). Padayachee notes that international loans contracted by South Africa in 1974–6 in response to the last dynamic burst doubled in value, fuelling inflation and then, once the boom collapsed, caused a severe credit crunch (Padayachee 1990, 101, 123). International loans became available on less and less favourable terms culminating in the Chase Manhattan loan refusal of 1985.

Two imperatives pushed the state: first, the necessity of moving economic activities to the borders of the so-called 'Bantustans' in line with the official ideology of racial partition and second, the growing emphasis on security coupled with a fear of international sanctions blocking access to markets and finance. This second tendency also went together with steep increases in military spending and military-orientated production. Both of these thrusts might in the abstract have contained developmental possibilities. As we have seen earlier, some industrialists thought that cheaply produced textiles had a great promise as a national industry using Bantustan labour. Other writers

[1] For an early assessment, see Gelb 1991. This collection tries to use the Lipietz model of Fordism as a means of understanding the South African system. This author has a chapter in it considering the gold mines.

might conceive that some operations of complex firms could take advantage of the cheap labour and subsidies in spatially reorganising different activities as was happening internationally. In reality, however, the potential from this spatial fix was quite limited and, with the protectionist regime dismantled from 1994, these new factories collapsed. The resources made available to the military certainly addressed technical problems so as to create viable industries. In Chapter 1 we mentioned Israel, very much South Africa's business partner from the late 1970s, as doing just this. In our discussion of the IDC, there was clearly an awareness of the critical potential in this regard. However, despite some impressive technological products, South Africa's military hardware hardly entered into international trade.

Turning to capital, in which the Afrikaner/English divide was of declining significance, it, too, was in a state of flux. The type of international regulatory system in place since the Second World War was being shattered and the scale of so-called 'globalisation' was such as to breach ideas about national capitalism and limit more and more what political economists have called import-substitution strategies: inward-looking capitalism aligned to particular states and national markets. South African big business became increasingly restless to move into a globalised future. It looked for opportunities through reaching out internationally and participating in global circuits, even while taking advantage of state imperatives for security and spatial decentralisation to take profits when it could in the short run.

In the last fifteen to twenty years of the apartheid system moreover, economic demands on the system pushed back towards the need to export minerals, albeit not necessarily the traditional pot of gold. Gold, in fact, was becoming harder and more expensive to come by, reducing increased productivity possibilities. Massive new investments would have been required to address this – which would only have been worthwhile if the price of gold was heading reliably upwards. Throughout the economy, this meant very large-scale expenditures (and loans, often international, requiring repayment) on base metal logistic and transport systems, for instance moving iron ore from Sishen in the Kalahari Desert to Saldanha Bay on the Atlantic coast north of Cape Town and moving coal across the Drakensberg to the new port of Richards Bay in northern Natal. This took priority in such a way as to re-enforce the old mineral-energy complex circuit quite powerfully.

Other economic impulses lost out. Closely related to this is the case of nuclear energy as already discussed in the previous chapter. Here vast resources were put into a weapon that was never used albeit with some ability to scare others while the peaceful use of nuclear power has proven to be fairly uneconomic compared to competitive sources of energy even today.

Amidst this turbulence, financial orthodoxy generally prevailed. The Reserve Bank continued to dominate policy here. The golden rule was that imports rose in good times calling for checks that would cut them, whatever the impact on industrial policy, in response to inflation. This would typically result in falls in exports as well (Mohr et al. 1989). This 'market-orientated money policy' targeted inflation above all; it could hardly be called a developmental policy (Padayachee and Rossouw 2011, S60). In itself this was successful enough so that national debt was reduced by 1985 to barely 30 per cent of GDP, a very low figure compared to most countries after rising for a time in the late 1970s as crisis first hit (Calitz et al. 2013).[2] However, it also set limits on development potential.

At the same time, prices ceased to operate predictably in a steady pattern that allowed for planning. The Americans cancelled the Bretton Woods agreement and the price of gold rose and fell precipitately. The old system whereby steel and electricity prices were controlled in South Africa and ESCOM and ISCOR were supposed to avoid taking profits tottered under these circumstances (Marquard 2006, 142 ff, for ESCOM). This could no longer be the basis of planning for industrial development.

Decentralisation

Because of its close links to the politics of apartheid, the homelands economic policy has been written about extensively. In an unpublished dissertation, Daryl Glaser traces its evolution from the Smuts era desire to establish consumer goods industry based on cheap labour near to the African locations in the hopes of stemming black urbanisation onwards

[2] Debt was raised as a big issue in the negotiations period of the 1990s but much of this had to do with one-time transfers that cannot be evaluated conventionally. The apparently steep rise then was ephemeral (Calitz et al. 2013).

(Glaser 1988). Under Hendrik Verwoerd, this policy intensified, more resources were thrown into it and industrial zones were created within the homeland entities directly. Measures, culminating in the Physical Planning Act of 1967 which appeared to try to force industry out of the Witwatersrand, were resented by most businesses although it has been argued, for instance from the example of Philip Frame, that there were businesses which hoped to prosper from this spatial shift, again especially in the manufacture of cheap clothing. The Afrikaanse Handelsinstituut, the voice of Afrikaner-run business, also reacted positively, cleaving as it did to apartheid ideology until very late. Yet negative reactions were strong.

As a result, in the 1970s and 1980s, emphasis began to be placed on creating a business linked environment to promote these new industrial zones. Mike Rosholt of Barlow Rand called this 'a welcome realism by the government, and an acceptance by it of the vital role of free enterprise' (Glaser 1988, 121). The creation of the Development Bank of South Africa in 1979, which also promoted regional investments, was an important move in this regard (Glaser 1988, 105). The bank secured for its directorships top industrialists such as John Maree of Barlow Rand, Gerrie Muller of Nedbank, John Plumridge of Gold Fields and A.P. Scholtz of Noord Westelike Kooperasie, (thus in effect a representative of corporate agriculture) (Glaser 1988, 220). Glaser shows that big business was more and more implicated in forging regional development policies. Large incentives were offered to firms to operate in these zones, incentives so generous that in fact most big companies indulged themselves this way to some extent. These included tax holidays, direct loans, preferential treatment in tender offer considerations as well as rebates for harbour and rail transport (Glaser 1988, 67). If foreign investors afraid of sanctions repercussions stayed away, there was at least investment from the black sheep – Taiwan and Israel (Glaser 1988, 221). Certain initiatives were more favourably located and did enjoy some success. In 1980, decentralised businesses hired 113,000 workers, of whom only 13 per cent were white. Some R1.195 m. was invested (R396 m. from the IDC) in 647 concerns, a modest but real presence (*Finance Week* 1980).

Some growing firms found it possible instead of expanding in the old way to divide up functions leaving some properties to operate profitably far from headquarters but the idea that blacks in large numbers would be lured to multi fold chances of employment far from the cities on this basis proved chimerical. At this very time, big business in South Africa began more and more rapidly to shed industrial jobs as well as jobs in agriculture and mining nationally. Moreover, the policy swallowed up large parts of the budget (Scerri 2009, 172). The IDC spent one-quarter of its budget in the 1980s on homelands industry, almost comparable to what it spent on chemicals, largely SASOL (de Waal 1982). One research team estimated moreover that twice the money spent on actual development projects in the homelands was being used for salaries and bureaucratic infrastructure (Macro-Economic Research Project 1993, chapter 6). In this context, one can refer to Dan Smit's incisive comments on so-called 'inward industrialisation'. To succeed generally, this would have had to incentivise expanding the market and promoting consumerism in a realistic way for the black majority and this not only did not happen; it regressed in good part as a sea of urban unemployment, despite the beginnings of differentiation, expanded (Smit 1989). Harry Oppenheimer never was convinced of the economic value of decentralisation and in fact, after the incentives disappeared in the new dispensation of 1994, both industrial and other developmental initiatives disappeared, leaving dramatic devastation in almost all of these locales.

Total Strategy

With regards to the military related economy, Dan Henk of the US Air War College provides a classic assessment:

> Still another interesting (if obvious) characteristic of the South African defense industry was the relatively small community of its senior leaders, scientists and engineers. For most of the *apartheid* era, the industry drew its top personnel from the white population, and largely from the even smaller subgroup of Afrikaners. This meant that industry insiders, key military leaders and top government officials came from the same limited population, attended many of the same schools and were strongly connected by bonds of ethnicity, family, church, school and social life. This did not attenuate significant cultural differences or eliminate deep feuds and grudges . . . but did promote a certain uniformity of world-view and common approach to problems. It also enabled industry, government and military leaders to resort to informal connections to communicate, influence decisions

and solve problems. On the other hand, it contributed to a culture of secretive decision-making lacking transparency and accountability. (Henk 2006, 6)

The military impetus reached a new level with the creation of Armscor in 1983 out of the Armaments Board and the Armaments Development and Production Corporation. Armscor defined itself as aiming at 'upgrading, modifying and modernising' existing weapons (McWilliams 1989, 101). Padayachee signals Armscor and the arms industry as the one area of manufacturing growth of importance in the last decade of the old regime (Padayachee 1990, 112–13).

The presidency of P.W. Botha, a very dynamic former Minister of Defence, was a critical element pushing the manufacture of military hardware forward (Grundy 1986). Armscor interacted intensely and on a very large scale with hundreds of private sector firms. Peter Batchelor estimated their number at 2,000 by 1984 and Dan Henk 3,000 in 1989. Henk also refers to how accomplished some figures in this world became at relevant industrial espionage (Henk 2006). Grundy considers this activation of the business world fundamental to Botha's strategic vision. For several years, Armscor was actually headed by John Maree seconded from Barlow Rand, a top figure in the corporate world (O'Meara 1996, 226). Botha stood for the dominance of business methods in administrative procedures but that did not mean that he was interested in undermining apartheid. It was rather a question of bringing corporate power in to ensure their commitment to fighting the ANC and keeping white South Africa intact.

Grundy and McWilliams agree that the chief co-ordinating body, which took over as forging a central direction for the South African state, was the State Security Council (Grundy 1986, 49). In addition, there was extensive interaction between the military and important bodies we have examined above such as the parastatals, the CSIR and even the HSRC (Grundy 1986; Henk 2006, 11–12; McWilliams 1989, 11, 61). At peak, approximately 10 per cent of measurable R&D was in the military sphere (Batchelor 1998, 102). Henk also estimates that as much as 9 per cent of manufacturing may have had a military foundation (Henk 2006, 17). Scerri estimates that 2 per cent of all military expenditure was on R&D; indeed there was little R&D expenditure in the public sector, i.e. the parastatals, otherwise (Scerri 2009, 15, 190). A large part of what high technology exports there were had a military purpose, largely ammunition and militarised ground vehicles (Scerri 2009, 192). The number of employees essentially dependent on the military was perhaps 150,000 including 2,000 engineers and scientists. Of these, in 1989 McWilliams estimated an Armscor workforce alone of 23,000 (McWilliams 1989, 106).

Grundy claims that South Africa eventually ranked tenth in the world as an arms manufacturer. Up to a point, this expansive side of the economy succeeded in replacing imports with home-grown hardware at an impressive rate but, as sophisticated weapons made their appearance, this process was if anything reversed. The Atlantis diesel engine project completed in 1981, to which reference was made in an earlier chapter in connection with IDC business and special radial tyre manufacture for lorries, was an expensive initiative that made no sense apart from the fears of being cut off from foreign markets (Grundy 1986, 46). Technically the engine was considered inadequate in quality by the South African Defence Force itself, although it had some civilian use (Duncan 1992, 86). South Africa also failed to get accepted into the elite club of international arms exporters with connections. At best, one partner (France and Italy were earlier significant partners), Israel, seems to have actually gone in for some joint military production. Exports never quite reached 1 per cent of production.[3] Thus the arms industry, despite the effort to export, was otherwise limited to an often uneconomical local market; moreover, the arms industry generally did not develop in such a way as to allow for adaptation to civilian use despite, as we have seen in our IDC example, some attempts in this direction (Henk 2006, 17).

The Technological Frontier

Those who have looked for South African participation in the kinds of manufacture that were taking off in the third quarter of the twentieth century note regression and qualitative decline with consequent dependence generally on foreign technology (Black 1991). A classic perspective was provided by David Kaplan in looking at telecommunications (Kaplan 1990). Here state initiatives mainly led by the Post Office gave way to investment by a small number of profitable firms with little interest in export. Later exports became somewhat more significant but

[3] For a similar perspective, see Seegers 1996.

were not clustered anywhere and seemed to depend on particular firm connections rather than having the logic of regional markets or sales to industrialising countries (Kaplan 1983). With the arrival of digital telecommunications, technology became difficult to sustain nationally and local innovation of little account. An obsession with self-sufficiency remained but became harder to realise. The local market was itself limited; the provision of telephony outside the white minority came late and on a small scale. By 1984 the state had organised a high-powered committee to formulate and implement a strategy for developing electronics but it cannot be said to have been particularly successful (Scerri 2009, 201). Finally by the late 1980s, there was a growing acceptance that the state should abandon efforts to interfere much with industrial policy. While low skills and the limited regional market were salient, the failure of the state to develop expertise here and promote sophisticated new capital goods products was even more important (Kaplan 1991). In particular, the computerisation of capital goods began to leave South Africa behind as a competitive producer (Kaplan 1986).

Automobile manufacture expanded enormously in the 1960s and 1970s with the entry of German and Japanese firms to rival the existing US and fading British models. In terms of employment and scale, this was a key industry that engendered an enormous parts and service activity. It was governed by a self-sufficiency drive that promoted under high levels of protection considerable industrial expansion. Local content, at first measured in volume but then in value, rose from 55 per cent in 1971 to 66 per cent in 1977 and applied from just cars to commercial vehicles in 1980 (Duncan 1992, 56). This system of regulation indicates how vital the state was in the expansion of the automobile industry (Duncan 1992, 66). These figures proved achievable and profits attracted more manufacturers although new car sales peaked in 1981 (Duncan 1992, 56). This growth certainly also had links to the military but they were hardly vital to its existence. However, R&D depended on imported technology and once again exports were of little importance (Duncan *c.* 1992).

As Peter Draper pointed out, this was nonetheless a relatively positive outcome compared to the computer industry. Despite an interest promoted in the IDC and the CSIR, there was virtually no R&D here until the very late 1980s with even less interest than in telecommunications (Draper 1996).[4] The IDC formed a state committee for electronics aimed at providing terminals but little else. He concluded that building technological capacity in hardware was essentially a failure. This meant dependence for crucial parts fell on foreign sources, even for the military.

At the same time, industry was hooked on imperatives which involved returning to the quandary of energy provision and the construction of big projects, not all of them sensible investments (Marquard 2006, 67). Van Eck's last dream was the harnessing of the Zambesi through the Cabora Bassa Dam, an expensive undertaking that in the end proved worthless to South Africa once Portuguese rule in Mozambique came to an end and the FRELIMO government was beleaguered by RENAMO guerrillas (who ironically fought with South African state sponsorship) (Marquard 2006).

A key landmark was the establishment of the Department of Minerals and Energy and the beginnings of an attempt to create a consistent energy policy (Marquard 2006, 70). Thus in the 1980s natural gas was discovered off Mossel Bay in the Indian Ocean. However, its extraction via the Mossgas project that went into effect in 1987 was far too expensive were it not for the obsession with security (Marquard 2006, 307).

The development of Richards Bay was more tenable. As we have seen, it required the complex rail link from the eastern Transvaal to allow for coal exports. It was tied into an export project – Alusaf – which used South African power to manufacture aluminium (Marquard 2006, 107). The technological know-how in Alusaf came from a Swiss partner. No effort was made to use this opportunity to manufacture aluminium products. A writer aware of the developmental state paradigm pointed out that 'as a consequence of shortsightedness, South Africa is producing aluminium ingots, T-bars and sheet metal, while South Korea is producing video recorders' (Ramburuth 1997, 71). Without subsidisation, Alusaf would in fact have ceased being profitable after 1994 were it not for the private sector Hillside refinery also in Richards Bay sharing the raw mineral import. Capital and intermediate goods dominated South Africa's

[4] It is true that Draper sees some interesting developments just beginning towards 1989, 85–6, especially involving the CSIR, the new firm of Altech and Barlow Rand with uncertain involvement by international giant IBM.

imports and did not fall in importance (O'Meara 1996, 172). Heavy industry remained dominant. According to Avril Joffe, between 1972 and 1990, chemicals and base metals rose from 40.4 per cent to 59.8 per cent of new investment in industry (Joffe 1993).

In both these areas, one classic aspect of the developmental state remained: the tight mesh of closely aligned and powerfully motivated figures who were often deeply committed to their work. 'It was, first and foremost, a system which took the general dearth of human capital as given and concentrated instead on a limited human resource development programme which applied at the higher end of the skills spectrum' (Scerri 2009, 180; see also Marquard 2006, 129).

South African Business Looks Outward

As Henk or Pretorius point out, some aspects of the developmental state remained intact. While business-state relations might be argued never to have been closer, especially given the fading of the English/Afrikaner divide, in fact, what was happening was that the state, notably P.W. Botha (very dramatically in the Carlton and Good Hope conferences) tried to persuade and push capital, especially finance and manufacturing capital, to serve its strategic and military priorities (Pretorius 1996).[5] From the view of capital, this was frustrating if profitable in the short term. It is possible to discern a movement of capital out of South Africa despite the efforts of the state to make this difficult – foreign disinvestment – but also, where possible, shifts of domestic capital overseas. The Soweto Crisis of 1976 had provoked this for a short time. US banks stopped lending to South Africa, notably Chase Manhattan. However, within a few years, they were back (Padayachee 1990, 234). Nevertheless the trend intensified in the following decade. Anglos was able to use its control of MINORCO, which represented the past investment interest in Zambian copper shifted to Canada and thus outside national control in this regard (Padayachee 1990, 128ff). This fed in to general pressures to reduce state controls in the economy and fall in with conventional liberal finance orthodoxy emphasising freed-up markets.

[5] Pretorius is right that the state more or less abandoned its commitment to white labour and, to some extent, agrarian interests, as witness the rise of the breakaway Conservative Party, which at peak mustered more than half the Afrikaner vote.

A.D. Wassenaar, an Afrikaner, was managing director of SANLAM from 1966 to 1985. In 1977 he published a book whose title translated into English was 'Assault on Free Enterprise; The Freeway to Communism' (Wassenaar 1977). This book outraged then Prime Minister B.J. Vorster (O'Meara 1996, 195) Wassenaar used Koeberg as one example of bad decision-making by the state and he rounded on the growing number of useless bureaucrats who threatened to stifle the system. The state, in other words, was crowding out the private sector.

> While the IDC has been and still is prepared to encourage and finance private enterprise, its main function has been the encouragement of other state enterprises. It has earned its wings in no uncertain way as an empire-builder and as an investment and industrial conglomerate in competition with private enterprise. (Wassenaar 1977, 142)

Wassenaar's answer to this was 'privatise, privatise, privatise'. He was only to a limited extent a free enterprise champion. He still favoured deals where the state cut in the private sector and he still obviously was very interested in joint initiatives. Nevertheless, his book became a bible for conservatives tired of state planning into which business could at best fit in. The Thatcher Big Bang on the London Stock Exchange was scripture for many of South Africa's money makers.

SANLAM, along with Rupert's Rembrandt empire, lay at the heart of the most powerful structure created by Afrikaners in tandem with the National Party in power. Now this power was able to challenge the state on some matters:

> The National Party government actually promoted the transition to monopoly capitalism in a number of ways. The state-owned Industrial Finance Corporation and Industrial Development Corporation both encouraged 'rationalisation' through amalgamation and mergers in various industries. Tariff protection and tax and fiscal policies all favoured efficient firms. The fostering of a merchant banking sector, a money market and the overall centralisation of credit and finance encouraged the trend towards concentration and centralisation. (O'Meara 1996, 81–82)

O'Meara argues that Wassenaar and his colleague Tienie Louw (true as well of Rupert) had a poor relationship with Verwoerd, who supported smaller businesses. It was the smaller fish, however, who effectively dominated the Afrikaanse Handelsinstituut, still a retro voice for high water-mark apartheid, by the 1970s (O'Meara 1996, 226).

Restlessness at the boundaries state regulation imposed, even in decline, grew steadily, marked in time by the visit of top representatives of capital to the ANC in exile. Morris noted in 1991 that while some parts of big business still cleaved to an inward-looking model that favoured close ties to the state, others, nurtured over time by state policy, were itching for more freedom and a globally acceptable regime (Morris 1991). Set against this was the mounting problem of credit. If US banks were becoming problematic,[6] it is true that South Africa, as we have seen in an earlier chapter, could turn to Germany, Switzerland and elsewhere but no longer at such favourable rates. South Africa lacked the capital that facing the so-called 'total onslaught' seemed to require. SASOL had been financed largely at government expense but with the creation of SASOL 2 and SASOL 3, it, too, began to be dependent on big foreign loans (Sparks 2015). The military imperative, the need to establish very expensive infrastructure that would allow for the flow of minerals out of the country, the huge demands of the parastatals, all created a credit squeeze that can only be evaluated as an important factor in why the regime was finally prepared to negotiate its way out of existence from 1990 (Padayachee 1990).

The Late Apartheid Years in the Vaal Triangle

What about the physical site of the ISCOR and SASOL plants near the Vaal and environs? Let us turn for a bit from the purely economic to the social and political. Earlier we examined the planning and implementation of housing in Vanderbijlpark and Sasolburg, the infamous Sharpeville Massacre near Vereeniging and the growth of Soweto of the South – Sebokeng. The state now began to establish ties with a rising black elite through the agency of the new Bantu urban advisory councils. The Verwoerdian dream of a homogenised black population of migrant labourers with families strewn elsewhere in the country was not working. Industry rather wanted a differentiated labour force while the political system was meeting serious resistance, notably in the 1976 violence that turned the massively expanded black township schools into turmoil. Moreover, in the 1970s a new insurgent trade union movement began to spread through the Witwatersrand. ISCOR

[6] Chase Manhattan spectacularly refused South Africa further credit in 1985, Padayachee 1990, 240.

was affected by strike action from 1980 and forced to sign a contract with MAWU, the Metal and Allied Workers' Union, in key plants, notably the USCO factory in the old, established municipality of Vereeniging, by 1985 (Hlatshwayo 2003, 107; Maller 1983, 100; Tom 1985, 54–5). To achieve stability, complicated and often contradictory administrative restructurings were coupled with a growing number of successful requests for exceptions to the rule, for increased amenities for black townships, for the character of self-government to be upgraded and for the councils of these townships, notably of Sebokeng, to be acknowledged respectfully as junior partners of the regime.[7]

Returning to the case of Zamdela outside Sasolburg, a township which was not in the sights for any white business or residential project, the construction of the clinic – bereft of luxury – was followed by the erection of a library, a community room, a crèche, a filling station, premises made available for a black physician and substantial extension of electrification.[8] By around 1980, the relevant file contains various letters where officials supported bending the rules – to allow a respectable African with Section Ten rights to buy a house where none was available to rent, to convert part of a hostel to housing for families and lodgers. In 1981, a new business centre for Zamdela with consideration for traffic and space for a small supermarket was being planned as well as 200 houses to be self-built by new owners.[9]

The slow pace and official unsteadiness manifested itself in stops and starts. Thus while Sharpeville was considered the most miserable location in the Vaal, there were worries about the cost of its upgrading and

[7] Admittedly Sebokeng had an influential white town clerk.

[8] NA, BAO 3/2365, D.C. Ganz, Chief Director, Administration Board, Oranje-Vaal to Chief Commissioner, Johannesburg, 25 February 1980; Chief Bantu Commissioner, Orange Free State to Director-General, Dept. of Co-operation and Development, 28 July 1980, NA, BAO 3/1969, A6/5/2/S10 pts 1–2, J.C. Knoetze, Chief Director, Vaal Triangle Bantu Affairs Administration Board to T.L.B. Prinsloo, Secretary, Bantu Administration and Development, 24 September 1976; J.C. Knoetze, Chief Director, Bantu Affairs Administration, Vaal Triangle, to T.L.B. Prinsloo, Chief Commissioner, Bantu Affairs, Johannesburg, 17 January 1978.

[9] NA, BAO 3/1969, A6/5/2/S10 pts 1–2, A. Schoeman, Oranje-Vaal Administration Board to Chief Commissioner, Bloemfontein, 9 December 1981, NA, BAO 3/2365, A6/6/2/S10/3, H. Nezar, Director-General, Co-operation and Development, to Director-General, Community Development and Government Auxiliary Services, 14 May 1981.

whether the master-plan would allow for it to be considered more permanent. The provision of essential services at Sharpeville, particularly water-borne sewerage and an improved electrical supply had been under consideration for a very long time, but firm decisions kept being postponed, because of the very considerable costs involved and uncertainty about the ultimate removal of Sharpeville. There was plenty of surveillance electric light but only 200 houses were supplied with it.[10] The determination to remove Sharpeville faltered from 1972 as funds were ceasing to be plentiful.[11]

The conversion of adjoining Evaton to leaseholds proceeded slowly and in 1986 there remained 700 owners amongst 2,700 stands. This would prove the point where the pressure eased and it was finally accepted that freeholds in this old, unplanned settlement could remain through granting black owners the right to sell to other black purchasers although leasehold arrangements were still pursued.[12]

The state dithered about all that did not fit. Thus a lengthy correspondence ensued starting in 1976 but stretching far into the 1980s about an 'onwettige dorp' (illegal village). The farm Cyferpan on the road from Vereeniging to Randfontein and Potchefstroom was an extreme example of how peri-urban development was stretching out of state control. Here were found a caravan park, houses, a transport business, filling station, nursery, cafe and a couple of shops! One inhabitant was connected to the power grid, got water from a borehole and did a bit of farming and had pasture as well as owning a general store, and of course there were *bantoe wonings* – Bantu habitations. There were legal white owners resident in, amongst others, Vanderbijlpark and Vereeniging. Despite the questionable legality of the *onwettige dorp,* the decision was taken to allow continuation for three years, later renewed. The apartheid spatial order began to be shattered.[13]

Back in town, there was a move to legalise 'Bantu eating houses' in the centre of Vanderbijlpark. It was conceded that black workers and

10 NA, BAO 3/2395, A6/6/2/V4, Administrative Committee, Bantu Administration, Vaal Triangle, 23 August 1978.
11 D.C. Ganz to Secretary, Ministry of Co-operation and Development, 26 March 1980.
12 NA, BAO 3/3079, A8/11/V4 pt. 1.
13 NA, 7337/PB4/3/2/34, Director of Local Government to Transvaal Council for the Development of Peri-Urban Areas, 9 October 1976.

shoppers had to be able to eat in the town. While insisting that such premises be far from white schools, churches and homes, effectively permission was given for the development of what might be called the poorer and sleazier end of the town to take on life under the law.[14] In 1980 officials continued to worry about the illegal presence of at least fifty Indian traders in Sebokeng but by 1982 they designated a district to set up businesses in white Vanderbijlpark for them (a Section 19 trading area).[15] The growing reality was the need to promote business where properties lay unused in a long phase of economic stagnation. In 1986 a free trading area was proclaimed in the business district of Vanderbijlpark and in 1987 the whole of industrial Vanderbijlpark was 'deproclaimed' for whites. Still later, an Indian resort with attractive holiday homes on the Vaal was given consent although still without Indians having the right to make a permanent home in the vicinity.[16]

More dramatic yet than Cyferpan and a little later, was the rapid transformation of another farm, in this case between the ever-threatened community of Evaton and expanding Sebokeng, owned by a firm named Weiler & Weiler but known eventually as Wheelers or Weillers Farm. Black tenants became more numerous and in the mid-1980s plans to annex this in a systematic way to the neighbouring African areas were overwhelmed. By 1986, liquidator of this property Leslie Cohen reported that 'the number of squatters on the Farm has now reached alarming figures and the position requires to be resolved as a matter of extreme urgency'.[17] By this time there were 10,000 squatters in Evaton alone.[18] The state abandoned any effort to eliminate them and compensated the Weiler estate.

Differentiation, as well as the contradictions in the state, was the context for the birth of class politics amongst black people in the Vaal Triangle. By 1981, Sebokeng was being fitted with an artisan centre,

14 NA, BAO, A7/6/2/V4/1, H.P. Joubert, Secretary, Bantu Administration and Development to Town Clerk, Vanderbijlpark, 1 November 1978.

15 NA, BAO 3/1281, A6/2/V4, Secretary, Gemeenskaapbou to Secretary, Department of Co-operation and Development, 3 June 1980.

16 NA, JGB 120, 13/1/3/5030.

17 In a letter to the Ministry of Constitutional Development and Planning, 14/11/86.

18 NA, BAO 3/3079, A8/11/V4 pt. 1. For massive squatting by this time around Evaton and Sebokeng and the 'Weiller' Farm story, see also Beavon 2004 and notably his useful map on 232.

community centre (Section 10) with swimming pool, soccer field, tennis court, bowls field, clubhouse and attached bar, crèche and kindergarten, space for doctors' offices and plans to reduce the flow of traffic reminiscent of the automobile obsession of Kirchhofer. Section 10 was described as an 'elite' community in the making.[19]

Whereas the Vaal region had been relatively quiescent in 1976, in 1984 it was for an important moment an extremely violent site of a new, raw form of class politics. In the effort to pay for creating amenities and services in Sebokeng, the Urban Council raised rentals to a level higher than anywhere in the country. This served the interests of an emerging class of professionals and sub-professionals, employees in the municipalities, health and education workers, security service personnel but also those with some status in the private sector while a small business sector based in the townships grew. However, this added up to only a relatively small minority.

The Marole case whose description hinges on an article in the black Johannesburg newspaper, *The World* in 1977, exemplified new circumstances. M.K. Marole was a member of the African Chamber of Commerce in Sebokeng. He stood by the government's reform policy permitting blacks to build and own shops but complained about the harassment of their employees for pass books and about white shopkeepers selling fresh produce on the border of the township while of course Africans could not trade in white areas. It turned out that the Maroles had a grudge against the state. They owned an automobile and their son had been arrested for driving without a licence. However, the policeman who ticketed him was black – and had on another occasion been highly praised by Marole, a Sebokeng councillor. The point was made as well that much trade in the township went on illicitly. Marole also wanted to own a licensed gun; he was worried about 'hooliganism' in the township.[20]

In 1966, a survey of 1,180 black (presumably male) youths in Boipatong and Bophelong (of whom few probably had secondary

[19] NA BAO 7/1862, E12/3/3/516 v. 4 and v. 5 etc., Section 10 plan by P.J. Coetzee and partners, 1982 inter alia. Here reference is to a particular Sebokeng neighbourhood. This is not to be confused with the Section Ten residential rights that loom large in discussions of African residential rights in apartheid South African towns.

[20] NA, BAO, A7/6/2/V4/1. Dlamini (2017) mentions the issue of guns to such officials which in fact was fairly standard by 1984.

education) found a mere 2.6 per cent were unemployed.[21] A memorandum of 1979 still pointed to far lower unemployment rates compared to further north in Soweto and the capacity to pay higher rates as a result.[22] This changed rapidly in the economically stagnant 1980s. By then a younger generation with limited political outlet and very little chance for mobility increasingly experienced unemployment on a big scale. In the Triangle townships, there was nowhere for a more educated rising generation to go; it became impossible to eliminate growing numbers of spontaneously erected shacks (Frankel 2001; Munnik 2012, 140). Moreover, at ISCOR there was the rising influence of the MAWU promoting anti-capitalist ideas.

In the Vaal Rising of 3 September 1984, (a culmination of growing agitation and unrest) representative figures of the new order, including a Sebokeng town councillor, were brutally attacked and killed – symbols of privilege and the state (Rantete 1984; Munnik 2012; Dlamini 2017). The councillor was killed brandishing a gun outside his house where a crowd went to look for him. Most councillors fled to an army base for safety and sixty-six people died in violent clashes within a week; the whole of the Vaal Triangle was up in arms.[23] This intensified the sense of *laager*, of siege, amongst whites in the region and the importance in strategic industries of security concerns (Frankel 2001). It was in fact the touchstone of a growing grassroots movement refusing to pay rents (actually consisting largely of service charges).[24] Business and trade union representatives became voices looking for some kind of accommodation but the state was unprepared to consider a withdrawal of control until change finally came at a national level in 1990.

[21] NA, BAO 1995, A20/1709, Bantu Advisory Board, Bophelong and Boipatong, 22 September 1966.

[22] NA, BAP 3/2035 A6/S2/V4, C. Beukes, Town Clerk, Community Council, Vaal Triangle Memo presented to Piet Koornhof on his visit to the area as Minister of Co-operation and Development, 26 November 1979.

[23] Chaskalson et al. 1987, 57. However ISCOR executives reported that the hostels were quiet. Sasolburg was also much less affected than the Transvaal townships. ISCOR Unconfirmed Minutes, 29 August 1984, NA, MPP 17, A3/1/6/4/4 pt. 1.

[24] This is the nub of Chaskalson et al. 1987. The September events are still commemorated in Sebokeng. Some radicals look back with nostalgia on what appears to be a self-organisation of community control that emerged as the council collapsed (Payn 2017).

However, reform also continued to influence how people lived. An example was the fate of the now miniature township of Bophelong, which had long ago been the brainchild of van der Bijl and Kantorowich. It now bestrode the plans for a new highway to the Vaal. On the far side of the highway a white suburb was emerging, for the first time to the north of Vanderbijlpark on the basis of promises that Bophelong, unwanted by the suburbanites, would be removed and its people packed off to Sebokeng. In October 1980 it was decided that Boipatong (population 12,416) and Sharpeville (population 42,000) would stay as they were – meaning that the existing home ownerships in place could continue to operate. They had actually already in contradictory manner been provided with certain improvements despite their supposed future fates.[25] However, Bophelong (population 10,590) was doomed.[26] Unsurprisingly, it was also a site of destruction and violent attacks on authority in 1984. According to the testimony of the Vanderbijlpark Town Clerk, admittedly eager for its destruction and perhaps exaggerating, it lay at the heart of the Rising. By his account, the beer hall, administration building, post office and bottle store were burnt down and inhabitants rushed out to attack vehicles on the Golden Highway.[27]

The archival records suggest that after the Rising, it was the initiative of the Lekoa Council, centred in Sebokeng, which issued the decisive memorandum pointing out that the Bophelong population included many pensioners, ISCOR veterans. Those working at the plant were still able to walk to the factory as planned from the start. The money involved in rehousing them, it was argued, was a waste, especially given that homeowners would have the legal right to have new houses built for them and money would be better spent on relocating 1,600 not

[25] NA, BAO 3/2035, A6/S2/V4, Report of a Meeting Convened by Minister M.C. Botha with political and administrative representatives, 12 November 1976.

[26] NA, JGB 120, 13/1/3/5030, Cabinet Memorandum, Ministry of Co-operation and Development, n.d. but certainly 1980; BAO 7/1862, E12/3/3/516 v. 4 and v. 5 etc., Planning Co-ordination Meeting of the Oranje-Vaal Administration with Co-operation and Development, 26 May 1980 and BAO 3/2035, A6/S2/V4, D.C. Ganz, Chief Director, Oranje-Vaal Administration Board to Secretary, Department of Co-operation and Development, 23 May 1980.

[27] NA, BAO 3/2035 A6/S2/V4, C. Beukes, Town Clerk, Vanderbijlpark to Hernus Kriel, Minister of Planning and Provincial Affairs, 5 March 1990. The heart of the rising was Sebokeng. For the impact on Sharpeville, see Tom 1985.

unwilling lodgers from Sharpeville and Boipatong in Sebokeng.[28] After this memorandum was sent, the official mood changed and authorities began to back off from the removal policy, even though Vanderbijlpark suburban homeowners, who had bought houses in the new suburb of Bonanne on being promised the extinction of Bophelong, were very annoyed and continued to demand that the policy be reinstated, astonishingly even after Nelson Mandela's release from gaol.

In effect the black local authority was allowed to overrule the white one. Slowly, top officials (especially the reform minister Gerrit Viljoen), who were devoted to considering these problems until the final days of the apartheid government, moved to 'saving Bophelong'.[29] One official noted that the potential political damage of destroying it was not worth it. Another wrote very positively about this relic from the model town designs. Most houses were very neat and clean, it was stated, the township had many trees and well-lined roads, a beer hall, three churches, a community hall, an administrative building, three schools and sixteen shops, a soccer stadium, a tennis court, a clinic, a post office and a courtroom. All houses had water reticulation and electricity.[30] The point had been reached where the voices of white fear and reaction could actually be rejected. Bophelong still stands today.

In the reform era, creating a homogeneous white society with a strong safety net began to be less critical and was increasingly difficult to prop up as companies shed labour and some unemployment and real poverty licked the edges of the white population of the Vaal (Prinsloo 1993). For some, employment in the parastatals and the amenities offered by the new towns had been a step-ladder to social mobility but for others, there was no longer an easy road to a better life. By 1986, one

[28] NA, JGB 120, 13/1/3/5030, Town Clerk, Lekoa to Chief Commissioner, Department of Co-operation and Development, 26 February 1985.

[29] NA, BAO 3/2038, A6/5/2/V4 pt. 5, Chief Commissioner, Orange Free State Department of Co-operation and Development to Director-General, 24 December 1984; BAO 3/3079, A8/11/V4 pt. 1, Notes of a Meeting on the Future of Bophelong, 25 November 1986; BAO 3/2038, A6/5/2/V4 pt. 5, Chris Ballot MP to Chris Heunis, Minister for Community Development and Planning, 6 November 1985 and 28 January 1986. Chris Heunis, one of the best-known reformers, was the relevant Minister of Constitutional Development and Planning.

[30] NA, BAO 3/2038, A6/5/2/V4 pt. 5, Memorandum, Department of Constitutional Development and Planning, early 1986? Presumably some of these features had been reconstructed after 1984.

estimate reported that there were 20,000 unemployed whites in the area. The picture was one of substantial alcoholism, an unusually high divorce rate with many broken homes and high numbers of school dropouts. (Ibid., 171) This was part of the process which allowed smallholders to feel free to protest at ISCOR policies and ISCOR pollution. This was the social context in which in 1989 debt-burdened and no longer profitable ISCOR steel-making plants were sold to Mittal.

By this time, the apartheid rules were beginning to be breached increasingly. A substantial Indian resort on the Vaal with fairly expensive homes? Fine. A meeting of sales representatives not all white in town? Fine. These transgressions increasingly formed part of a less and less coherent social structure before the political break. Since 1994, it is capital that rules the roost and chooses, as it were, the successes and failures of the new order. There are no more racial rules. However, there is a social and spatial inheritance and also one that comes very much as a dead weight from the physical environment that began to be laid out in the middle of the last century. Those blacks who were able to take advantage of the reform phase of apartheid and their children, it may be posited, have become the cornerstone of the new black middle-class of post-1994 South Africa, while the poverty of the majority often remains intense.

The Parastatals to 1990

But what had become of the trademark parastatals? ESCOM had, if anything, detached itself from the others and indeed from much of the state. P.W. Botha struggled to rein it in as it had become a law unto itself. SASOL, which was privatised in 1979, remained a great favourite because it tied into the obsessive concern with security. Expansion in the early 1970s seemed justified by the oil 'shock' of 1973 when prices rose quite precipitately for a while (see Figure 10.1). At peak, it provided a large percentage of South African vehicle fuel. SASOL 2 and then SASOL 3, huge plants far bigger than the one in Sasolburg, were erected at Secunda, far to the east of Sasolburg in the eastern Transvaal, now Mpumalanga Province (Crompton 1994, 140; Sparks 2016). SASOL 2 was paid for 60 per cent by the fuel levy, 25 per cent by export credits and 15 per cent as a direct parliamentary grant. Moreover, the state was

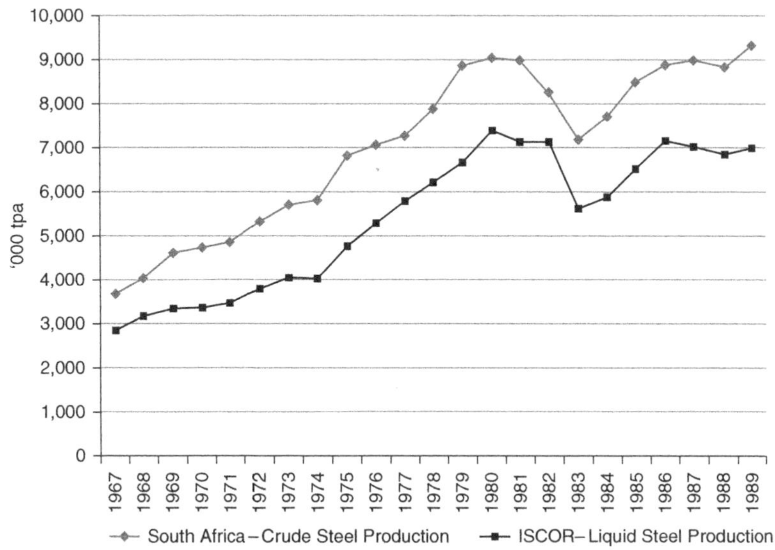

Figure 10.1. South African and ISCOR Crude Liquid Steel Production, 1967–89 (millions of tons per annum)
Source: Steel Statistical Yearbook, World Steel Association, International Iron and Steel Institute, ISCOR Annual Reports. Borrowed from Zalk 2017.

also then prepared to authorise a State Oil Fund (Marquard 2006). Andrew Marquard describes the two Secunda investments as planned 'despite the market' and characterises them as over-investment (Marquard 2006, 348). SASOL also expanded effectively in the chemicals industry as the price of oil fell in the late 1980s given its dominance of chemical feedstocks and used the end of apartheid to develop increasing international ties (Crompton 1994, 174). As of writing (2017), it has a huge investment under construction in the US state of Louisiana while remaining South Africa's largest taxpayer. Crompton has expressed the view that SASOL, too, held back essentially rather than get involved in plastics, the final product where there were far more possibilities for smaller producers and further industrial development of the consumer economy. However, SASOL has long since been an oligopoly with many tentacles and hardly a developmental agent.

The story of ISCOR is quite a different one. ISCOR enjoyed a generation of growth and prosperity in the 1950s and 1960s. It faced the sometimes intense dilemma then of choosing between

Table 10.1. *Number of ISCOR Workers*[34]

1972/73	37,901
1981/82	62,381
1985/86	48,234

Source: Prinsloo 1998, 111.

exporting steel and meeting its requirements for local provision at a price set by the state. On this basis too, it financed the long line of rail between Sishen, the greatest national source of iron ore, and Saldanha Bay at the start of the 1970s.[31] A third plant at Newcastle in Natal, close to the KwaZulu homeland with its chief labour resource was constructed and opened. Despite its poor productivity figures, ISCOR still was a very competitive cheap producer of steel.[32]

However, once done, conditions in the world steel market changed dramatically for the worse. With unpredictable ups and downs, ISCOR incurred major debts in the 1970s and depended on government bail-outs, noticeably the sale of the Sishen-Saldanha railway in 1976.[33] Costs took over from any other analytical consideration despite, as the figure shows, growing volumes of production.

Things did not improve in the final decade of the old government after a last gap of prosperity in 1979–81 in conjunction with the brief rise in gold prices.[35]

Eventually in 1985, the old system of fixed pricing came to an end; ISCOR could charge a market price for its product. It became more efficient, producing more steel while starting to shed jobs but far more investment in modernisation was needed (see Table 10.1). The state was

[31] NA, MPP 44, A3/10/9; HR/12/1 pt. 4 1971–73, v. 5; Zalk 2017, 125.

[32] NA MPP 233 H/4 12 vol. 3, Minister Owen Horwood speech to ISCOR personnel selected, V, 13 September 1974, issued by Department of Information.

[33] NA, A3/10/9, Meeting with Ministry, 8 October 1976, Pistorius Committee Report and views of the Ministry of Industries, final report of committee 25 May 1977; MPP 50, Draft Annual Report 1978; MPP 45 A3/10/9 pt. 1 Annual Report 1977; Zalk 2017, 130.

[34] The drop in Vanderbijlpark was 11.8 per cent of the workforce, less than elsewhere but still very substantial.

[35] NA MPP 47, A3/10/9, ISCOR Annual Report 1980; *Beeld* 22 February 1984.

anxious to sell and finally found a buyer in Mittal, the international steelmaker headquartered in Luxembourg and ultimately powered by an Indian magnate with vast holdings on several continents. This was the end of state control over the key industry that did so much to generate South Africa's metal sector. For Nimroad Zalk, this represents the irreversible retreat from state ownership of a major resource (Zalk 2017). It is a fitting marker for the closing of the developmental state phase in South Africa.

Conclusion

In bringing this study to an end, we can first reiterate the main points of the preceding chapter. A developmental state will involve a deeply embedded partnership between the state and at least parts of capital in pursuit of common projects leading to economic growth. One would expect the state to give direction in significant ways. In South Africa, starting in the 1960s and then intensifying, the state re-orientated itself towards entrenching the apartheid racial divisions into a national partition and became obsessed with security issues. This made purely economic and developmental goals far less important unless attached to those priorities. Neither were fruitful directions with long-term positive consequences on any scale pursued.

Capital also changed. Unlike many otherwise comparable situations, South Africa by 1940 already had a strong mining/financial sector focused on gold with Anglo-American the locally based premier firm. To some extent, more comprehensive industrial development meant winkling out resources from that sector to benefit the economy more generally. The South African developmental state at first enjoyed much success in this regard. However, this bred new actors with considerable power and autonomy. Key figures such as Tienie Louw of SANLAM or Anton Rupert of Rembrandt saw themselves as rival Oppenheimers (Oppenheimer was the master of Anglos), not as dependent on the state in the long run. From the late 1970s, capital generally was restive and eager to reach out to a changing, deregulated investment world.

One limitation of South African economic development was the very weak role of manufacturing sales internationally. For this, there were several reasons difficult to disaggregate. Cheap and plentiful black labour was coupled, notably in industry but also in gold mining, with expensive white supervisory/skilled labour and the total sum was not cheap and did not encourage great gains in productivity as Charles

Feinstein rightly insisted. South Africa, unlike the Asian development icons, was isolated from other major trading economies; it was a giant compared to its neighbours and very far away from interesting markets on any real scale. South Africa from the 1970s needed to spend large sums on high technology if it was to produce new competitive products; there was not a sufficient community of practitioners with which to build a relevant platform. As a result, South Africa's import bill was often problematic and gold mining, the cash cow on which the people around J.C. Smuts had begun planning, ceased to be a reliable substitute for other exports. The emergence of SASOL, ISCOR and others did lead to substantial industrial growth in general but the heavy industry that ensconced itself on the East Rand, the Vaal Triangle, the port of Durban and elsewhere, held little export potential. In fact, it harmonised with the huge mining sector.

The most obvious exception to this today is the automobile industry. Its ability to export Mercedes, BMW and other cars especially to the USA depends on the African Growth and Opportunity (AGOA) legislation in the USA intended to help Africa to industrialise. This is not at all part of free market ideology, of course. In fact, the German carmakers certainly constrain severely the South African ability to do more than follow the blueprints designed in Germany. In the end, moreover, the South African motor industry imports in value somewhat more than it exports.

As a result, from 1975 South Africa increasingly depended not on the manufacturing sector that provided so many jobs but rather on the growing sale of other minerals such as manganese, platinum, iron ore and coal. Thus industrial growth really fitted fairly well a characteristic import substitution industry behaviour pattern as in Latin America even if South African industry tended to be linked to local economic empires rather than being branch plants of foreign firms. Just as in Latin America, however, moving up the value chain led to the need for more expensive capital goods imports. Only diversified mineral export made this possible. South Africa was squeezed by foreign banks to pay back loans, amongst other things on the infrastructure that allowed minerals in remoter parts of the country to be brought to the seacoast efficiently. One can consider the 1980s therefore as a period of almost permanent financial crisis despite overall a rather modest national debt level.

In the interests of achieving coherence, I have not peppered this book with citations to Ben Fine and Zavareh Rustomjee's 1996 study, *The*

Political Economy of South Africa: From Minerals-Energy Complex to Industrialisation. This is certainly the most important book on the South African economy published in recent years, given that twenty years have already passed since it came out. The subtitle is something of a misnomer. The basic argument that the authors make is that South African industrialisation has a character to it, based on massive use of coal-fired electric power and feeding the needs of gold and other kinds of mining, that is fundamentally unlike the industrialisation of the East Asian tigers. Indeed the book starts with a lengthy chapter on South Korea, by implication thus making the comparison with developmental states, Korea being a classic example. The authors then argue that even before 1940 these characteristics were dominant in South Africa.

This book essentially rests on that set of insights. The creation of the parastatals, the Second World War era planning exercises and documents, the new institutions such as the IDC that emerged only served to re-enforce this structure and add to it through the rise of the big oligopolies in branch after branch of the economy. Here I would add that the developmental state after 1940 did try to widen the terrain for economic diversity and economic growth to a significant extent but in the end, the circumstances from the middle 1970s caused changes in direction largely to fall by the wayside, almost forgotten today. Fine and Rustomjee defined the mineral/energy complex 'not merely as a core set of industries and institutions but as a system of accumulation and one that has varied in its nature over time' (Fine and Rustomjee, 1996, 10). Much of their analysis revolves around reading statistics of that time which we have not repeated here as it seems to make more sense just to refer the reader on to their study (see Fine and Rustomjee 1996, 77, 83–4, 91 for striking statistical evidence). Moreover, this book is one essentially of history which concerns itself with places, individuals and with precisely the variation over time while Fine and Rustomjee are above all economists.

Moreover, they were writing just at the start of the new democratic era when policymaking seemed open in a way that it no longer does. The Fine/Rustomjee model of mineral-energy dependence in the economy, which in my view this study bears out, was proving an iron cage once some advantages were exhausted. The achievements of the nascent developmental state were not such as to allow an escape from that enclosure. There is a certain ambiguity in their study in that it is not clear whether they seek to wean South Africa off its classic sources of wealth or to propose further growth within the cage. They argue against the once conventional wisdom that manufacturing was overtaking/had overtaken mining as a core economic activity. It is true that more people are employed in manufacturing and that manufacturing still has a considerable importance in South Africa but nobody would propose that 1996 mainstream economists' wisdom anymore in any case.

One problem brought to the fore was South Africa's massive use of energy in the form primarily of electricity fired by coal. This was indeed a postulate of the development planning of the 1940s just as they hoped somewhat later to take advantage of the relatively prolific presence of the rare mineral, uranium, to develop uses for nuclear energy. Just as the latter has proven to be a largely empty promise, the former is also an environmental hazard. The good growth years at the start of our present millennium suddenly brought to the fore the rapid consequent need for energy. It was necessary to commission huge new power plants and the country went through a severe power shortage in 2013–14. How to organise energy applications remains an unresolved major planning dilemma. There was also growing recognition, as we have seen for the Vaal Triangle, of the environmental costs of the massive energy demands of the economic system.

The political transition brought about still another major change. Up to 1990 it was still possible to write that a committed, technically expert elite, with similar formation, goals and a common sense of community, existed at the top in South Africa. It is striking that a range of writers not sympathetic to apartheid were struck in their research by this phenomenon and have commented on it approving at least the probity, sense of dedication and ability to find ingenious solutions to technical problems in the past (Ballim, Fig, Henk, Scerri, Sparks). This is not to say that corrupt practices had not long penetrated into many parts of the government such as the homelands development. In 1990, President F.W. de Klerk began the process of negotiations, unbanned the ANC in particular and undid key apartheid legislation. This initiated almost four unsteady years of political negotiations. By the end of that time, it was clear that the dominant elite had been thrust aside and would have no part in the future political dispensation.

Indeed, as I have argued elsewhere (Freund 2013b), the ANC dominated government bought into a free market ideology hook, line and sinker. This included the convinced views of those from within such as the Minister of Finance Trevor Manuel and the second ANC president, Thabo Mbeki. Tariff barriers collapsed, deregulation and privatisation ruled the day for the remainder of the 1990s. At the same time, the trade unions particularly put their weight behind the Reconstruction and Development Programme (RDP). The RDP raised a myriad of aspects of poverty and under-development experienced by most of the black African majority as key problems blamed on apartheid racism. For a time from 1996, the former Congress of South African Trade Unions (COSATU) General Secretary Jay Naidoo was supposed to be a super-cabinet minister co-ordinating RDP based policy shifts and allocations of funds. It was never really empowered or financially supported, however, to this end. The cabinet, notably Manuel in charge of the Ministry of Finance, asserted itself and got rid of the awkward RDP unit and of Naidoo after a short time.

The original RDP, in any case, had been strong on an assortment of social issues. The link to economic means of addressing problems was always missing. In succeeding years, the state has indeed addressed many specific issues of the RDP. Universal pensions, the child grant, disability allowances, the roll-out of free drugs to counter the damage caused by the wide prevalence of HIV/AIDS and the massive construction of little 'RDP' houses handed out without charge, were all big benefits to the poorest part of the population. What was lacking was the kind of transformative element that the old developmental state had at one time promised white South Africans.

The anti-apartheid movement and most of those who believed in it and supported it understood what they were doing as a kind of crusade against racism. With the ascendancy of the ANC to power in 1994, all legislation based on race – apart from policies intended to benefit those self-defined as previous racial victims – was abolished. For all the many good results of this profound normative shift, society is far from entirely transforming in consequence. The extent to which the yawning inequalities and human differentials in South Africa could be ascribed to the racialisation of citizenship was certainly exaggerated in a movement that tried seamlessly to unite liberal and left militants. There are two areas where it is hoped that this study can be seen as having continuing, not merely historic, value. The first is that it has tried to provide shading and dimension to the narrowly racial understanding of the old social and economic structure of the country. Here we have tried to explain that structure in ways that were always intended to harmonise with racial division but had very much their own character and life. The second is to propose that, unlike the defunct racial laws, deeply embedded social and economic practices continue and cannot be reduced to racism however one defines this analytically loose term.

It is certainly possible to look at South African economic history in terms of the exploitation or oppressive labouring conditions of the black majority. In mining, in agriculture and in industry, especially heavy industry, this has been the case, as so many studies attest. However, this book puts its emphasis on another aspect, exclusion, which has certainly played a huge role in carving the gaps in education, skill and income between black and white that still exist. One thing that can be learnt from this historic experience concerns that. It was not so easy turning whites with no urban skills and despised by the leaders in society into a working class that had a foundation which allowed some social mobility and a road to a better life. Simply being white was rarely sufficient in this respect. Training of individuals and economic restructuring affecting collective experience were critical. To the frustration of many black South Africans, as a result whites are largely able to cope with their loss of access to state employment surprisingly well today. This was an achievement nonetheless and there are others, such as the promotion of scientific experimentation and institutionalisation. This side of human upliftment could certainly be applied to the population at large by an inclusive government were it determined enough.

It has been suggested that the black economic empowerment drive of the government (central now, for instance, to the work of the expanded IDC) is an attempt to create co-operative black partners in capital. Mbeki as president consulted with big business but took the important step of permitting several of the biggest, notably Anglos, to shift their headquarters to London, possibly to rid himself of their influence and power. In fact, as we have seen, while powerful Afrikaner capitalists eventually emerged, for a long time it was only a few in what remained a largely English language world in the private sector who really succeeded. It was a long, hard process for this situation to alter. Whether BEE could or will succeed in this regard is very open to question. There was an apparent equivalent, when Anglos began to unbundle in 1999, of the 1964 deal that created Gencor and opened the gates for the biggest Afrikaner business network at SANLAM to enter the mining field, but the market soon crashed leaving a big debt burden for the new black mine magnates instead of the vaunted economic power. Later efforts, connected to new tendering procedures in, for instance, power stations and coal mines, continued along these lines and found more traction. However whether that power goes with any capacity for entrepreneurial creativity, for taking the development further and addressing its problems, is so far an open question.

Mbeki liked to call his regime a democratic, developmental one. With good prices reigning in the minerals world for a while, the economy grew significantly for the first time in twenty years and some foreign investment arrived. However much of it has just involved foreigners buying into South African firms and inevitably subordinating them to global strategies. Of the big metal-working firms, Bateman is owned by an Italian company, Boart is part of a larger enterprise headquartered in Salt Lake City, while Deswick is headquartered in Australia. White goods are under the control of Turkish capital, and tyres, Indian capital, just like ISCOR. This is true to a massive extent. Reconstructing a developmental state in South Africa would be hard. How would it be financed given the dominance of fiscal orthodoxy? It would also need to base itself on new technology leaders. The most remarkable entrepreneurs in this rubric, such as Elon Musk, Patrick Soon-Shiong or Mark Shuttleworth, have emigrated far away. Finally it is not clear that it would solve in itself the basic, elemental problem of mass unemployment (coupled with a big shift that has taken place towards making jobs contractual, and thus short-term and precarious) that swept the country from the late 1980s. Global capitalism generally is orientated towards economic processes that are labour-saving and reducing or eliminating many classic forms of large-scale labour recruitment. This is not to say, as note the revival of the CSIR, now liberated from an onerous market-dominated regime, or the expansion of the IDC, facts do not indicate that the state continues to try, undoubtedly with some successes, to save and support worthwhile business endeavours. What is so far missing, however, is what we could call overall planning. The extant National Development Plan is just a rather indigestible wish list of considerable length.

If we return finally to the developmental state paradigm, however, it might be noted that not much is written on the dissolution or dissipation of the developmental state. The models presented by Chang and others focus on its birth, rise to importance and key features in place. There is an unsaid assumption that once certain conditions come into being that they were to stay in place ad infinitum potentially. However, the more recent history of Japan or Korea does not suggest that this is how things have worked in real life. These are countries that were transformed into industrial powerhouses over particular periods of time but this did not preclude subsidence into problematic blockages and stagnation. Whether South Africa has potential in the future to become a different sort of developmental state again with transformed or new state institutions and new forms of industrialisation is an open question.

Bibliography

Adams, Randall (2011/12). 'Die ver-Suid-Afrikanerisering van die Suid-Afrikaanse ekonomie: 'n studie van SANLAM 1918–80'. Unpublished MA thesis, University of Stellenbosch.

Ake, Claude (1981). *A Political Economy of Africa*, London: Longmans.

Allen, Robert C. (2003). *From Farm to Factory: A Reinterpretation of the Soviet Industrial Revolution*, Princeton, NJ: Princeton University Press.

Allen, V.L. (1992). *Mining in South Africa and the Genesis of Apartheid 1871–1948*, Keighley: Merlin Press and Moor.

Ally, Russell (1994). *Gold and Empire: The Bank of England and South Africa's Gold Producers 1886–1926*, Johannesburg: Witwatersrand University Press.

Amin, Samir (1973). *Neo-colonialism in West Africa*, Harmondsworth: Penguin.

Amin, Samir (1974). *Accumulation on a World Scale: A Critique of the Theory of Underdevelopment*, New York: Monthly Review Press.

Amsden, Alice (1989). *South Korea and Late Industrialism*, Paris and New York: Oxford University Press.

Annecke, Wendy (2003). One Man, One Megawatt: One Woman, One Candle: Women, Gender and Energy in South Africa. Unpublished PhD thesis, University of Natal, Durban.

Annecke, Wendy (2009). Still in the Shadows: Women and Gender Relations in the Electricity Sector in South Africa. In David McDonald, ed., *Electric Capitalism: Recolonising Africa on the Power Grid*, London, Sterling, VA and Cape Town: Earthscan and HSRC Press, PP. 258–320.

Ballim, Faeeza (2017). Evolution of Large Technical Systems in the Waterberg Coalfield from Apartheid to Democracy, Unpublished DPhil Thesis, University of the Witwatersrand.

Barker, H.A.F. (1963). A Comment on Textile Development in South Africa. *South African Journal of Economics*, **31**(4).

Barker, Theo (1996). Pilkington Glass in South Africa 1882–1992. *South African Journal of Economic History*, **11**(2), 285–303.

Batchelor, Peter (1998). South Africa's Arms Industry: Prospects for Conversion. In Jacklyn Cock and Penny McKenzie, eds., *From Defence to Development: Redirecting Military Resources in South Africa*, Cape Town and Ottawa: David Philip and IDRC.

Beavon, Keith (2004). *Johannesburg: The Making and Shaping of the City*, Johannesburg and Leiden: UNISA Press and Brill.

Bell, M.M.S. (1978). The Politics of Administration: A Study of the Career of Dr. D.L. Smit, with Special Reference to his Work in the Department of Native Affairs 1934–45, Unpublished MA thesis, Rhodes University.

Bell, Trevor (1986). The Role of Regional Policy in South Africa. *Journal of Southern African Studies*, **12**(2), 276–92.

Bezuidenhout, Andries and Cock, Jacklyn (2007). Corporate Power, Society and the Environment: A Case Study of Arcelor Mittal South Africa. *Transformation*, **69**, 81–105.

Biesheuvel, Simon (1943). *African Intelligence*, Johannesburg: South African Institute of Race Relations.

Black, Anthony (1991). Manufacturing Development and the Economic Crisis: A Reversion to Primary Production? In Stephen Gelb, ed., *South Africa's Economic Crisis*, London and Cape Town: Zed and David Philip, pp. 156–75.

Botha, D.J.J. (1973). On Tariff Policy: The Formative Years. *South African Journal of Economics*, **41**(4).

Bozzoli, Belinda (1981). *The Political Nature of a Ruling Class: Capital and Ideology in South Africa 1890–1933*, London, Boston, MA and Henley: RKP.

Bozzoli, G. (1997). *Forging Ahead: South Africa's Pioneering Engineers*, Johannesburg: Wits University Press.

Brayshaw, B.C. (n.d.) *The IDC, Its Work and Influence 1940–1965*, Self-published.

Brennan, James and Rougier, Marcelo (2009). *The Politics of National Capitalism: Peronism and the Argentine Bourgeoisie 1946–76*, State College, PA: Pennsylvania State University Press.

Brenner, Robert (1993). *Merchants and Revolution: Commercial Change, Political Conflict and Overseas Traders 1550–1653*, London and New York: Verso.

Brewer, Anthony (1980). *Marxist Theories of Imperialism: A Critical Survey*, London: Routledge & Kegan Paul.

Brown, Karen (2005). Tropical Medicine and Animal Diseases: Onderstepoort and the Development of Veterinary Science in South Africa 1908–50. *Journal of Southern African Studies*, **31**(3), 513–30.

Browne, G.W.G. (1965). Investment in the Public Sector of South Africa. *South African Journal of Economics*, **33**(4), 279–92.

Browne, G.W.G. (1971). The Application of the Economic Development Programme in the Public Sector of South Africa. *South African Journal of Economics*, **39**(4), 261–70.

Bruwer, A.J. (1923). *Protection in South Africa.* PhD thesis, University of Pennsylvania, Stellenbosch: Pro-ecclesia.

Bruwer, A.J. (*c.* 1934). *Kapitalisme, Party Politiek en Armoede*, Bloemfontein: self-published.

Busschau, W.J. (1955). The Capital and Economic Policy in the Union of South Africa. *South African Journal of Economics*, **33**(3), 179–88.

Calitz, Estian, du Plessis, Stan and Siebrits, Krige (2013). *Fiscal Sustainability in SA: Will History Repeat Itself?* University of Stellenbosch Bureau of Economic Research, Stellenbosch Economic Working Papers 7/13.

Cartwright, A.P. (1971). Die Nywerheids-Ontwikkelings Korporasie van Suid-Afrika Beperk, translated into Afrikaans, Johannesburg: n.p.

Chakrabarty, Dipesh (2000). *Provincialising Europe*, Princeton, NJ: Princeton University Press.

Chang, Ha-Joon (1992). *The Political Economy of Industrial Policy*, London: Macmillan.

Chaskalson, Matthew (1986). The Road to Sharpeville: A History of Vereeniging's African Townships in the 1950s, African Studies Institute Paper, University of the Witwatersrand.

Chaskalson, Matthew, Jochelson, Karen and Seekings, Jeremy (1987). Rent Boycotts and the Urban Political Economy. In Glen Moss and Ingrid Obery, eds., *South African Review 4*, Johannesburg: Ravan, pp. 53–74.

Chibber, Vivek (2003). *Locked in Place: State-Building and Late Industrialization in India.* Princeton, NJ: Princeton University Press.

Chibber, Vivek (2013). *Postcolonial Theory and the Spectre of Capital*, London and New York: Verso.

Chipkin, Ivor (2016). The Decline of African Nationalism and the State of South Africa. *Journal of Southern African Studies*, **42**(2).

Chisholm, Linda and Morrow, Sean (2007). Government, Universities and the HSRC: A Perspective on the Past and Present. *Transformation*, **63**, 45–67.

Christie, Renfrew (1984). *Electricity, Industry and Class in South Africa*, London: Macmillan.

Clark, Nancy (1993). The Limits of Industrialisation under Apartheid. In Philip Bonner, Peter Delius and Deborah Posel, eds., *Apartheid's Genesis 1936–62*, Johannesburg: Ravan and Wits University Press.

Clark, Nancy (1994). *Manufacturing Apartheid: State Corporations in South Africa*, New Haven, CT: Yale University Press.

Cloete, Nico, Muller, Johan and Orkin, Mark (1986). How We Learned to Stop Worrying and Love the HSRC. *Psychology in Society*, **6**, 29–46.

Coase, Ronald (1937). The Nature of the Firm. *Economica*, **4**, 16, 386–405.

Cock, Jacklyn (2004). Connecting the Red, Brown and Green: The Environmental Justice Movement in South Africa. Unpublished paper for the University of KwaZulu/Natal Globalisation, Marginalisation and New Social Movements in Post-Apartheid SA Project.

Coronil, Fernando (1997). *The Magical State: Nature, Money and Modernity in Venezuela*, Chicago, IL: University of Chicago Press.

Coupe, Stuart (1995). Divisions of Labour: Racist Trade Unions, in the Iron, Steel, Engineering and Metallurgical Industries of Post-War South Africa. *Journal of Southern African Studies*, **21**, 3, 451–72.

Coupe, Stuart (1996). Testing for Aptitude and Motivation in South African Industry: The Work of the National Institute for Personnel Research 1946–73. *Business History Review* **70**, 1, 43–68.

Crompton, Roderick (1994). The South African Commodity Plastics Filière: History and Future Strategy Options. Unpublished PhD thesis, University of Natal, Durban.

Crompton, Rod (15 November 2016). 'SA Needs to Get Out of its Petrochemicals Cul de Sac', *The Conversation* Newsletter (internet).

Cronje, F.J.C. (1952). The Textile Industry in the Union of South Africa. *South African Journal of Economics*, **20**, 1, 23–30.

Cross, Tim (1994a). Afrikaner Nationalism, Anglo American and ISCOR: The Formation of the Highveld Steel & Vanadium Corporation, 1960–70. *Business History* **36**, 3, Kl-99.

Cross, Tim (1994b). Britain, South Africa and l'entente internationale de l'acier. *South African Journal of Economic History*, **9**, 1–12.

Crotty, Ann (30 May 2013). In *Business Day*.

Davies, Robert (1979). *Capital, State and White Labour in South Africa 1900–1960*. Atlantic Highlands, NJ: Humanities Press.

Davies, Robert et al. (1976). Class Struggle and the Periodisation of the State in South Africa. *Review of African Political Economy*, 7, 4–30.

de Kock M.H. (1922). *Government Ownership in South Africa.* Cape Town: Juta.

de Kock, M.H. (1963). Review of the Financial and Economic Situation in South Africa. *South African Journal of Economics*, **31**, 3.

Denoon, Donald (1983). *Settler Capitalism: The Dynamics of Dependent Development in the Southern Hemisphere*, Oxford: Clarendon.

de Vries, Jan (1994). The Industrial Revolution and the Industrious Revolution. *Journal of Economic History*, **54**, 2, 249–70.

de Waal, Marius (1982). Why Have an IDC . . . After Forty Years? *Journal of Business Management*, **13**, 2.

Dlamini, Jacob (2017). The Death of Jacob Dlamini. In Christopher Ballantine et al. eds., *Living Together, Living Apart?: Social Cohesion in a Future South Africa*, Pietermaritzburg: UKZN Press, pp. 183–94.

Dommisse, Ebbe (2011). *Sir David Pieter de Villiers Graaff, 1st Baronet of de Grendel*, Cape Town: Tafelberg.

Dooling, Wayne (2008). *Slavery, Emancipation and Colonial Rule in South Africa*. Athens, OH: Ohio University Press.

Draper, Peter (1996). Limits to Indigenous Technological Capacity in the South African Computer-Hardware Industry. *South African Journal of Economic History*, **11**, 75–97.

Dubow, Saul (1997). Colonial Nationalism, the Milner Kindergarten and the Rise of South Africanism 1902–10. *History Workshop Journal*, **43**, 57–85.

Dubow, Saul (2000). A Commonwealth of Science: The British Association in South Africa, 1905 and 1929. In Saul Dubow, ed., *Science and Society in Southern Africa*, Manchester: Manchester University Press, pp. 66–99.

Dubow, Saul (2001). Scientism, Social Research and the Limits of 'South Africanism': The Case of Ernst Gideon Malherbe. *South African Historical Journal*, **44**, 99–142.

Dubow, Saul (2005). Introduction. In Saul Dubow and Alan Jeeves, eds., *South Africa's 1940s: Worlds of Possibilities*, Cape Town: Double Storey, pp. 1–19.

Dubow, Saul (2006). *A Commonwealth of Knowledge: Science, Sensibility and White South Africa 1820–2000*, London and Cape Town: Oxford University Press and Double Storey.

Dubow, Saul and Jeeves, Alan, eds. (2005). *South Africa's 1940s: Worlds of Possibilities*, Cape Town: Double Storey.

Duncan, David (1992). Foreign and Local Investment in the South African Motor Industry 1924–92. *South African Journal of Economic History*, 7, 2, 53–8.

Duncan, David (*c*. 1992). 'We Are Motor Men': Management Culture and Consciousness in the South African Motor Industry. Unpublished ms.

Duncan, David (1995). *The Mills of God: The State and African Labour in South Africa 1918–48*, Johannesburg: Wits University Press.

Edwards, Paul and Hecht, Gabrielle (n.d.). Technopolitics in the Construction and Destruction of Apartheid South Africa. Unpublished, ms. Itala Park Conference workshop.

Engineers' Liaison Committee of Pretoria (1963–72). Hendrik van der Bijl Lesings-Lectures (1967 Address by T.P. Stratten; 1971 Address by G.S.J. Kuschke; 1972 Address by P.E. Rousseau). IDC Infocentre.

Evans, Peter (1995). *Embedded Autonomy: States and Industrial Transformation*. Princeton, NJ: Princeton University Press.

Esterhuyse, Willie (1986). *Anton Rupert: Advocate of Hope,* Cape Town: Tafelberg.

Feinstein, Charles (2005). *An Economic History of South Africa: Conquest, Discrimination and Development*, Cambridge: Cambridge University Press.

Fig, David (1998). Apartheid's Nuclear Arsenal: Deviation from Development. In Jacklyn Cock and Penny McKenzie, eds., *From Defence to*

Development: Redirecting Military Resources in South Africa, Cape Town and Ottawa: David Philip and IDRC, pp. 163–80.

Fig, David (2005). *Uranium Road, Questioning South Africa's Nuclear Direction*, Johannesburg: Jacana.

Fig, David (2009). A Price Too High: Nuclear Energy in South Africa. In David McDonald, ed., *Electric Capitalism: Recolonising Africa on the Power Grid*, London, Sterling, VA and Cape Town: Earthscan and HSRC Press, pp. 180–201.

Finance Week (1980). IDC Special Survey 22–8 June.

Finance Week (2014). 17 October.

Fine, Ben and Rustomjee, Zavareh (1996). *The Political Economy of South Africa: From Minerals-Energy Complex to Industrialisation*, London: Hurst.

Fleisch, Brahm (1995). Social Scientists as Policy Makers: E.G. Malherbe and the National Bureau for Educational and Social Research. *Journal of Southern African Studies*, **21**, 3, 349–72.

Frank, Andre Gunder (1969). *Capitalism and Underdevelopment in Latin America*, New York: Monthly Review Press.

Frankel, Philip (2001). *An Ordinary Atrocity: Sharpeville and Its Massacre*, New Haven, CT: Yale University Press.

Frankel, Rudy (1988). *Tiger Tapestry*, Cape Town: C. Struik.

Frankel, S. Herbert (1938). *Capital Investment in Africa*, London: Oxford University Press.

Frankel, S. Herbert (1947). Whither South Africa? An Economic Approach, *South African Journal of Economics*, **XV**, 1, 27–39.

Frankel, S. Herbert (1992). *An Economist's Testimony*. Oxford: Oxford Centre for Postgraduate Hebrew Studies.

Freund, Bill (1985). Modes of Production: A Debate in African Studies. *Canadian Journal of African Studies*, **14**, 1, 23–9.

Freund, Bill (1989). The Cape during the Transitional Era 1795–1814. In R. Elphick and H. Giliomee, eds., *The Shaping of South African Society 1652–1820*, Cape Town: Maskew Miller Longmans, revised edition, pp. 324–58.

Freund, Bill (2001). Brown and Green in Durban: The Evolution of Environmental Policy in a Post-Apartheid City. *International Journal of Urban and Regional Research*, **25**, 4, 717–39.

Freund, Bill (2007a). South Africa as Developmental State?, *Africanus*, Pretoria, **37**, 2, 191–7.

Freund, Bill (2007b). South Africa as a Developmental State? Changes in the Social Structure since the End of Apartheid and the Emergence of the BEE Elite. *Review of African Political Economy*, **114**, 661–78.

Freund, Bill (2009). The Significance of the Mineral-Energy Complex in The Light of South African Economic Historiography. *Transformation* **71**, 3–26.

Freund, Bill (2012). The South African Developmental State and the First Attempt to Create a National Health System: Another Look at the Gluckman Commission of 1942–44. *South African Historical Journal*, **64**, 2, 170–86.

Freund, Bill (2013a). Swimming against the Tide: The Macro-Economic Research Group in the South African Transition 1991–94. *Review of African Political Economy*, **138**, 519–36.

Freund, Bill (2013b). A Ghost from the Past: The South African Developmental State of the 1940s. *Transformation*, **81–2**, 86–114.

Freund, Bill (2014). Nationalisms Inclusive and Exclusive: A Comparison of the Indian Congress Movement and the African National Congress of South Africa. *Transformation*, **86**, 5–29.

Freund, Bill (2016). The Keys to the Economic Kingdom: State Intervention and the Overcoming of Dependency in Africa: A Comparison of South Africa and Black Africa before the Crisis of the 1970s. *Theoria*, **147**, 44–60.

Freund, Bill and Padayachee, Vishnu (1998). Post-Apartheid South Africa: The Key Patterns Emerge. *Economic and Political Weekly (Bombay)*, May 16, **33**, 20, 1173–80.

Garrett, G.G. and Clark, J.B. (1992). Science and Technology in Transformation in South Africa. *Transformation*, **18/19**, 12–21.

Garson, Noel. (2007) Smuts and the Idea of Race. *South African Historical Journal*, 57, 1, 153–78.

Gelb, Stephen (1990). Democratising Economic Growth: Alternative Growth Models for the Future, *Transformation*, **12**, 25–41.

Gelb, Stephen, ed., (1991). *South Africa's Economic Crisis*, London and Cape Town: Zed and David Philip.

Giliomee, Hermann (1979). The Afrikaner Economic Advance. In Heribert Adam and Hermann Giliomee, eds., *Ethnic Power Mobilized: Can South Africa Change?* New Haven, CT: Yale University Press, pp. 145–76.

Glaser, Daryl (1988). *The State, Capital and Industrial Decentralisation Policy in South Africa 1932–85*. Unpublished MA thesis, University of the Witwatersrand.

Grundy, Kenneth (1986). *The Militarization of South African Politics*. London: I.B. Tauris.

Hallowes, David (2010). Environmental Injustice through the Lens of the Vaal Triangle: Whose Dilemma? In Bill Freund and Harald Witt, eds., *Development Dilemmas in Post-Apartheid South Africa*, Scottsville: University of KwaZulu-Natal Press.

Hallowes, David (2011). *Toxic Futures: South Africa in the Crises of Energy, Environment and Capital*, Scottsville: University of KwaZulu-Natal Press.

Hamilton, Alexander (1934). *Alexander Hamilton's Papers on Public Credit, Commerce and Finance*, New York: Columbia University Press.

Hamilton, Nora (1982). *The Limits of State Autonomy: Post-Revolutionary Mexico*, Princeton, NJ: Princeton University Press.

Hancock, W.K. (1968). *Smuts: The Fields of Force 1919–1950*, Cambridge: Cambridge University Press.

Headlam, Cecil, ed., (1931, 1933). *The Milner Papers*, London: Cassell & Co., 2 vols.

Hecht, Gabrielle (2009). *The Radiance of France: Nuclear Power and National Identity after World War II*, Cambridge MA: MIT Press.

Hendrik, Johannes van Eck (1902–70). *South African National Biography*. (1929–), Cape Town and Pretoria: South African National Library. v. 4.

Henk, Dan (2006). *South Africa's Armaments Industry: Continuity and Change after a Decade of Majority Rule*, Lanham, MD: University Press of America.

Herwitz, Daniel (2003). *Race and Reconciliation: Essays for the New South Africa*, Minneapolis, MN: University of Minnesota Press.

Hindson, D. (1987). *Pass Controls and the Urban African Proletariat*. Johannesburg: Ravan.

Hirson, Baruch (1989). *Yours for the Union: Class and Community Struggles in South Africa*, Johannesburg and London: Witwatersrand University Press and Zed Books.

Hlatshwayo, Mondli (2003). The Politics of Production and Forms of Worker Response at the ISCOR Vanderbijlpark Works 1965–73, Unpublished MA thesis, University of the Witwatersrand.

Hobsbawm, Eric (1968). *Industry and Empire*: London: Penguin.

Hodge, Joseph (2007). *Triumph of the Expert; Agrarian Doctrines of Development and the Legacies of British Colonialism*, Athens, OH: Ohio University Press.

Houghton, D. Hobart (1967). *The South African Economy*, 2nd edition, Cape Town: Oxford University Press.

Houghton, D. Hobart and Dagut, Jennifer, eds. (1972). *Source Material on the South African Economy 1860–70*, v. 3 1920–70, Johannesburg: Oxford University Press.

Human Sciences Research Council, assorted Research Reports.

Hurtado, Diego (2010). *La ciencia argentina: un proyecto inconcluso 1930–2000*, Buenos Aires: Edhasa.

Hutt, W.H. (1943). A Critique of the First Report of the Social and Economic Planning Commission. *South African Journal of*

Economics **11**, 48–62 with later reply by J. Reedman of the University of the Witwatersrand.

Hyslop, Jon (1988). State Education Policy and the Social Reproduction of the Urban African Working Class: The Case of the Southern Transvaal 1945–76. *Journal of Southern African Studies*, **14**, 3, 445–76.

Innes, Duncan (1984). *Anglo: Anglo American and the Rise of Modern South Africa*, Johannesburg: Ravan Press.

Jacobs, Alice (1948). *South African Heritage: A Biography of H J van der Bijl*, Pietermaritzburg: Shuter & Shooter.

Jaglin, Sylvy and Dubresson, Alain (2015). *Eskom: Électricité en pouvoir en Afrique du Sud*, Paris: Karthala.

Jaffee, Georgina (2001). *Joffee Marks: A Family Memoir*, Johannesburg: Sharp Sharp Media.

Jeeves, Alan (2005). Delivering Primary Health Care in Impoverished Urban and Rural Communities: The Institute of Family and Community Health. In Saul Dubow and Alan Jeeves, eds., *South Africa's 1940s: Worlds of Possibilities*, Cape Town: Double Storey, pp. 87–107.

Jeffrey, Ian (1991). Cultural Trends and Community Formation in a South African Township: Sharpeville 1943–85, Unpublished MA thesis, University of the Witwatersrand.

Joffe, Avril et al. (1993). Meeting the Global Challenge: A Framework for Industrial Revival in South Africa. In Pauline Baker, Alex Boraine and Warren Krafchik, eds., *South Africa and the World Economy*, Cape Town, Washington DC and Aspen, CO: David Philip, IDASA, Brookings Institution Press and the Aspen Institute, pp. 91–126.

Johnson, Chalmers (1982). *MITI and the Japanese Miracle: The Growth of Industrial Policy 1925–75*, Stanford, CA: Stanford University Press,

Johnstone, Frederick (1976). *Class, Race and Gold: A Study of Class Relations and Racial Discrimination,* London, Henley and Boston, MA: Routledge & Kegan Paul.

Kahn, Ellison (1943). Whither Our War-Time Native Policy? *South African Journal of Economics*, **10**, 2, 126–52.

Kahn, Ellison (1959). Public Corporations in South Africa: A Survey, *South African Journal of Economics*, **27**, 4, 279–92.

Kantorowich, Roy (1958). Civic Design. *South African Architectural Record*, **33**, April 1958.

Kaplan, David (1976). The Politics of Industrial Protection in South Africa 1910–39. *Journal of Southern African Studies*, **3**, 1, 70–91.

Kaplan, David (1983). The Internationalization of South African Capital: South African Direct Foreign Investment in the Contemporary Period. *African Affairs*, **82**, 465–94.

Kaplan, David (1986). Towards an Analysis of the South African Capital Goods Industry: Some Evidence from a Study of the South African Machine Tool Industry in Comparative Perspective. Unpublished paper, University of Edinburgh Centre of Technology and Social Change.

Kaplan, David (1990). *The Crossed Line: The South African Telecommunications Industry in Transition*. Johannesburg: Witwatersrand University Press.

Kaplan, David (1991). The South African Capital Goods Sector and the Economic Crisis. In Stephen Gelb ed., *South Africa's Economic Crisis*, London and Cape Town: Zed and David Philip, pp. 175–97.

Kaplan, David and Morris, Mike (1976). Labour Policy in a State Corporation. *South African Labour Bulletin*, **2**, 6, 8, 21–33, 2–21.

Kaplan, Mendel with Solomon Kaplan and Marion Robertson (1979). *From Shtetl to Steelmaking: The Story of Three Immigrant Families and a Family Business*. Cape Town: Kaplan-Kushlick Foundation.

Kelsall, Tim and Booth, David (2010). Developmental Patrimonialism? Questioning the Orthodoxy on Political Governance and Economic Progress in Africa, University of Sussex, Africa Power and Politics Programme Working Paper 9.

Khan, Mushtaq and Sundaram, Jomo Kwame (2000). *Rents, Rent-seeking and Economic Development: Theory and Evidence in Asia*. Cambridge: Cambridge University Press.

Kilvington, Ken (1996). A Second 1820s Settlement: British Textile Manufacturers and South Africa Post-1945. *South African Journal of Economic History*, **11**, 2, 218–50.

Kingwill, D.G. (1990). *The CSIR: The First Forty Years*, Pretoria.

Kirchhofer, Max (1958). Sasolburg OFS: Report on the New Town. *South African Architectural Record*, **43**, March.

Kok, Leon (2009). *South African Corporate Legacies*. Melrose Arch: ABC Press.

Koorts, Lindie (2014). *D.F. Malan en die opkoms van Afrikaner-nasionalisme*, Cape Town: Tafelberg.

Kooy, Marcelle and Robertson, Hector (1966). The South African Board of Trades and Industries. *South African Journal of Economics*, **34**, 3, 205–44.

Krige, Sue (1997). Segregation, Science and Commissions of Enquiry: The Contestation over Native Education Policy in South Africa, 1930–36. *Journal of Southern African Studies*, **23**, 3, 491–506.

Krige, Sue (1999). 'Trustees and Agents of the State', Missions and the Formation of Policy towards African Education, 1910–20. *South African Historical Journal*, **40**, 74–94.

Kuschke, G.S. (1969). South African Industrial Expansion. IDC Infocentre.

Laite, Harold J. (1943). *Portrait of a Pioneer: The Life and Work of William James Laite 1863–1942*, Cape Town, Johannesburg and London: South African Publishers.

Landes, David (1998). *The Wealth and Poverty of Nations: Why Some Are So Rich and Some So Poor*, New York: W.W. Norton.

Lewis, Jon (1984). *Industrialisation and Trade Union Organisation in South Africa 1924–55: The Rise and Fall of the South African Trades and Labour Council*, Cambridge: Cambridge University Press.

Lloyd, Philip (Energy Institute, Cape Peninsula University of Technology). (2014). Letter to the editor, *Business Day*, 23 March.

Lodge, Tom (2011). *Sharpeville: An Apartheid Massacre and Its Consequences*, London: Oxford University Press.

Lomas, P.K. (1955). Some Aspects of Profit Re-investment in the Union. *South African Journal of Economics*, **23**, 4, 287–98.

Lombard, J.A. and Stadler, J.J. (1967). *Die Ekonomiese Stelsel van Suid-Afrika*, HAUM.

Luiten van Zanden, Jan (2012). *The Long Road to the Industrial Revolution: The European Economy in a Global Perspective 1000–1800*, Leiden and Boston: Brill.

Mabin, Alan (2000). Varied Legacies of Modernism in Urban Planning. In G. Bridge and S. Watson, eds., *A Companion to the City*, Oxford, UK, and Malden, MA: Blackwell, pp. 555–66.

Macro-Economic Research Group (1993). *Making Democracy Work: A Framework for Macroeconomic Policy in South Africa*, Bellville: Centre for Development Studies, University of the Western Cape.

Mager, Anne (1999). *Gender and the Making of a South African Bantustan: A Social History of the Ciskei 1945–59*, Cape Town, London and Portsmouth, NH: David Philip, James Currey and Heinemann.

Mager, Anne (2010). *Beer, Sociability and Masculinity in South Africa*, Bloomington, IN: Indiana University Press.

Malherbe, E.G. (1980). *Never a Dull Moment*, Cape Town: Howard Timmins.

Maller, Judy (1983). Tseretetsi Bopelong ba Basebetsi: Health and Safety for Workers: A Study of Conditions of Health and Safety in the Metal Industry in the Vaal Triangle, Unpublished BA (Hons) dissertation, University of the Witwatersrand and DSG/Critical Health Dissertation Series, No. 4.

Marais, J.S. (1961). *The Fall of Kruger's Republic*, Oxford: Clarendon.

Marks, Shula and Trapido, Stanley (1979). Lord Milner and the South African State. *History Workshop Journal*, **8**, 50–80.

Marquard, Andrew (2006). *The Origins and Development of South African Energy Policy*, Unpublished DPhil thesis, University of Cape Town.

Marseille, Jacques (1984). *Empire colonial et capitalisme français: histoire d'une divorce*, Paris: Albin Michel.

Martin, William (1990). The Making of an Industrial South Africa: Trade and Tariffs in the Interwar Period. *International Journal of African Historical Studies*, **23**, 2, 59–86.

McDowell, James (2000). A History of the South African Textile Industry: The Pioneering Phase 1890–1945, Unpublished University of Natal, Durban MA thesis.

McWilliams, James (1989). *Armscor: South Africa's Arms Merchant*, London: Brasseys.

Mendelsohn, Richard (1991). *Sammy Marks 'The Uncrowned King of the Transvaal'*, Cape Town and Athens, OH: David Philip and Ohio University Press.

Meyer, F. (1952). The Development of the Iron and Steel Industry in South Africa. *South African Journal of Economics*, **20**, 2, 101–12.

Meyer, Norman (1963). The Development of the Footwear Industry in South Africa 1947–61. *South African Journal of Economics*, **31**, 4, 220–40.

Mkandawire, Thandeka (2001). Thinking about the Developmental States in Africa. *Cambridge Journal of Economics*, **25**, 3, 265–88.

Mohr, Philip, Botha, Mariana and Inggs, John (1989). South Africa's Balance of Payments 1946–85. *South African Journal of Economic History*, **5**, 1, 37–54.

Moll, Terence (1990). From Booster to Brake. In N. Nattrass and E. Ardington, *The Political Economy of South Africa*, Cape Town: Oxford, pp. 73–87.

Moore, Barrington Jr. (1966). *Social Origins of Dictatorship and Democracy: Lord and Peasant in the Making of the Modern World*, Boston, MA: Beacon.

Morrell, Robert (1986). Farmers, Randlords and the South African State: Confrontation in the Witwatersrand Meat Market 1920–23. *Journal of African History*, **21**, 3, 513–32.

Morrell, Robert and Padayachee, V. (1991). Indian Merchants and Dukawallahs in the Natal Economy 1875–1914. *Journal of Southern African Studies*, **17**, 1, 71–102.

Morris, Mike (1991) State, Capital and Growth: The Political Economy of the National Question. In Stephen Gelb, ed., *South Africa's Economic Crisis*, London and Cape Town: Zed and David Philip, pp. 33–58.

Morris, Mike and Hindson, Doug (1992). South Africa: Political Violence, Reform and Reconstruction, *Review of African Political Economy*, **53**, 43–59.

Munnik, Albert Victor (2012). Discursive Power and Environmental Justice in the New South Africa 1996–2005. Unpublished PhD thesis, University of the Witwatersrand.

Nattrass, Nicoli (2005). Economic Transformation and Growth in the 1940s. In Saul Dubow and Alan Jeeves, eds., *South Africa's 1940s: Worlds of Possibilities*, Cape Town: Double Storey, pp. 20–43.

Nel, Graham E. (1982). *Analysis and Formulation of a Strategy for Bateman Equipment Ltd.*, Unpublished M Business Leadership thesis, University of the Witwatersrand.

Nell, Dawn (2000). For the Public Benefit: Livestock Statistics and Expertise in the Late 19th century Cape Colony 1850–1900. In Saul Dubow, ed., *Science and Society in Southern Africa*, Manchester University Press, pp. 100–15.

Nishiura, Akio (2012). Industrial Concentration and Business Groups in South Africa: A Comparison with the Japanese Zaibatsu. Unpublished paper, World Economic History Conference, Stellenbosch 2012.

O'Meara, Dan (1983). *Volkskapitalisme: Class, Capitalism and Ideology in the Development of Afrikaner Nationalism*, Johannesburg: Ravan.

O'Meara, Dan (1996). *Forty Lost Years: The Apartheid State and the Politics of the National Party, 1948–94*, Athens, OH and Johannesburg: Ohio University Press and Ravan.

Oppenheimer, Harry F. (1950). *The Future of Industry in South Africa*, Johannesburg: South African Institute of Race Relations.

Padayachee, Mahavishnu (1990). South Africa's International Financial Relations, 1970–1987: History, Crisis and Transformation. Unpublished PhD thesis, University of Natal, Durban.

Padayachee, Vishnu and Rossouw, Jannie (2011). 'Reflecting on Ninety Years of Intermittent Success: The Experience of the Reserve Bank with Inflation since 1921'. *Economic History of Developing Regions*, **26**, supplement 1, S53-72.

Palmer, G.F.D. (1954). Some Aspects of the Development of Secondary Industry in South Africa since the Depression 1929–32. *South African Journal of Economics*, **22**, 148–59.

Parnell, Susan (1987). The Slums Act: Racial Segregation in Johannesburg 1934–40. *South African Geographical Journal*, **70**, 2, 112–26.

Parnell, S. and Mabin, A. (1995). Rethinking Urban South Africa. *Journal of Southern African Studies*, **21**, 1, 39–61.

Paton, Alan (1965) *South African Tragedy: The Life and Times of Jan Hofmeyr*. New York: C.S. Scribner's Sons.

Payn, Robert (2017). Asinamali! Building a United Front of Communities and Workers: Contemporary Struggle, Neoliberalism and the 1984–85

Vaal Uprising. Unpublished paper, Southern African Historical Society conference paper, 21 June.

Polakow-Suransky, Sasha (2010). *The Unspoken Alliance: Israel's Secret Relationship with Apartheid South Africa*, New York and Johannesburg: Pantheon and Jacana.

Pomeranz, Kenneth (2000). *The Great Divergence: China, Europe, and the Making of the Modern World Economy*. Princeton, NJ: Princeton University Press.

Posel, Deborah (2005). The Case for a Welfare State: Poverty and the Politics of an Urban African Family in the 1930s and 1940s. In Saul Dubow and Alan Jeeves, eds., *South Africa's 1940s: Worlds of Possibilities*, Cape Town: Double Storey, pp. 64–86.

Pretorius, Louwrens (1982). Interaction between Interest Organisations and Government in South Africa. *Politieia*, 1, 1, 1–30.

Pretorius, Louwrens (1996). Relations between State, Capital and Labour in South Africa: Towards Corporatism. *Journal of Theoretical Politics*, 8, 2, 255–81.

Prinsloo, P.J.J. (1993), redakteur, Yskor: Vanderbijlpark-Werke 1943–93, Unpublished ms., Potchefstroom. Potchefstoom Universiteit vir Christelike Hoër Onderwys.

Ramburuth, Shan (1997). The Financing of Megaprojects in the Mineral-Energies Complex. Unpublished University of the Witwatersrand M. Management Comm. thesis.

Randall, R.J. (1942). Full Employment in Wartime. *South African Journal of Economics*, 10, 2, 121–5.

Rantete, Johannes (1984). *The Third Day of September: An Eye-Witness Account of the Sebokeng Rebellion of 1984*, Johannesburg: Ravan.

Reader, W.J. (1976). *Metal Box: A History*, London: Heinemann.

Rembrandt Tobacco Company (1977). *Quality Above All*, privately printed.

Richards, C.S. (1940). *The Iron and Steel Industry in South Africa*, Johannesburg: Wits University Press.

Richards, C.S. (1942). Fundamentals of Economic Policy in the Union, *South African Journal of Economics*, 10, 42–72.

Richards, C.S. (1949). Some Thoughts on the Union's Economic Outlook. *South African Journal of Economics*, 17, 2, 142–54.

Richards, C.S. (1957). The Growth of Government in South Africa since Union. *South African Journal of Economics*, 35, 4, 259–63.

Richards, C.S. and Piercy, Mary (1962). Economic Budgeting in South Africa: A Comment. *South African Journal of Economics*, 30, 4, 310–26.

Rosenthal, Eric (1960). *Industrial Development Corporation of SA Ltd 1940–60: The Story of Its First Twenty Years*, Johannesburg: IDC.

Rosenthal, Eric (1961). *As Pioneers Still 1911–61, An Appreciation of Lever Brothers' Contribution in South Africa*, Unilever.

Rosenthal, Eric (1981). *The SARMCOL Story*, Sarmcol.

Rostow, W.W. (1960) *The Stages of Economic Growth: A Non-Communist Manifesto*, Cambridge: Cambridge University Press.

The Round Table. volumes 15, 21, 30, 33, 34, 36.

Rupert, Anton (1967). *I Plead for my Country and All Its Peoples*. Self-published.

Rustomjee, Zavareh (2012). *Maximising the Developmental Impact of the People's Mineral Assets: State Intervention in the Mining Sector*, unpublished paper for the ANC Policy Institute.

Sagner, Andreas (2000). Ageing and Social Policy in South Africa: Historical Perspectives with Particular References to the Eastern Cape. *Journal of Southern African Studies*, **26**, 3, 523–54.

Scerri, Mario (2009). *The Evolution of the South African System of Innovation*, Newcastle: Cambridge Scholars.

Schirmer, Stefan (2008). The Contribution of Entrepreneurs to the Emergence of Manufacturing in South Africa before 1948. *South African Journal of Economic History*, **23**, 1/2, 184–215.

Schirmer, Stefan (2009). Manufacturers and the Formulation of Industrial Policy in 1920s South Africa. *African Historical Review*, **41**, 2, 1–27.

Schoeman, Beaumont. (1980). *Die Geldmag*, Pretoria: (n.p.).

Scholtz, G.D. (1974). *Dr. Hendrik Frensch Verwoerd, 1901–66, 2de Band*, Johannesburg: Perskor.

Seegers, Annette (1993). Towards an Understanding of the Afrikanerisation of the South African State. *Africa*, **63**, 4, 477–97.

Seegers, Annette (1996). *The Military in the Making of Modern South Africa*, London and New York: I.B. Tauris.

Seekings, Jeremy (2005). Visions, Hopes and Views about the Future: The Radical Moment of South African Welfare Reform. In Saul Dubow and Alan Jeeves, eds., *South Africa's 1940s: Worlds of Possibilities*. Cape Town: Double Storey, pp. 44–63.

Seekings, Jeremy (2008). The Carnegie Commission and the Backlash against Welfare State Building in South Africa 1931–37. *Journal of Southern African Studies*, **34**, 3, 515–37.

Seekings, Jeremy and Nattrass, Nicoli (2005). *Class, Race and Inequality in South Africa*, New Haven, CT: Yale University Press, 2005.

Selwyn, B. (2009). An Historical Materialist Appraisal of Friedrich List and His Modern Day Followers. *New Political Economy*, **14**, 2, 157–80.

Senor, D. and Singer, S. (2009). *Start-Up Nation: The Story of Israel's Economic Miracle*. New York and Boston, MA: Twelve.

Sitas, F., Douglas, Allison, J. and Webster, E.C. (1989). Respiratory Disease Mortality Patterns among South African Iron Moulders. *British Journal of Industrial Medicine*, **46**, 310–15.

Smit, Daniel (1989). The Political Economy of Urban and Regional Planning in South Africa 1900–1985: Towards Theory to Guide Progressive Practice, Unpublished PhD thesis, University of Natal, Durban.

Smit, Dan and Mabin, Alan (1997). Reconstructing SA's Cities? The Making of Urban Planning 1900–2000. *Planning Perspectives*, **12**, 2, 193–223.

Smuts, J.C. (1917) The Future of South and Central Africa. In *Wartime Speeches, A Compilation of Public Utterances in Great Britain*, London: Hodder and Stoughton, pp. 79–96.

Smuts, J.C. (1966). *Selections from the Smuts Papers*, W.K. Hancock and Jean van der Poel (eds.), Cambridge: Cambridge University Press, v. 2 and (1973) v. 7.

South Africa Department of Information (n.d.). *Gedecentraliseerde Nywerheids-Ontwikkeling in Suid-Afrika*.

South African Journal of Economics (2002). *Special Issue in Honour of Presidents of the South African Economics Society*, **70**, 3.

Sparks, Stephen (2012). Apartheid Modern: South Africa's Oil-from-Coal project and the Making of a Company Town. Unpublished DPhil dissertation, University of Michigan, Ann Arbor.

Sparks, Stephen (2015). Dependence, Discipline and the Morality of Consumption: An Intellectual History of the SASOL Project. Unpublished paper.

Sparks, Stephen (2016). Between 'Artificial Economics' and the 'Discipline of the Market': SASOL from Parastatal to Privatisation. *Journal of Southern African Studies*, **42**, 4, 711–24.

Sparks, Stephen (n.d.). An Act of Faith: The Establishment of the SASOL Project, unpublished paper.

The Star 23.9.77, 18.3.80.

The State, X, September 1909, p. 300.

Styger, Paul and Saayman, Andrea (2011). The Economic Architecture of the Two de Kocks. *Economic History of Developing Regions XXVI*, supplement 1, S21–52.

Sunday Express (1981) 2 August.

Sunday Times (1969) 26 January.

Swanson, Maynard (1996) The Joy of Proximity: The Rise of Clermont in Paul Maylam and Iain Edwards, eds., *The People's City; African Life in*

Twentieth-Century Durban, Portsmouth, NH and Pietermaritzburg: Heinemann and University of Natal Press, pp. 274–98.

Terreblanche, Sampie (1973). *Vernuwing en Herskikking: op pad na nuwe ekonomiese instellings en prioriteite in Suid-Afrika*, Cape Town and Johannesburg: Tafelberg.

Thompson, Leonard M. (1960). *The Unification of South Africa 1902–10*. Oxford: Clarendon.

Threlfall, S.D. (1946). Some Comments on Secondary Industry in South Africa. *South African Journal of Economics*, **14**, 4, 288–304.

Tom, Petrus (1985). *My Life Struggle*, Johannesburg: Ravan.

Transvaal Chamber of Industries 1910–1960: An Historical Review.

Trapido, Stanley (1986). A History of Tenant Production on the Vereeniging Estates 1886–1920. In Stanley Trapido, William Beinart and Peter Delius, eds., *Putting a Plough to the Ground*, Johannesburg: Ravan, pp. 337–72.

Turrell, Robert (1987). *Capital and Labour on the Kimberley Diamond Fields 1871–90*. Cambridge: Cambridge University Press.

van Eck, H.J. (1951). Some Aspects of the South African Industrial Revolution, Speech to South African Institute of Race Relations, Johannesburg: Hoernle Memorial Lecture.

van Eck, H.J. (1961). The Growth of Industry since 1911. *The Certified Engineer*.

van Eck, H.J. (1966). The Possibilities of Power and Water Development, speech, South Africa Club dinner, Savoy Hotel, London, 25 October, IDC Infocentre.

van Eck, H.J. (1967). Industrial and Economic Development, 75th Anniversary symposium, South African Institution of Mechanical Engineers, University of the Witwatersrand, 30 June 1967. IDC Infocentre.

van Niekerk, Robert (2007). Social Policy and Citizenship in South Africa: The Development of Inclusive, Deracialised Policies in the Periods 1939–61 and 1989–98. Unpublished DPhil thesis, Oxford University.

van Onselen, Charles (1982). Randlords and Rotgut 1886–1903. In *A Social and Economic History of the Witwatersrand, 1886–1914 I: New Babylon*, Johannesburg, Ravan, pp. 44–102.

van Wyk, R.J. (1967). The Relationship between Scientific Research and Economic Growth and its Possible Implications for Policy in South Africa. *South African Journal of Economics*, **36**, 1, 32–44.

Wallerstein, Immanuel (1976). *The Modern World System*, New York: Monthly Review Press.

Wallis, P.F.D. (1953). The National Finance Corporation. *South African Journal of Economics*, **21**, 4, 394–417.

Walwyn, D. (2013). Political Economy, State Institutions and Policy: The Transformation of the CSIR, unpublished paper.
Walwyn, D. and Scholes, R.J. (2006). The Impact of a Mixed Income Model on the South African CSIR: A Recipe for Success or Disaster?, *South African Journal of Science*, **102**, May/June, 239–43.
Wassenaar, A.D. (1977). *Assault on Private Enterprise: The Freeway to Communism*. Cape Town: Tafelberg.
Webster, Eddie (1981). Servants of Apartheid: A Survey of Social Research into Industry in South Africa. In John Rex, ed., *Apartheid and Social Research*, Paris: UNESCO, pp. 85–113.
Webster, Eddie (1985). Cast in a Racial Mould: Labour Process and Trade Unionism in the Foundries. Johannesburg: Ravan.
White, Carolyn (1992). Can the HSRC Join in the Future? *Transformation* **18/19**, 22–31.
Winkler, Harald (2009). *Cleaner Energy, Cooler Climate: Developing Sustainable Energy Solutions for South Africa*, Cape Town: UNISA Press.
Woo-Cumings, Meredith, ed., (1999). *The Developmental State*, Ithaca, NY: Cornell University Press.
Worger, William (1987). *South Africa's City of Diamonds: Mineworkers and Monopoly Capitalism in Kimberley, 1867–95*, New Haven, CT: Yale University Press.
Wylie, Diana (2001). *Starving on a Full Stomach: Hunger and the Triumph of Cultural Racism in Modern South Africa*, Charlottesville, VA, University of Virginia Press.
Zalk, Nimrod (2017). The Things We Lost in the Fire: The Post-Apartheid Restructuring of the South African Steel and Engineering Sectors. Unpublished PhD thesis, School of Oriental and African Studies, London.
Zipp, Samuel (2010). Manhattan Projects: The Rise and Fall of Urban Renewal in Cold War New York. London: Oxford University Press.

Government Reports

Agreement between SAR and ISCOR, Ann 665–1934.
Conditions of Trade and Industries ... (Cullinan) Commission 1910, UG 10 1912.
Customs Tariff (Holloway) Commission 1934/35 UG 5/1936.
UG 37–1935 Industrial Legislation Commission Report (van Reenen)
Customs Tariff Commission (Holloway 1936).
UG-27, 1940, Rural Industries Commission Report.
UG 40/1941 3rd interim report, Industrial and Agricultural Requirements Commission (van Eck).

UG 42/1941 Native Affairs Commission (Reitz).
UG 9/1943 Social and Economic Planning Council Report 1, Re-employment, Reconstruction and the Council's Status.
UG 14/1944 Social and Economic Planning Council Report 2, Social Security, Social Services and the lNational Income.
UG 30/1944 National Health Services Commission. Report on the Provision of an Organized National Health Service for All Sectors of the People of the Union of South Africa 1942–4.
UG 34/1944 Social and Economic Planning Council #5 Regional and Town Planning.
UG/10 1945 Social and Economic Planning Council, #4 The Future of Farming in South Africa, H.J. van Eck, chair.
UG 53/1948 Social and Economic Planning Commission, Report 13. Economic and Social Conditions of the Racial Groups in South Africa.
Union Statistics for Fifty Years, Bureau of Census and Statistics, Pretoria, 1960.

South Africa. National Archives (NA)

ARB, A153/103
BAO, A7/6/2/V4/1
BAO 3/1281, A6/2/V4
BAO 3/1969, A6/5/2/S10
BAO 3/2035, A6/S2/V4
BAO 3/2365, A6/6/2/S10/ v.1–2
BAO 3/2365, A6/6/2/S10/3
BAO 3/2395, A6/6/2/V4
BAO 3/3079, A8/11/V4 pt. 1
BAO 7/1862, E12/3/3/516 v. 4 and v. 5
BAO 1747, A19/1603 v. 1
BAO 1995, A20/1709
BAP 3/2035 A6/S2/V4
BTS 01/132/5/5 v.1
'Aspects of Post-War Planning', 1942 [van Eck?]
BTS 01 132/5/5 v. 8
Summary of Report 5: Town and Regional Planning
1945 Annual Report
BTS 01/132/10
1948 Report on Banking (12)
BTS 01/132/10/30
Full Employment in SA

BTS 28/8/1
HEN 29, 28, 477/2/6/1 v. 1/2
HEN 2927 Post-War Planning
HEN 3511
HR/12/1 pt. 4 1971–73 v. 5
7337/PB4/3/2/34
JGB 120, 13/1/3/5030
MES 21, H46/ v. 1 and H47
MES 236, H4/12/1 pt. 3
MES 244, H4/4/12/3 v. 2
MPP 17, A3/1/6/4/4 pt. 1
MPP 23, A3/10/1 pt. 1
MPP 29, A3/10/4 v. 5/6
MPP 31, A3/10/4
MPP 44 A3/10/9
MPP 45, A3/10/9 pt. 1
MPP 47, A3/10/9
MPP 233, H4, 12S v. 3
MSB 52, 1/11/1/1
RNH 68, NH 4/11/17 pt. 1
SEC 2 Correspondence, Social and Economic Council
  1946 Extract from meeting: 25 February 1946
  Memorandum from Smuts 21 October 1948
SEC 3
  Industrial and Agricultural Requirements Commission.
  Reserves Report (9) 1946
SEC 48
  Report 7. Taxation and Fiscal Policy.
SES 0 A1/79
TES 9007, 161/11/1 v. 1
TES 9008, 161/11/1A
TES 9009, 161/11/1 v. 2
TES 9011, 16/11/1 v. 3
TES 9012, v. 7/8, 7
TES 9013 v. 9/10, 9
TES 9014, 161/11/2
UOD 2812, E296/ v.1/Social and Economic Planning Council
  Social and Economic Planning Council, 17–19 September 1947; Summary of Planning Report 9 on the Reserves, 1947

ISCOR FILES

AES 13, AM 7/7 pt. 1
AFE 29, E4/12/1 pt. 1

AFE 30, E4/12/3
BTS no volume, 8/19/5
MES 232, H 4/12 pts ½
MPP 233 H/4 12 v. 3
MES 234, HR/12 v. 4
MES 235, H4/12/ v. 1 and 2
MES 235, HE/12/3/12/1
MES 236, H4/12/1 pt. 3
MES v. 236 sys 01
MES 244, H4/12/3 v. 2
MES 245, H4/12/3/ v. 3–4
MES 245, H4/12/3 pt. 4, HR/12/1 pt. 4 1971–73
MMY 107, M4/6 pt. 1
MPP 14, A 3/1/2/4/4 v. 2 and A3/1/6/3
MPP 17, A3/1/6/4/4 pt. 1
MPP 23, A3/10/1 pt. 1
MPP 29, A3/10/4 vols 5/6
MPP 31, A3/10/4
MPP 44, A3/10/9
MPP 45, A3/10/9 pt. 1
MPP 47, A3/10/9
MPP 48, A3/10/9 Verslae en Notules
MPP 49, A3/10/9
MPP 50, A3/10/9
MPP 51, A3/10/9
WW 289, K 12/84
SASOL FILES
AES 10, AM 7 and AM 7/3, 3660
HEN 605, 80/29/30
HEN 3357, 506/1/4/1 v.1–3 1951–56
HEN 3660, 539 pts 1–3
HKE 139, H7/54 v. 2 AND H7/55
MES 218, H 46/6 v. 1 and 46/7
WW 36, K2/11A/2

Other Unpublished Sources

University of the Witwatersrand Libraries. Cullen Library

F.W. Lucas Papers

SASOL Papers AG 2207

B1

Preliminary report on Sasolburg, Max Kirchhofer, 31.1.51
Interview with Director, Native Labour 23.7.51
D.F. de Villiers to Max Kirchhofer, 18.12.51
A. Brink (SASOL Construction Manager) to Max Kirchhofer, 22.11.52

B4

Notes on the Planning of Sasolburg by Max Kirchhofer, February 1957
Max Kirchhofer to D.P. de Villiers, 3/8/57
Max Kirchhofer to Cecil Hersch, architect, 18/9/65

C 22

T.J.D. Fair and B.G. Boaden, *SASOL II-The Regional Setting: Population Growth and Shopping Structure,* Urban and Regional Research Unit, 1975, University of the Witwatersrand

D1

P.S. Reinecke, *Site Planning for Low-Cost Housing*, 1963
The Star, 23.9.77

F18

Vanderbijl Park, The Planned Industrial City, Vanderbijl Park Estate Company, 1948

F21

P.R. Nell, compiler, *An Historical Review of the Town of Vanderbijl Park for the Period 1941 to December 1951*, Van Riebeeck Festival Committee, Vanderbijl Park

F22

Natural Resources Development Council, *A Regional Survey of the Orange Free State Goldfield,* 1954, Government Printer, Pretoria

F30

Mallows, Louw and Hoffe, Vanderbijlpark Riverside: A Proposed Development Plan for the Vaal River Front, 1973

K1 SASOL/Secunda

E.N. Mallows and Max Kirchhofer, *Motivation Report on the Need and Desirability of the New Town Secunda, Eastern Transvaal, 1/6/76*
L.J. Oakenfull, *The Need and Desirability for the Township Secunda Extension 6 for SASOL, Motivation Report*
M.C. Tisdall, Manager, Production, Co-ordination and Despatch to General Manager, SBD, SASOL, 16/7/76

Rhodes University

Douglas Smit papers, Albany Museum, Rhodes University, Grahamstown
Address for Ciskei 13/9/37
Speech to Rotary Club, Pietermaritzburg, 13/11/41
Speech at Bantu Social Club, 27/10/44
SA Outlook 1/1/47
Notes on Future Development of Native Councils: 24/3/47

Industrial Development Corporation
Correspondence with Sandock-Austral Ltd., Boksburg, 1979

Interviews

Interview with Roy Kantorowich [by Alan Mabin], 13 July 1991
Interview with Samson Mokoena, Vaal Environmental Justice Alliance, Vanderbijlpark, 3 March 2015
Interview with Rolf Stumpf, ex-HSRC head 1990–99, 28 February 2014, Pretoria

Index